Busines *Success Secrets* should be on the bookshelf of every entrepreneur, regardless of how long you've been in the game! The insight and wherewithal with which this amalgamation of professionals relate their stories is unparalleled in its usefulness. A fantastic read for the rookie and veteran alike!

**James White | Former CEO,
Jamba Juice; Executive Coach & Speaker**

"The Formatting of *Business Success Secrets* makes it an easily accessible book to all, offering the distilled wisdom of professionals from nearly every kind of industry you can imagine. It is evident that a great deal of thought was put into which authors would participate in this project, as every single one of them has an original and creative story to tell."

**Monica Smiley | Editor & Publisher of
Enterprising Women**

Busines *Success Secrets* should be on the bookshelf of every entrepreneur, regardless of how long you've been in the game! The insight and wherewithal with which this most impressive group of professionals relate their stories is extraordinary in its usefulness. A fantastic read for the rookie and veteran alike!

Walter Hill | CEO, Icon Blue; Author of the forthcoming book, *Think Red Flags: A Proactive and Profitable Approach for Your Small Business*

Anthologies like *Business Success Secrets* are great for two reasons: they provide a nearly limitless supply of motivation when going through the trials and tribulations of business, but even more importantly… whatever your problem currently is, more likely than not one of these entrepreneurs has gone through it before and has the answer you're looking for.

Shawn Johal | Business Growth Coach and author of *The Happy Leader*

"Riveting from the very first chapter! Once you get the pages turning, it's very difficult to put this book down. Each author is so unique, and yet, so many of the lessons learned can be extrapolated and applied to whatever professional endeavor you've always dreamed of spearheading."

Reggie Van Lee | Partner and Chief Transformation Officer, The Carlyle Group

Congratulations on the important book: *Business Success Secrets* by women and men entrepreneurs who pour out their hearts and souls with valuable insights. I urge each of you to read the stories and delve deep into the answers to the piercing questions and see the perseverance, ingenuity and candid assessments. Their learnings are invaluable. No need to reinvent the wheel!

Edie Fraser | CEO, Women Business Collaborative (WBC); Enterprising Women Hall of Fame and founding member of C200; Founder, Million Women Mentors (MWM)

Business Success Secrets does an excellent job of driving home the notion that you don't have to belong to the family of a wealthy industry tycoon to go out there and make your dream a reality. Tempered with practical and pragmatic wisdom from a charming selection of entrepreneurs of all ages, races and backgrounds, it was a highly informative literary journey.

Sanjay Jaybhay | Bestselling author of *Invest and Grow Rich*

If there was one thing that struck me as particularly noteworthy about *Business Success Secrets*, it was the rawness of the contributing authors. There was no gussied up language or fanatical blueprints to fame and fortune. It was simple, understandable and highly actionable pieces of advice from real people – just like you and I – who have been there and done it all before.

Michael Flory | CEO, Director & Board Member, MRFH, LLC

It was downright rejuvenating and inspiring just to see how many top-tier companies are now being run by successful, empowered and business-oriented female professionals all around the world! An excellent addition to any entrepreneur's personal library.

Mark Nureddine | CEO, Bull Outdoor Products and bestselling author of *Pocket Mentor*

Business Success Secrets delivered even more than I had anticipated. Offering invaluable insight and awareness of the challenges associated with striking out on your own, each personal narrative is primed with nuggets of hard-earned wisdom, just waiting to be plucked.

Sid Mohasseb | Transformational and Motivational Speaker, and bestselling author of *You Are Not Them!: The Authentic Entrepreneur's Way*

BUSINESS SUCCESS SECRETS

ENTREPRENEURIAL THINKING THAT WORKS

Dr. Tamara L. Nall • Victor Agapov • Patrick Borlik
Trudy Bourgeois • Karen Cole • Denita R. Conway
Melanie Cook-McCant • Euran S. Daniels • Lawrence M. Drake II, Ph.D.
Rachel Dunbar, Ph.D. • Julian Frederick • Jennice Gist, DNP, CRNA
David Greene III, SMP, CPCC • Karen Marieke Heine
Tomeka B. Holyfield • Dawn M. Houle • Robert Merrill Jefferson
Rashi Arora Khosla • Lianne Lami, PE, CEM, CEA
Chef LaToya Larkin, MBA, CCE • Elisabete Miranda • Chukwuka C. Monye
Jessica Moseley • Nish Parikh • Lynn K. Petrazzuolo • Kimberly Rath
Dr. Angela D. Reddix • Ryan A. Rickert • Dr. Carrie Singer
Jonathan Sparks, Esq. • Solomon Thimothy
Theresa R. Williams-Harrison, MBA, PMP, CSM • Diedre L. Windsor • Pokin Yeung

Leaders
Press

Leaders
Press

Copyright © 2021 Dr. Tamara L. Nall

Published in the United States by Leaders Press.
www.leaderspress.com

ISBN 978-1-63735-052-2 (pbk)
ISBN 978-1-943386-92-5 (ebook)

SIMON &
SCHUSTER

Print Book Distributed by Simon & Schuster
1230 Avenue of the Americas
New York, NY 10020

Library of Congress Control Number: 2021904356

Contents

What Man Has Done, Man Can Do

Victor Agapov

Victor Agapov founded Wallo Brands LLC in 2013 to bring his invention to the market. Wallo Brands is comprised of two divisions: Wallo, which engineers, manufactures, and distributes commercial and residential construction products and Midwest Biotech Supply, which was established in 2017 as a contract research biotech division that provides a full scope of custom protein process services and high-quality protein products for biotech and pharmaceutical applications. The company is based in Madison, Wisconsin, and information can be found online at wallobrands.com.

Tell us about you as the owner/founder. What's your story that made you the entrepreneur you are today?

My story actually begins in the former Soviet Union, now Belarus, where I was born and lived until I immigrated to the United States at the age of twenty-three. Growing up in the USSR, my family had very little. I didn't get my first taste of Coca-Cola until the age of sixteen, and didn't get a driver's license until several years after my move to the United States. I attended college for a few years but my life of scarcity continued during my two years of mandatory service in the Russian military shortly after the fall of the USSR. Severely depleted by the upheaval, the military's resources were all but nonexistent.

My experiences with turmoil and scarcity in the former Soviet Union were, I think, some of my earliest lessons in entrepreneurship. With so little available in terms of means and resources, I was often forced to think creatively and practice resourcefulness in order to get what I needed. Such ingenuity has been critical in growing my company, even from the very first days when I created my first product to solve a construction issue in my own home.

I immigrated to the United States in 1996. As a young man in my early twenties, unable to speak English and with only a few hundred dollars to my name, my early days in the United States were little more than an exercise in survival. I took any odd job I could find, working in a lumber yard, acting as a security guard, and washing dishes in a restaurant. I was not afraid to work and was, in fact, grateful for any opportunity to earn an income and establish a life for myself.

During this time, I graduated from college and worked as a systems administrator for several companies and universities. After so many years of harboring no aspirations other than survival, I was hungry for a better life. With stable employment and a more substantial income, it finally seemed within my means to build exactly the life I wanted.

Years later, I was at last a homeowner and encountered a small problem while remodeling our basement. After the ceiling was drywalled, the building inspector informed me that we had to provide permanent access to all the HVAC air dampers concealed behind the drywall to be in compliance with the latest building codes. I wanted to use something aesthetically appealing as an access panel, preferably with a circular shape to match our speakers and other round fixtures, but when I browsed the stores I was unable to find the type of solution I was looking for. Determined to achieve the aesthetic I wanted, I designed and made my own round access panel.

In the midst of what could perhaps be described as an early midlife crisis, I channeled all of my untapped energy into cultivating my newly developed product into a full-blown business. Shortly after creating that first prototype, Wallo Brands was born.

I feel that my journey into entrepreneurship is reflected in the nineteenth-century proverb "what man has done, man can do." I don't consider myself special or believe there is anything exceptional about me. I don't think I have any unique talents or extraordinary abilities. I simply started. I felt that I could be successful in business, just as many other men before me had been successful, if I was just willing to invest the hard work and the time. Such is the case for anyone – if you are willing to put in the effort, you can also accomplish what I accomplished.

What have been the key factors to your success and why?

I owe my success in large part to luck, patience, and support from my family and friends. The key factor to my success, however, was simply my willingness to start without hesitation. From the moment I created that first prototype, I never hesitated in my decision to take it to the next level. Though I did thorough research on the development of and market for my product, I never second-guessed my decision to go into business in the first place. I didn't give consideration to reasons why I might fail. By pressing forward without pause, I was able to avoid the inclination to lose interest or change my mind, two mindsets that have derailed many a good idea.

Though establishing the business was easy in the beginning and things just seemed to fall into place, I continued to press on even when things became more challenging. With no background or education in marketing and business management, I had no idea how best to grow the business and, as a result, my sales were flat for a number of years. Instead of getting discouraged or assuming that this lack of growth meant there was no market for my product, I continued to believe in the merits of my creation and searched for ways to expand my reach. I did my own market research, took marketing classes, and started networking in an attempt to make connections that could get the product in front of other companies.

In my experience, the secret to success is to have unwavering confidence in your initial idea, to press forward with fearlessness, and to remain persistent in the face of challenges. You must overcome the impulse to second-guess or lose interest if you hope to even get your idea off the ground and you must be resourceful to overcome setbacks and disappointments. Anyone who can do these things can, in my opinion, be successful in business.

What has been your worst decision and how did you bounce back and still get to where you are today? How did this failure prepare you for your current success?

In the first year of my business, I botched a big client negotiation and lost the opportunity to gain a significant new customer. Ahead of the negotiations, I had already painted a picture of the outcome in my mind, but their initial offering did not match my expectations. I was initially unwilling to compromise on my ideal outcome and by the time I was ready to make some sacrifices nearly six months later, the key decision maker had left the company and was no longer interested in pursuing a relationship. I came away none the richer for my time investment but did learn a significant lesson about the proper approach to negotiations. From that day forward, I adopted the mantra "a bird in the hand is worth two in the bush" and realized that I would need to be willing to make some concessions if I ever hoped to establish relationships with larger clients.

In contrast, my conversations with Menards, one of the largest players in the home and garden space, included the appropriate amount of give and take to establish a mutually beneficial relationship. The Menards team were tough negotiators that put forward a very low-ball initial offer. I rejected their first offer but countered with the best possible price I was able to accommodate. They accepted my counteroffer, and today my products are sold in Menards stores across the country. To reach a successful outcome, I had to be willing to compromise but also brave enough to stand my ground on the non-negotiables, say no, and risk losing the opportunity. In the end, I found that striking a balance between concession and resolution is crucial to effective negotiation.

What has been your best decision and why?

My wisest move in the early days of my business was to trust my instincts and remain persistent in my efforts to grow my customer base and market my product. Rolling out a completely new-to-the-customer product essentially meant creating an entirely new market space. With a low-price product and thin margins, there was no room to hire broker representatives to put the product in front of potential customers, so I was on my own in creating a market space.

To establish a customer base, I needed to leverage social and traditional media to spread the word and build demand among potential customers. I had no inkling as to the "proper" way to accomplish this, so I simply tried multiple strategies and continued with the methods that produced results. I was constantly shipping out samples to potential customers and following up on social media. As these prospective clients tried the product and realized that it worked, I began to receive more and more positive feedback. Several small, local contractors became customers, and I began to develop a reputation as a trusted supplier in my local area and then nationally.

Though I built a sizeable customer base all across the United States and Canada, including some high profile customers, it still took nearly four years before I was able to break into my first retailer. Several years after my first rejected application, I was finally invited to a company's headquarters to demonstrate the product's effectiveness and superior aesthetic. Upon seeing what I had to offer, the buyer was interested and willing to give the product a try.

In the beginning, I could have decided that my lack of marketing expertise would make it impossible to sell my product. With no ability to leverage the assistance of brokers, I could have determined that I would never be able to grow my customer base. Instead, even with my broken English and a disability that causes me to stutter, I was able to create a marketing plan leveraging nothing more than my own instincts and trial and error, establish connections with prospective customers, and build a reputable brand. If I was able to accomplish this despite my limitations, I am convinced that anyone can do so.

What is an unusual habit you have as an entrepreneur that helps you succeed?

I am a bit of a contradiction in that, though I jumped into starting my company without hesitation, when confronted with a new idea or problem I prefer to act slowly and take a few days or even a few weeks to sleep on it. I learned the benefits of this approach in my work as a systems administrator. In managing IT systems, if you are delayed in addressing a problem the user will often find a solution themselves. In managing my own business, I often have similar experiences with my customers and employees. If I am unable to respond to an issue immediately, the customer or employee is often able to find the solution or answer on their own. I believe this demonstrates that problems are oftentimes not as daunting as they initially seem, which is why I like to slow down and create some space between myself and the situation. If you give yourself enough time and distance to gain some perspective, you can often find simple solutions to seemingly complicated situations.

With the knowledge and experience you have now, what would you have done differently if you were to start your entrepreneurial journey again?

If I were to start again, I would change my approach to introducing additional products to my offering. After the success of my first product rollout, I became overeager and overconfident in introducing my next couple of products. I didn't invest sufficient time in performing market research, and as a result I didn't take notice of the challenging competitive landscape and other issues that would inhibit my ability to sell the products. When I attempted to introduce a few products on Amazon, they didn't perform as expected and were eventually taken down. From this failure, I learned that no matter how successful you have been in the past, you must remain diligent and conscientious. It is of critical importance to do your research and get a firm grasp of the current environment before stepping into a new venture.

What do you do when you feel demotivated and overwhelmed?

I believe life always has ups and downs, so when I feel like everything is working against me, I try not to fight it. Instead of resisting the hard times and dwelling on the added stress, on any given day I simply focus on completing the tasks before me. To do this most effectively, I break down whatever is on my plate into small, simple steps and do them one by one. By breaking my to-do list into smaller pieces, I prevent myself from worrying about every task all at once. I think of this exercise as something like mental yoga – it calms me down and eliminates any negative thoughts so I am able to get the work done.

Discuss a crisis situation (2008 depression, 9/11, COVID-19) that you/your company were in and how you overcame it.

COVID-19 is the first real crisis our company has faced. Fortunately, we did not suffer as severely as many other suppliers. Our construction products division has even experienced a moderate increase in sales during the pandemic. That said, amid the shutdowns it became nearly impossible to expand our reach to new customers. We eventually stopped reaching out to prospective customers altogether, as many of them had a large portion of their workforce on furlough and no one was available to respond to our inquiries. Even as the economy reopens, we are struggling to make connections as these companies are too overwhelmed with their own internal issues to make time for us. In light of these challenges, we have simply had to maintain our patience and accept that situations such as this are out of our control.

What is that one secret to your business success that would be helpful to current and aspiring entrepreneurs?

Create something of real value that fills a void or satisfies some need for your customers. Don't get ahead of yourself – be diligent and do lots of research, planning, and testing before jumping in.

What's your advice for entrepreneurs who are still struggling?

Patience is king, especially in product development and marketing. The sales cycle can take years to complete and sometimes the wait feels unbearable. If you maintain faith in your product, the payoff will eventually come.

Did you have to deal with tough barriers to entry?

Yes, barriers to entry are very typical when trying to break into a market as a young company with a new product or service. To overcome those barriers, I simply focused on gradually building a good reputation, which I then leveraged to pursue larger and larger customers. Once you've gotten your foot in the door with a few influential clients, never be afraid to drop those big names, even if you worked with them minimally or their orders were relatively small.

With my disability, I faced an additional barrier to entering the market and growing my business. For years I hated interacting with people over the phone or in person. The entire concept of networking was made more difficult because of my aversion to speaking with others. At one point, a business associate pointed out that I was hiding from talking to customers because of my disability, making it much harder on myself to run my business. He suggested that I pursue the Disability-Owned Business Enterprise (DOBE) certification and obtaining that designation has opened doors and emboldened me to verbally interact with customers more freely.

A Thirst for Learning

Patrick Borlik, CPT, CH, LMT

Patrick Borlik is a certified personal trainer, boxing coach, licensed massage therapist, nutritional consultant, and certified hypnotist with over ten years of experience. He launched Pillar2Wellness to help people understand and achieve their true mind and body potential. Pillar2Wellness is a wellness business which utilizes multiple modalities and angles to develop programs that help clients progress both mentally and physically. The company is based in Mt. Airy, Maryland, and information can be found online at www.facebook.com/ Pillar2Wellness.

Tell us about you as the owner/founder. What's your story that made you the entrepreneur you are today?

I took a strong interest in fitness and the gym lifestyle at a very young age. I began working out at ten-years-old and had absolutely no idea what I should be doing. I began by mimicking what I saw in the gym and learning as much as I could through training during high school sports. Improper technique plagued me with severe back pain throughout high school. I went to several doctors and chiropractors and was eventually told to schedule an appointment with an orthopedic surgeon.

Despite the discomfort I continued to weight lift as heavy as possible with what now seems as little knowledge as possible. Strength training intrigued me, so after high school I began studying to become a personal trainer. After learning basic principles on posture and how it affects the body's ability to handle stress, my back pain began to disappear. It amazed me how simple it actually was to resolve after I had spent years in pain. I began my career in wellness at the age of nineteen when I landed my first job as a personal trainer. I worked in a few different gyms and was amazed by how much of a difference I could make in my clients' lives with very little experience.

It was also quite different, being just out of high school and instructing current teachers what to do. It was a whole new dynamic for me. It was thrilling and I liked it! While I saw a very high rate of success with fitness and nutrition only, I saw gaps where some principles didn't seem to work on certain people. Certain clients experienced limitations during exercise due to fascial restrictions. Their issues led me to attend massage school to become a massage therapist three years later. After learning an entirely new outlook and mode of treatment, I began using a combination of massage and personal training to build my own business. This helped me achieve an even higher rate of success and client retention.

My next goal was to specialize in a sport so I could develop training programs specific to certain athletes. I began studying and learning boxing at a local boxing club. They soon hired me, and I trained for eighteen months before competing in, and winning, my first boxing tournament. Boxing provided me and my clients an amazing workout as well as lasting stress reduction. My training seemed to help in creating such great fitness and wellness programs, but I still felt there was something missing within wellness.

I knew there was great potential within the mind; I just never knew how to address it. Working myself to absolute fatigue provided great stress reduction, but only for so long. I knew I still had more I could be doing in order to reach my full potential. I would often think, "If a subconscious perception is causing me stress, is fatiguing myself addressing the problem or the symptom?" I have seen many people use exercise, easily one of the greatest medicines ever utilized, and end up causing damage to their bodies due to lack of knowledge and excessive training.

In my experience, this could be because they are addressing a discrepancy of mind by using a physical modality. This led me to hypnosis. Learning how to address certain false perceptions of the subconscious mind is almost never addressed in fitness protocols. After training for boxing over an eighteen-month period and using hypnosis to increase my self-confidence and overcome fears, I won my first boxing tournament, going 4-0. Using the modalities of fitness, nutrition, massage, boxing, and hypnosis, I created Pillar2Wellness.

What have been the key factors to your success and why?

I am a lifelong learner. One major factor that has helped me progress is my desire to continuously improve the quality and effectiveness of my product. I saw people make incredible progress by adding exercise into their lives, but I knew there was more. I have continued to increase my knowledge base and skill set by learning more modalities. Boxing, massage, hypnosis, nutrition, and fitness training have all helped me develop the skill set to make a wellness program unique. I continue to learn more on each subject as well as have the openness to look for even more potentially effective skills.

What has been your worst decision and how did you bounce back and still get to where you are today? How did this failure prepare you for your current success?

My worst business decision was in 2015 when I decided to leave my existing business and move to California for a fresh start. This all began when I went to California on vacation and received offers from multiple gyms in the area. After relocating, I realized it was not the landscape I was looking for. Six months later I left California and came back East. By that time, most of my previous business had moved on and I felt like I was starting all over again. Starting all over allowed me the time and energy to experiment on myself and others with different fitness and massage protocols to learn more through trial and error.

What has been your best decision and why?

My best decision was taking a leap of faith by combining all of my experience and knowledge to create Pillar2Wellness. I had been an entrepreneur for years, keeping a relationship with some fitness facilities as an independent contractor. It was not until I relied solely on myself and created my own business that I saw significantly more potential.

What is an unusual habit you have as an entrepreneur that helps you succeed?

One unusual habit that has helped me succeed is my total abstinence from alcohol. I do not believe this to be some universal rule that can benefit everyone, but it has worked for me. In my experience, not drinking alcohol has granted me increased clarity and self-awareness. I began drinking at a young age and developed an emotional reliance on it. I was using it to mask feelings that I was trying to suppress, and it led to an unhealthy relationship with alcohol. I stopped drinking before I was even legally able to drink and I am very grateful for that decision. It has allowed me to stay focused and become a much more effective and successful entrepreneur.

With the knowledge and experience you have now, what would you have done differently if you were to start your entrepreneurial journey again?

If I had a chance to begin my entrepreneurial journey over again, I would start by spending more time studying hypnosis and massage therapy. I've found that expanding my base of knowledge has allowed me to carry new information and insight into multiple aspects of my profession. When I first entered my profession, I only focused on fitness and was unsure of what else, if anything, I needed to study. I now know that an ever-changing career such as fitness requires some level of flexibility and innovation to stay effective and ahead of the curve.

For instance, people are frequently given different advice or varying diagnoses from different doctors because the body is so complicated, and perspectives are so different. The more points of reference you have the better your understanding and ability to create new and effective change. This is how I eventually moved on to incorporate boxing, massage therapy, and hypnosis into my practice, which led to a stronger, more well-rounded approach.

What do you do when you feel demotivated and overwhelmed?

There will always be ups and downs in business and life. When I do feel demotivated, I notice that there may be some imbalance with the way I have spent my time lately. Typically, it is either not spending enough time with my close friends and family or that I am not staying on top of my business goals. While I don't live to work, not being productive can be mentally detrimental. There is a balance between the two that varies from person to person, and that balance can be achieved through a combination of mindfulness, hypnosis, taking a few days off to refocus, and fitness. It may take some trial and error but finding the balance that works for you can increase self-awareness regarding your mental state.

Discuss a crisis situation (2008 depression, 9/11, COVID-19) that you/your company were in and how you overcame it.

COVID-19 has been the biggest crisis Pillar2Wellness has faced, due to the temporary shutdown of fitness/wellness facilities. One-hundred percent of my business was impacted immediately. Within a week I was able to pivot most of my business and continue offering virtual services. I started an online fitness subscription service and I was able to offer hypnosis sessions via live video and pre-recorded tapes. Thankfully that pivot allowed me to continue with eighty percent of my business. Now that everything has been partially opened, I have also added outdoor training classes, massage, and hypnosis while maintaining social distancing guidelines. It has led me down the path of establishing a semi outdoor wellness space that could adhere to safety guidelines while being very cost effective. Both my flexibility and creativity have allowed me to get through the pandemic and even benefit in some ways.

What is that one secret to your business success that would be helpful to current and aspiring entrepreneurs?

Entrepreneurs in the service industry, especially those in fitness, need to have the desire and creativity to adapt. Whether it is using multiple modalities with a client or having flexibility in your own business to adapt to changes, you must put yourself in your client's shoes and view your product within their potentially limited knowledge of the field.

Additionally, you need to decide what success means for you. I never want to be an absentee business owner; I get a lot of satisfaction out of the work I do. For me, success means working twenty or so hours per week along with offering a lot of benefit to my clients and employees while providing adequate income, security, and freedom. You can never expect to have a one-hundred percent success or retention rate, but you should always aim to increase it. Having a unique and effective product makes selling and retaining a client base much easier.

What's your advice for entrepreneurs who are still struggling?

All people experience ups and downs in business and in life. One thing to remember is to persevere and focus on self-care. Keeping yourself healthy, calm, and rested will keep you in the game. You will be much better suited to handle stress if you spend time focusing on yourself. I frequently see this firsthand as the stress relieving benefits of exercise, massage, and hypnosis are a large part of my business. It is common for those in the wellness industry to focus more on taking care of others than themselves. It may be what makes them effective and compassionate workers, but it will also take a toll and be detrimental in the long run.

What is the best investment you've made and why? (Can be an investment of money, time, or energy.)

My best investment has been on myself. By spending time and energy on expanding my knowledge base and offering services that complement each other, I view the return on my investment to be exponential. Putting myself through massage school while not working for almost a year severely limited my income, but it has paid off in the long run. Trading billable time with clients for training in the boxing gym multiple times per week also cut back on my income during that time. Additionally, it has allowed me to expand my services and generate more revenue. Becoming a hypnotist was no different. Taking the time to learn each practice area has greatly expanded my ability to reach a wider variety of clientele. It was my constant thirst for learning that led me to see the long-term gain in investing in myself. I subscribe to a unique vision that is unmatched and the sky's the limit for me.

The Courage to Fly on Your Own

Trudy Bourgeois

Trudy Bourgeois is the founder and CEO of The Center for Workforce Excellence, a global leadership development company dedicated to developing inclusive leaders who create inclusive cultures to drive better business results. The company is located in Prosper, Texas, and information can be found online at WorkforceExcellence.com.

Tell us about you as the owner/founder. What's your story that made you the entrepreneur you are today?

I never thought that becoming an entrepreneur was even possible for a black woman born into segregation and growing up during the Jim Crow era. I wanted to become president of a company and people would tell me to consider attending a trade school instead. I wanted a seat at the table, to be a senior level manager, and to impact strategy and culture.

There are several defining experiences that caused me to lean into becoming an entrepreneur. I began working at a larger consumer goods organization and quickly learned that a black woman was not welcomed into the good old boy network and would not automatically receive support. I was interested in moving beyond an individual contributor into a people manager position. When I asked my manager for help for career advancement, he informed me that he was currently grooming two Caucasian males. Maybe after he was done with getting them to the point that he wanted them to be, then he would give some consideration to my request.

The leaders that were "at the table" with power and authority were all Caucasian males. I began to act like them but soon I did not like what I saw in the mirror. This dissatisfaction with my reflection motivated me to build my own models for success since there were no books available at that time. I spent two years researching, studying, and questioning how I could serve as a catalyst for meaningful changes in the workplace. I did not want other women to experience what I had experienced. I told myself, "Trudy, if things are going to change, then you need to embrace personal empowerment, personal responsibility, and personal accountability." My success was born out of this recognition to become the architect of my own career. I am not saying that you can do it all by yourself. I am saying that you have to step out and create your own opportunities with the help of others.

It was a scary, intimidating, overwhelming, yet inspiring time in my life. I knew that I wanted my life to be different but what would I do and how would I do it?

What would a perfect day look like, a perfect week, a perfect month, a perfect quarter? What is the story that I wanted to share at the end of the year? I knew that I loved helping people, making changes happen, researching, and collaborating on projects. How could I leverage this passion and my capabilities to form a business? I wanted to be a part of creating a business world in America where everyone would be welcomed and included – not belittled or invisible. Inclusion and diversity management did not exist then. As I reflect on what made me who I am today, I would say that there were at least three events that influenced my decision to begin a company on my own. I will share those with you here.

The first defining moment that advanced my decision to leave corporate America came when my husband and I attended the Kentucky Derby with my colleagues at a company-sponsored event. The company hired a bus for a private party of fifty people and my husband and I were the only two black people included. That morning we visited the museum and a country club, and then attended the Derby. Once we finished gift shopping, the group was to meet at the bus which was scheduled to leave at 3:00 pm. My husband and I arrived at the designated location at 2:45 pm, but upon arrival, we did not see the bus. I thought, since the Coliseum is round, maybe I made a mistake with the location, so we hustled to the other side. We still could not find the bus. I called the meeting coordinator and, after a series of conversations with her and the SVP, we all realized the obvious: the bus left without us. We just stood there feeling invisible and rejected. That no one considered our absence as an issue made us feel excluded, belittled, and rejected. I could not help but to think of how wrong the entire situation was. It was at that moment that the shift began in my mind to consider other career opportunities.

Another defining moment happened when I was working from home and my daughter had a Saturday volleyball tournament. The many responsibilities and pressures of work caused me to be late. My daughter said to me, "I do not want to be like you when I grow up." She spoke truth to me and it stung. We were living in Plano, Texas, but we had moved eight times for my corporate career and none of those locations were near family. My non-stop drive to do better was taking a toll on my family and my daughter's statement brought that to my attention. After much reflection, I was too scared to venture out on my own and thought I would just find a job in Dallas. My husband said, "No, hang a shingle and do what you want to do in your heart." With that advice and support, the business was born. We have been busy every day since then.

The last example that stands out in my mind as a defining moment is when colleagues heard the news that I was on the market. I got a call from James White, who was a VP of Sales at Purina Pet Care at the time. We had met a year before and had become reciprocal mentors. James offered to hire me to work for him. I was done with Corporate America and politely turned down the offer. He then asked if he could hire me as a consultant to help build up six future female leaders located across the country. Quite the ambitious and optimistic thinker, James thought that all six could get to the C-Suite. This is how the coaching pillar of my business began. I am happy to say that five of the six made it. God used James to allow me to build a track record as an executive coach. Based upon this success, referrals started pouring in. It was here that the company expanded!

What have been the key factors to your success and why?

A key factor to my success has been having a level of humility. I did not know what I did not know. I had been in a rotational cycle for a vice president position, so I knew how corporate worked. It was just a matter of me having to relearn, study, and have the discipline to develop models and new approaches on my own. It was important for me to have confidence that they would work. Since I had never done any of this before, there were no proof points for me to use as a litmus test. There were so many long hours that I spent researching everything I possibly could to assist me in my journey. My first book, *The Corner Office*, was born from the fact there was nothing written about new approaches and models before. I had a willingness to learn, to stay focused on the needs of the consumer/customer, and to be practical. This was not a "pie in the sky" belief. I needed confidence to develop innovative solutions and to not go the traditional route. That does not work. The proof is in the pudding – the clients that I worked with had inclusive leaders.

What has been your worst decision and how did you bounce back and still get to where you are today? How did this failure prepare you for your current success?

A bad decision was putting myself at the center of everything. I ran the entire business and although I had put together contracts worth billions of dollars before, it was different once I was on my own. I learned that I could not keep working fifteen hours a day and do it all. Slowly but surely, I started trusting people that shared my values and beliefs and added those people to my team around the world. To invest in client development, I took classes at Cornell and Dartmouth because I had a thirst for knowledge. Those classes were helpful in acquiring practices and approaches that would be successful. One of the things I realized late in the game is that I did not have a mindset to scale immediately and build an infrastructure that would allow me to touch more people. It was necessary for me to study other businesses to see what their strategies were with supplier diversity and it took me close to ten years to get to where I wanted to be.

What has been your best decision and why?

My best decision has been hiring Karen, my executive assistant. She is my chief of staff and a project manager. She is also a trusted advisor and enables me to focus on the business development that was critical to growth. I chose her based on her character components, not just productivity. I trust her implicitly to the point that I would leave my children with her. I know how honest and trustworthy she is in every facet. I have made mistakes in the past by hiring on skill set and not on passion or character. Karen's passion is customer focused while mine is customer obsessed. Karen did not have all of the experience of being a Chief of Staff at first, but she is a quick learner and so trustworthy. You cannot put a price on being able to trust someone with everything that you build. Having Karen on my team allows me to focus on process improvement and scaling to bring in other clients. Karen focuses on other processes and we can collaborate. I am more than blessed to have her!

What is an unusual habit you have as an entrepreneur that helps you succeed?

A habit I have is that I cannot start my day without reflection time. I gather my thoughts (usually while in the shower) and then have my quiet time. I did not realize the value of this until much later. It will soon be twenty years since this journey began. Now that I think about this a bit more, I would not say that it is unusual. Rather, it is just the routine that I have which might be different from what others choose to do. I begin my mornings with prayer and then I take a shower. This is where all of my thoughts come to me. It is like a deposit of creative energy that I take while I am in my quiet space and then I can take those thoughts with me to the office with a pioneering mindset. Somehow, I get the confidence and creative energy to keep jumping the "S curve," knowing that what goes up, must come down. We have to continue to be innovative in the way that we serve others. While I am in the shower,

I wash away my doubts, letting go of negative energy and buying into thinking that has limitless possibilities. We all have an "itty bitty committee" of doubt that can choke the life out of our businesses if we let them. While I reflect in the shower, I actually wash away that doubt.

With the knowledge and experience you have now, what would you have done differently if you were to start your entrepreneurial journey again?

We all have to answer the question about what we would do differently based upon the knowledge that we now have. I think that I would go to a deeper level of self-discovery while still in the corporate world. I would conduct more interviews and build more relationships. Instead of doing this the first time, I had the mindset to keep my head down and do good work. Building relationships is absolutely critical for success and this time around, I would know who my first five clients were going to be before I started. You must know your value and impact and be willing to serve as a sponsor. I would not put myself at the center of the business, but instead would hire consultants and delegate to their expertise. It is important to think about scaling from Day One. I am far more intentional about building an infrastructure that can be replicated. When you are doing everything by yourself at first, you have it all in your head rather than on paper. If someone comes to my company and sees what is on paper, they will know the heart of my business and why I do things this way.

Based upon the lessons I have learned, I would also automate my processes at the onset.

What do you do when you feel demotivated and overwhelmed?

I have not ever felt demotivated, but I have been overwhelmed. I think about what I want to do, and I find the courage to say no when necessary. It is not just about making money. I reach out to others who have expertise that I can draw upon and utilize other resources such as contract writers and technical experts on digital platforms. As an entrepreneur, I did not appreciate that I should have thought about scaling from the beginning. It was so overwhelming. What I realized is that I needed a plan of action that allowed for accomplishing goals and experience satisfaction versus emotions of stress and feeling overwhelmed.

Discuss a crisis situation (2008 depression, 9/11, COVID-19) that you/your company were in and how you overcame it.

I started my business in August 2001 and then 9/11 hit. We weathered the depression in 2008 and are now living during the COVID-19 times. We stayed clear about our values and the impact we could make. People are the greatest asset of any organization. Crisis is coming. We protected our investment, tightened our budget, and our track record speaks for itself. The team, which includes my husband, Mike, and my entire family, supported me in every decision. I am working from home more due to COVID-19 restrictions. I love working from home, but am now focused on making sure that I am more intentional about balancing the hours that I dedicate to work. It is easy to come into my home office at any time of the day or night.

What is that one secret to your business success that would be helpful to current and aspiring entrepreneurs?

The one secret revolves around having a 'centric' focus on various stakeholders. I would encourage that a customer-centric model be the focus. Always think about the value that you are adding. Use resources and find solutions. Then an employee-centric model should be followed. Do not do this alone. You need a good team. After that, be future-centric. What comes next? Study trends in leadership and focus on agility. Understand the needs of the consumer/customer. Survey clients to determine their ideas so that you can plan ahead to meet their needs.

When you started your business did you have support? How did you handle the naysayers?

The decision involved my husband, children, and extended family, but there were definitely naysayers. Several of my brothers and sisters were naysayers, as they were concerned and openly expressed their feelings. They warned me about the risk of leaving the security of a "good job" that provided a six-figure income and lots of benefits and perks. My mother cried and my siblings asked what I was doing since it did not make sense to them.

Because entrepreneurship was new to me, I conducted informational interviews with successful women to cut my learning curve. I was introduced to two women (one black and one white) by a senior executive at a large consumer company and they both gave me interesting and shocking advice. The Caucasian woman said that I should focus on black women since the Caucasian women were not ready to advocate for a woman of color. The black woman said that she had been to the "school of hard knocks" and that I, too, needed to go through that process. Rather than assist, she said that I was asking for proprietary information. Both of these conversations were disappointing to me.

Did you have to deal with tough barriers to entry?

Yes, I dealt with barriers. For one thing, I was not a household name. I was fortunate to have made some friends like James White, whom I mentioned earlier. When I was in corporate America, I was always focused on keeping my head down and delivering exceptional results, so I did not make the connections that I should have. I wished that I had a better understanding of the importance of strategic relationships. I also experienced stereotypes from clients, which meant that I always had to be twice as good as my competition. Dealing with daily microaggressions has been a part of my experience from the very beginning. I met challenges in trying to collaborate with other vendors on big projects. On one occasion, an owner of another consulting company actually stole my IP and represented the models that I had created as his own. No matter what professional path that you pursue, barriers will always be a part of the experience. I just remind myself that I cannot control the barriers, but I can control how I respond to them. I try hard to use experiences with barriers as teachable moments to make myself smarter, stronger and more resilient.

Barriers to entry will not always be professional. Sometimes they will be personal, so you have to remind yourself why you do what you do. My son was born with Down Syndrome. Rearing him has helped me to see that I am resilient and strong. We all will have dark days and it will not be easy to be an entrepreneur. You have to know what you are made of and draw on your life experiences to convince yourself that you can keep on going. You have to constantly be reminded of your purpose and why you do what you do. I wake up every day fighting for equity and equality. One of the reasons I do this is because of my amazing bi-racial granddaughter who is a double minority: she is female, and she is mixed race. I have a deep-seated passion to do what God has given me to do and part of that is to make sure that the ones I love are not directly impacted by biases. Yes, there may be some indirect consequences from hatred that others spew, but I can do my part to fight for equity.

The Disaster Lady

Karen Cole, CBCP, CISA, CRISC, MBCI

Karen Cole is the cofounder and CEO of Assura, Inc., a woman-owned cybersecurity services company that believes in the democratization of cybersecurity. The mission of Assura, Inc. is to secure the future one client at a time because dreams can be stolen by hackers and other threat actors. The company is located in Richmond, Virginia, and information can be found online at www.assurainc.com.

Tell us about you as the owner/founder. What's your story that made you the entrepreneur you are today?

Most people will say that they got into cybersecurity because they like the technology. My motivation came at a much earlier age when I was the victim of horrible bullying. As I grew up, I worked with crime victims early in my career and really focused on the need to help those who had been hurt to recover and find their new strength to overcome victimization. As my career evolved and focused on technology, I saw that there were also victims of heinous cybercrimes that needed my help. My motivation in this industry has always been to protect others from cybercriminals; they are nothing more than another type of bully.

What have been the key factors to your success and why?

I think one of the key factors to my success was not feeling as though I had to follow the same path as everyone else. I am somewhat of a unicorn in my industry. There are very few female CEOs of technology companies in the United States and there are even fewer in the cybersecurity field. When I started my first business, I had a lot of people tell me they thought I would be better served working for a large company because it was a safer path. When my business started to succeed, those same people then told me that my company should do what everyone else was doing and be an IT service integrator – in other words, my company should be a jack of all trades and master of none.

While that would probably have increased the top line of the business more rapidly, the lack of specialization would mean that we were just like everyone else. And I don't want my business to be like any other – I want it to be unique and stand for something special. This stance was validated by professors in top business schools who told me that to be competitive in the global market, you need to be specialized. For fifteen years, my focus has been to have a company that is the very best at what it does – which, in our case, is cybersecurity. We are reaping the benefits of specialization by acquiring and maintaining a portfolio of fiercely loyal clients who reward us with a ninety-five percent retention rate.

What has been your worst decision and how did you bounce back and still get to where you are today? How did this failure prepare you for your current success?

I have made my fair share of mistakes. However, one of the biggest mistakes I made was with my first business. My business partner was a close friend and she was ten-years-older than me and wanted to start a business sooner than later. I had two-year-old twins at the time and wanted to wait a couple of years. I decided to ignore my gut instinct and move forward with creating a business when I was not ready. I was also more apt to be enticed into making that decision because I was fed up with the company I worked for at the time.

After we started the company, I began to see warning signs that I had made the wrong decision to go into business with this person. However, I kept ignoring the warning signs and having the uncomfortable conversations because I wanted to be a good friend. When I finally got the nerve to deal with the situation, the business was overleveraged and underwater. This led to a horrible business divorce and, in the end, we lost not only the business but our close friendship as well. I learned that it is never a good thing to avoid dealing with a bad situation. Now I always make sure to face difficult situations head-on and not run just because something is uncomfortable. In fact, I've begun to joke that I'm the queen of uncomfortable conversations.

What has been your best decision and why?

The best business decision was to convince my husband to join the new firm I created and become my partner in business as well as in life. He is in the same industry and I needed someone who had the passion and drive that matched mine to make a difference in the cybersecurity field. As two professional risk managers, we went into business together *in spite of* being married and not because of it. It also helps that I know where he lives in case he doesn't want to show up for work! All joking aside, we have worked together for fifteen years and he has been the best right-hand person I could have ever asked for. We spent a lot of time in the beginning carving out an operating model that ensured our private life did not bleed into our professional life. We are so good at it that most of our employees and clients forget we are married.

What is an unusual habit you have as an entrepreneur that helps you succeed?

Even though I am a technologist and lead a tech company, I still have handwritten to-do lists of everything that needs to be done; I update my lists each day. The practice of handwriting a to-do list helps me calm my thoughts while jogging my memory about what needs to be done. If I use an electronic tracking tool, I tend to get overwhelmed and demotivated. Sometimes old-school pen and paper just work better. We use electronic project plans, but the stuff I need to do ends up on one of my paper lists.

With the knowledge and experience you have now, what would you have done differently if you were to start your entrepreneurial journey again?

I would have planned for five times the amount of capital needed to launch the company so that I did not drain my retirement to bootstrap the company in the early days.

What do you do when you feel demotivated and overwhelmed?

I write a list of all of the things I need to do and then check them off one-by-one.

Discuss a crisis situation (2008 depression, 9/11, COVID-19) that you/your company were in and how you overcame it.

As a certified disaster and continuity planner, I have dealt with my fair share of disasters not only for my business, but for my company and its clients. However, COVID-19 presented an unusual convergence of risk events that required me to think differently about not only how I operate the business, but also how I take care of my employees and give back to the community. As such, I created the persona of The Disaster Lady after getting that title one time at a speaking event. It is a labor of love to help other businesses and organizations get professional disaster management and recovery advice on how to keep their businesses afloat during crises. The Disaster Lady is now a nationally recognized resource (www.thedisasterlady.com) where people can go to find the latest information on disasters, find up-to-date information, and ask questions of The Disaster Lady (and her supporting staff of planners) offers her services for free. It feels good to use my 20+ years of experience to help those that would otherwise not have a resource to count on.

What is that one secret to your business success that would be helpful to current and aspiring entrepreneurs?

I used to spend a lot of time comparing myself to others and thinking that they had it all figured out. The secret I discovered is that we are all struggling, and we are all making it together. The real difference in achieving growth and success are the people you surround yourself with and making sure that those people truly believe in your vision for the company. After I realized that, I spent more time building up my employees and less time worrying about everyone else. Not that I ignore my competition, but instead of being envious, they spur me and my company to be better, to innovate and provide a much better customer experience.

What's your advice for entrepreneurs who are still struggling?

I remind myself that the largest number of millionaires and the creation of some of the biggest businesses we know today came during the Great Depression. It is a testament to the fact that out of crisis, there can be opportunity. It is our job as entrepreneurs to identify the opportunity and make it work to our advantage.

How would you describe the culture of your company? Did you develop your company consciously or did it just happen?

If you ask any of my employees that have been with us for any length of time, they will say that our values grew out of what used to be called "Karenisms." These were common things that I would say in our team meetings. About five years ago, we went through a strategic planning activity to take our business to the next level of growth.

During that time, we had our business coach act as an outside facilitator to have our staff complete an exercise where they revamped our company's written set of core values. It was important that these were developed by the staff, and not something that was pushed on them by me. Nothing was sacred and they could create a whole new set of core values if they chose.

I stayed silent during the exercise as I did not want to influence the outcome. To my surprise, the staff listed almost all of the original "Karenisms" as the values they wanted to keep. And, fortunately, they came up with a few more. When prospective employees and clients look at our core values, we regularly get compliments on their directness and honesty. Here are the five core values for Assura:

1. Eat our own dog food (i.e., use the products we represent and follow the same advice we give clients).
2. No a**holes allowed.
3. Walk the talk.
4. Sweat the details.
5. Own the outcome.

Who Says You Can't?

Denita R. Conway

Denita R. Conway, FMP, is president and CEO of PROVEN Management, LLC. The company was established in 2008 with one mission in mind: transforming complex facility challenges into clear, all-around successes. PROVEN specializes in providing turnkey consulting services in program management, space planning, interior design, furniture procurement, change and move management, and facility help desk services. The company is located in Washington, D.C., and information can be found online at www.provenmgmt.com.

Tell us about you as the owner/founder. What's your story that made you the entrepreneur you are today?

It was never my intention to start a business. I was happy with my work as a contract move manager at the Pentagon, but I began to get frustrated with constantly being at the mercy of contract changes. I didn't always like the way myself and other contractors were treated. One day in a meeting, a colleague told me I did great work and had proven processes and a management style that were impeccable. It was then that I began to fully appreciate what I brought to the table, and I decided in that moment that it was time to stop being an employee and become an employer.

Though I formed PROVEN in 2008, I didn't truly start the business until 2011. In the interim, I continued working with the Pentagon as a consultant and set out to learn everything there was to know about leading a business. I also spent those three years building relationships and securing my mentor group of accountants, attorneys, and others so that I would be ready when I earned my first contract.

When my consulting contract with the Pentagon expired in 2011 and the time came to start PROVEN, the transition from contracting as an individual consultant to contracting as a firm was relatively smooth. Because I had spent years developing a trusted reputation within the government space, government clients were more than willing to partner with me through PROVEN. I obtained several government certifications, secured my first major contract, and hired my first six employees to fulfill the contract. After years of planning and hard work, PROVEN was finally off the ground.

Though securing clients was relatively simple, starting PROVEN was by no means easy and required discipline, commitment, and, especially in the early years, an enormous amount of sacrifice. As a result of my initial move from employee to business owner, my income plummeted from $150,000 to $50,000 and my kids and I became very accustomed to eating bologna sandwiches. On top of the pressure of trying to manage a fledgling company, I was a single mother to two daughters, ages fourteen and seventeen, in 2011. I had no money, marginal credit from mistakes I had made in college and a limited support system as both of my parents were deceased and I had no siblings. Stretched between raising my two kids and managing and growing my business, I barely slept for years and the concept of "self-care" all but disappeared from my life.

With the many pressures I was facing and my disadvantages, I had to be very deliberate about setting priorities. While I was fully committed to the success of my business, I also committed to my children that I would never miss a PTA meeting, a family dinner, or a dance competition. Meeting all of these commitments required a lot of discipline and some very firm boundaries, but in the end, it helped me maintain some balance in my life.

Given my experience, I think it is important for budding entrepreneurs to understand that the decision to start a business should never be made lightly. Ensure you are one-hundred percent committed – and willing to make some serious sacrifices – before taking the plunge. If you consider your decision carefully, go in with both eyes open, and devote your full effort to your business, entrepreneurship will be an incredibly fulfilling experience.

What have been the key factors to your success and why?

I am always learning. In the early days, I knew nothing about business ownership though I had a formal education in business from Temple University, so self-education was absolutely necessary. But even after thirteen years in business, I still believe in education and am constantly seeking out new knowledge and skills.

When I started the business, it was an incredibly humbling experience to learn how to be a successful business owner from many wise and prominent mentors. My mentorship strategy was to focus on three to four people I wanted to be like and could mimic. I would then study their entrepreneurial journey and seek out their advice, tailoring their approach and tips to what worked for me and my business. Beyond mentorship, I would intentionally attend business events and identify speakers who were clearly subject matter experts. Today, I regularly complete formal training programs from organizations like Goldman Sachs, studying subjects that are out of my comfort zone or beneficial to my business. Most important, I have learned that failure is part of entrepreneurship, and have used my mistakes to develop the wisdom I need to be an effective leader and businesswoman.

What has been your worst decision and how did you bounce back and still get to where you are today? How did this failure prepare you for your current success?

My biggest misstep as a new entrepreneur was being too risk averse, letting fear dictate my decisions. For years, I remained conservative and shied away from taking steps that would ultimately lead to my success. I was afraid to go after big contracts out of fear of rejection. I did not hire the best and brightest talent out of fears that I was not large enough or organized enough. I did not want to expand beyond my initial business, move management, into something greater. Perhaps my worst decision was my hesitance to hire my number two person out of fear that they would not lead the company as I wanted it to be led. Gradually, all that changed as I gained confidence in my aptitude as a business owner and was far more willing to push the business and myself out of our comfort zones. Today, I often look to some sage words from former Walt Disney CEO Bob Iger's book *The Ride of a Lifetime*, for wisdom on courage and risk-taking: "The foundation of risk-taking is courage and in ever changing, disrupted businesses, risk-taking is essential, innovation is vital and true innovation only occurs when people have courage." I strive to live these words in the leadership of my business, and I have come to find that you realize the biggest payoffs when you direct your business with courage and a willingness to boldly innovate.

What has been your best decision and why?

Without a doubt, my best decision was the decision to become an entrepreneur in the first place. I get immense satisfaction and fulfillment from delivering value and great service to my clients, and the joy that comes with hiring someone and giving them a better quality of life cannot be explained. I am immensely grateful for the opportunity to touch so many lives through my business.

What is an unusual habit you have as an entrepreneur that helps you succeed?

This may not be particularly unusual, but I try to study and adopt the habits of highly successful people. In the early years of the business, I would stay up twenty hours out of a day, rarely took vacations, and spent all my money reinvesting in the company. Today, I am up by 6 a.m. every day and read a book weekly.

I am constantly on the hunt for proven habits and character traits. I regularly mine publications like *Forbes* and *Inc.* for stories about prominent businesspeople and how they found success. I also read business biographies, study my competitors, and listen to the advice of great mentors. Though PROVEN is still a small business, I can study the fundamental philosophies and practices of business titans like Warren Buffet and find a few tools to add to my toolbox.

With the knowledge and experience you have now, what would you have done differently if you were to start your entrepreneurial journey again?

One important lesson in business ownership is that sometimes you have to be okay with saying no. As a new entrepreneur, it can be highly tempting to take on every opportunity that presents itself, but if you don't have a plan or the infrastructure to support that opportunity, it is often wiser to be selective and say no than to bite off more than you can chew and underperform.

If I could restart my entrepreneurial journey, I wish I would have been able to set better expectations with my initial clients. They wanted it all, every amenity that I had to offer. On one hand that's great. On the other hand, I wasn't prepared. I learned that you can only support so many of these clients at the same time, and as a result my team and I were stretched too thin trying to accommodate expectations that we did not have the resources to meet. Had I been better prepared, I would have been better positioned to meet everyone's needs and fully satisfy each client without overextending my team.

What do you do when you feel demotivated and overwhelmed?

When I have a daunting task or I feel overwhelmed by the number of items on my to-do list, I usually try to complete the small, simple tasks first to give myself a sense of accomplishment and build momentum toward tackling the larger tasks. Even something as simple as filing a paper can give me a sense of calm and accomplishment because with less clutter on my desk, I can focus more on the bigger tasks at hand. When you start with the little things, you can invest minimal time and effort and yet still look at your to-do list and see that it is, for instance, thirty percent complete already. Psychologically, that goes a long way in making you feel capable of completing your objectives.

To fend off loss of motivation due to disappointment or rejection, I avoid putting all of my eggs into one basket and always try to have multiple goals or opportunities. If you have multiple irons in the fire, when you experience rejection you can simply turn your attention to one of your other opportunities and focus your energy there. Disappointment is an everyday phenomenon when you are an entrepreneur, so it is important to find ways to maintain your focus and motivation in the face of failure.

Discuss a crisis situation (2008 depression, 9/11, COVID-19) that you/your company were in and how you overcame it.

The most severe crisis my company experienced was the 2013 government shutdown. At the time, I was a new business owner, new employer, and fairly new to government contracting, so I was wholly unprepared to handle the shutdown of contracts, delayed payments, and having to cut my own pay and furlough employees. It was an extremely stressful time that slowed down the company's progress, and I knew I would have to think strategically to get through it. To make the best of the downtime, I continued to reach out to government agencies that were still operating to try to build relationships. I also worked with my remaining employees to rethink our processes and offered additional training opportunities. The fear surrounding this experience taught me that I needed to expand my client base and even venture beyond the government space, so I began to market to other federal agencies, added some commercial clientele, and began working nationally as opposed to just regionally.

My experience with the shutdown also prepared me to address the challenges presented by the COVID-19 pandemic. I was able to avoid layoffs through the entire pandemic and, as with the shutdown, was able to find constructive uses for the downtime created by the lockdowns. I again encouraged my team to pursue additional training opportunities offered by the Small Business Administration (SBA) and continued to meet with my team regularly to discuss strategy and maintain a sense of comradery. As a result of these efforts, we have been primed to hit the ground running as the economy begins to open up and business returns to a normal pace.

What is that one secret to your business success that would be helpful to current and aspiring entrepreneurs?

The secret to my success has been confidence in myself, backed by knowledge and perseverance.

How would you describe the culture of your company? Did you develop your company consciously or did it just happen?

The PROVEN company culture can be summed up with the word "fairness." In my experience, if I treat my employees with fairness and respect, they will be far more likely to give the same back to me. If we treat our clients fairly by providing excellent customer service and approaching our work with integrity, we will establish trust and our clients will be more interested in a long-lasting relationship. My mother used to say that in every situation, there are three possible choices – the good one, the bad one, and the right one. I lead my life by that philosophy, and it has become the cornerstone of the PROVEN corporate culture. We believe that by standing on what is right, regardless of the short-term ramifications, we will always come out ahead in the end.

The PROVEN culture was something that I very much developed consciously. From the beginning, I wanted to model our company's ethics on the relationship between myself and my girls – a ride or die partnership where we look out for one another, work hard for one another, and celebrate big together. As such, I don't micromanage and I treat each member of my team as though they are responsible for themselves. I expect one-hundred percent from them but also respect that family should be their number one priority. I support my team and they support each other in both their professional and personal endeavors. This culture is well-embraced by my team because they appreciate the environment of fairness, mutual respect, and support.

When you started your business did you have support? How did you handle the naysayers?

To put it plainly, I probably should have been voted "Most Likely *Not* to Succeed" in high school. I was a C student at best, with a spicy personality and a moderate case of Only Child Syndrome. This guaranteed me a few doubters and naysayers as I began to experience success. Because I believe in working quietly and producing loudly, I didn't tell many people that I planned to go out on my own and didn't publicize my early successes, so I avoided a lot of commentary from others early on. When I finally did share my step into entrepreneurship with someone, she told me my business would not last five years. Her assessment, I believe, was based on my lack of experience and leadership skills in that moment, not on a forecast of the businesswoman I would become. As more and more people in my circle learned of my successes, others began to share doubts as well, not necessarily because they intentionally wished to hurt me, but because their judgment was clouded by jealousy or apprehension.

I try to approach this kind of negativity empathetically, because it helps me to see that a person's naysaying is not necessarily an indictment of me as a person.

From ADD to Harvard

Melanie Cook-McCant

Melanie Cook-McCant is the CEO of Veritas Management Group, Inc. (VMG), a professional services company founded in 2016 which provides consulting services to government and commercial customers. The company focuses on public health, business process improvement, data management, communications, and IT services. It is one-hundred percent woman- and minority-owned. VMG is based in Alpharetta, Georgia, and information can be found online at veritasmanagementgroup.com.

Tell us about you as the owner/founder. What's your story that made you the entrepreneur you are today?

If you had peered at my life from the outside when I was a child, you would not have guessed that I would become a successful entrepreneur. When I was a child, I experienced difficulty completing my schoolwork. My peers seemed to breeze through their work. Undiagnosed ADD and dyslexia inhibited me from reading and comprehending the material. Even if the teachers had known about my learning disabilities, they lacked the knowledge and resources necessary to actually help.

By the end of my first year of school, I was officially "behind" in reading and math, and I flunked first grade. The school told my parents that I could progress to second grade only if I worked with a tutor over the summer and improved my reading and math skills. I vividly remember working with the tutor while my sisters and other friends went to Girl Scout camp and enjoyed their summer. I resented having to go to a tutor every day. I always wondered why I could not be like the other kids. Why couldn't I read and do math? Why was I the only one that was being punished by having to go to a tutor? In addition to my resentment, I was frustrated with my inability to learn. But I knew that the only way to progress to the second grade was to find a way to learn how to read. So, I did. I made myself find a way to make it work. I am not sure how I learned how to read. I think I memorized sounds and imitated what I heard when other people read.

That experience set the pattern for the rest of my life: one of seeing challenges not as obstacles that could keep me from succeeding, but as opportunities to find unique solutions and move forward.

To help me seize the opportunities that knowing how to read well might give me, my father made me read out loud at every chance, in Sunday school, every sign we came across – every billboard, street name, and storefront placard – was another chance for me to practice my skill. Despite my early struggles, I became a strong reader. Over time, I fell in love with reading. My father was trying to teach me how to read, but he also taught me to love speaking in public.

My mother sensed early in my life that I was destined to start my own business. It was less that she could sense my unrefined business instincts, and more that she could not see me working for someone else for very long. She thought my temperament would be best suited to be a boss instead of taking orders from someone else. When I was young, she told me that I would never work harder for anyone than I would work for myself. In the same way that my father helped me learn to read, my mother began to shape my young mind with business acumen. She dispensed a steady stream of advice and encouragement, planting tiny seeds of knowledge as we went about our daily lives.

On one family vacation, our room contained an autobiography of the hotel's founder, J.W. Marriott. I laughed at the apparent conceit and asked, "Who would want to read this?" My mother turned to me and said, "You should. If you want to be a business owner someday, you need to read about how other people have become successful."

When I was in high school, Reginald Lewis – who later became the first African-American to build a billion-dollar company – executed his first leveraged buyout. The company he purchased was the McCall Pattern Company, which sold sewing patterns. My mother had taught me to sew, and I loved it. When we saw the news story about the buyout, my mother turned to me and asked, "Melanie, if you were in that position, how would your background in sewing have helped you close the transaction?"

My parents' efforts caused me to believe that there was a good chance I would end up with a career in business. For my undergraduate, though, I pursued a degree in English from Spelman College, where I graduated with honors. My plan was to pursue a career in journalism.

Prior to graduating, I decided to forego a career in journalism in favor of going to law school. My mother became ill while I was still in college, and she died before I filled out my law school applications. To escape the pain of being at home, I began looking at out-of-state schools. The president of my college had gone to Harvard for graduate school and encouraged me to apply. I knew that if I wanted to have a shot at Harvard's competitive admissions process, I would have to understand precisely what the committee was looking for and strongly demonstrate that on my application. I found that above all, Harvard was looking for one thing: leaders. I leaned hard on my high LSAT score, an extensive history in leadership positions, and strong public service experience, and was admitted to Harvard Law School.

Going to law school set me down a path in law, Wall Street, and government contracting – a career full of learning, knowledge, and growth. It was still many years before I would start my own business. But each new position I took gave me another tool that I could eventually use to start my own company.

On September 11, 2001, I was working in New York City. In a day, the world changed. I wanted to get out of New York, and I did not want to face anything like that ever again. With no plan for my future, I returned home to Atlanta. Soon after, a contact from DC asked me to consult on a business he was launching in Atlanta. The initial three-month contract turned into fourteen years. During that time, my role within the company changed from being a consultant to a client to a sales and account manager, giving me a chance to learn every side of the intricacies of government contracting.

Over the years, I contemplated transitioning into my own business many times. But circumstances always pointed me in a different direction. In retrospect, I believe that God was protecting me, leading me toward where I am today in His perfect timing.

When I finally struck out on my own in 2016, I had the expertise and the experience to build my own business. From my parents gently prodding in the right direction to my professors imparting their own knowledge to my extensive work with government, businesses, and law firms, the pieces of the puzzle had all finally fallen into place.

After a difficult first year, my business has thrived. We have grown from just me and one other employee to thirty-two employees across three states. It was an overnight success that took decades of turning obstacles into opportunities. Because of those experiences, the understanding that came from them, and my own integrity and faith, I was able to grow VMG into the company it is today.

What have been the key factors to your success and why?

As a child with undiagnosed ADD and dyslexia, I could have easily fallen through the cracks. My learning disabilities damaged my self-esteem. I believed I was not smart and did not think I could achieve like my peers and older sisters. The support of my parents was the earliest key to my success. My parents had frequent meetings with my teachers and principals, pushing them to make sure I had the help I needed. At home, my parents tutored me, and I was encouraged to read constantly, write book reports, participate in public speaking contests, Girl Scouts, 4-H, Future Business Leaders of America, and every youth activity at church. The power of my parents was the first and most powerful key to my success.

The strengths that I developed due to ADD and dyslexia laid the foundation for my success. Having to work hard and figure things out gave me resilience and an ability to solve problems that has perpetually come into play throughout my life.

My faith has also impacted and shaped me every step of the way. It set the tone for the kind of person I wanted to be and the way I wanted to show up in the world. Integrity was at the forefront of every decision I made.

Together, these three things – my family, my faith, and my perseverance – helped me open doors, take chances, and find my path to success.

What has been your worst decision and how did you bounce back and still get to where you are today? How did this failure prepare you for your current success?

As an undergrad, I knew that I wanted to start my own company. My mother encouraged me to pursue my MBA to get a foundation in business. As I glanced over the courses I would need to take, I saw *calculus*. The mere sight of the word induced mental paralysis. My brain flashed back to when I was a child, and how dyslexia made me unable to make sense of simple equations.

I panicked and decided business school was not for me. I did not give up, though. If I was not going to go to business school, I knew I had to learn business skills and strategies somewhere else.

After law school, I worked for the Securities and Exchange Commission, where I learned a great deal about finance. Later, I worked as a senior policy advisor to the secretary of commerce, where I learned another side of business: government contracting. Finally, in my position at a small investment bank in New York, I learned the third side of business – the entrepreneurial aspect. I was inspired by how the founder and CEO of the investment bank leveraged his college basketball career and MBA into becoming one of the top investment bankers in the country.

What has been your best decision and why?

Working on President Clinton's re-election campaign was the beginning of my journey into federal contracting, which provided the foundation for my business.

What is an unusual habit you have as an entrepreneur that helps you succeed?

I use the power of visualization to focus and to combat ADD. So, at the start of every day, I form a visual picture in my mind for what the day will look like. I picture what every event, conversation, and meeting will look like, even how I will react when things go wrong, and how the day will build around it. This process and rational visualization reinforce my unstoppable attitude and combat the negative thinking associated with my ADD and dyslexia.

With the knowledge and experience you have now, what would you have done differently if you were to start your entrepreneurial journey again?

I would have outsourced jobs earlier. I spent too much time trying to do every position in my business. But as the CEO, I need to delegate tasks and free up my time to do the work to grow my business.

What do you do when you feel demotivated and overwhelmed?

I reflect on where I started, where I am now, and where I am headed. I reflect on how blessed I have been and how God has guided me every step of the way. Remembering that gives me energy, clarity, and focus that motivates me through the most difficult times.

Discuss a crisis situation (2008 depression, 9/11, COVID-19) that you/your company were in and how you overcame it.

The biggest crisis situation I faced ended up actually being the catalyst that helped me start my company. When I was ready to strike out on my own, I decided to acquire an IT company. It was a great IT company with an extensive customer list and enough revenue to sustain my lifestyle and be comfortable. I planned to supply my portion of the acquisition loan from my 401(k). In order to access those funds, I could no longer be an employee at the company I worked at. When the bank told me that the underwriting would be done in fourteen days, I realized I had to make a move immediately. I resigned from my job, ready to go all in.

The next day, I received a call from the bank. They had found some discrepancies in the seller's personal tax records and they could no longer supply the necessary amount of funding.

I did not know what to do. I suddenly had neither a job nor funding to acquire the company. I had to make the decision right then: either put my plan on the back burner or jump off a cliff.

I jumped.

It was a planned exit – just not the way I planned it. It ended up being the best thing that could have happened to me. My back was against the wall, and I had to hustle to make it. I had to find contracts, so I started subcontracting until I had enough experience to win prime contracts. Having an instant stream of revenue would have made my life comfortable, but that comfort would have made my lazy. I needed to be hungry enough to learn how to hustle. My husband humbles me when he reminds me of how difficult it was for me to change from an "every two-week paycheck" mentality to adjusting to the financial ebbs and flows of the entrepreneurial lifestyle.

I had to have the rug pulled out from under me to truly go after what I wanted. It was a planned exit, but that was not the way I planned it. Without that crisis, I do not know when or if I would have branched out and started my own company.

What is that one secret to your business success that would be helpful to current and aspiring entrepreneurs?

In Michael Gerber's book *The E-Myth Revisited,* he posits that three types of people get into business: the technician, the manager, and the entrepreneur.

The technician invents a product and then decides to go into business. The manager decides they can use their management skills to sell it themselves. The entrepreneur comes along and says, "I didn't make it, and I didn't manage it – but I'm going to sell it." Gerber believes that in order to truly succeed in business, you have to become the entrepreneur. The technician and the manager might have great, important skills, but they may not understand how to sell their products and grow their companies.

I read that book before I started my business and that is one of the secrets that I relied on – be the entrepreneur, not the manager or the technician. I saw this principle in action through the CEO of the company I worked for before I started my company. He focused on growing the business and making strategic decisions about the direction of the company. His focus helped grow his company to becoming one of the top small businesses in the country.

What's your advice for entrepreneurs who are still struggling?

Ask yourself if God is taking you through a challenge to prepare you for something greater. No matter how much you are struggling, learn everything you can. What may look like a failure is only a failure if you let it become one. If you can come away from an experience with new knowledge, new approaches, or new perspectives, then it was a success.

Did you have to deal with tough barriers to entry?

Losing my funding the day after I resigned from my full-time job was a tough blow. But it was not the only hard experience I had faced in life. By then, I knew that I had a choice: I could either let it stand in my way or allow it to propel me forward.

When you are challenged, you discover new things about yourself. You find out how you deal with stress and how you approach difficult situations. You find out how strong your faith is – in God, in other people, and in yourself. Most important, you receive the push you need to succeed.

The Fortune of a Childhood Dream

Euran S. Daniels

Euran S. Daniels is an entrepreneur, executive producer, and motivational speaker. His business ventures span a variety of platforms including entertainment, technology, tourism, and education. He is a native of Wilmington, North Carolina, and information about him and his multiple pursuits can be found online at www.EuranDaniels.com.

Tell us about you as the owner/founder. What's your story that made you the entrepreneur you are today?

I was born and raised in Wilmington, North Carolina. I was very fortunate to grow up in a household with two parents and an older brother, and they were supportive of me and all my endeavors. I was also fortunate to have parents and grandparents who were business leaders within the community in which I was raised. Currently, I live in Raleigh, North Carolina. I am married and have two children. My wife and children are also very supportive of all of my initiatives. Having strong family support has been very instrumental to balancing personal growth as well as business growth. Growing up as an African American male, there were always negative obstacles against me in life. My family instilled in me that I would always have to work twice as hard to be successful in life. In addition, whatever career path I chose in life, if I wanted to be a successful business owner, I needed to include everyone in the business plan, all races, genders, and cultures. As a child, I believed that if I kept these two family principles, the sky was the limit with whatever career path I decided to pursue!

As an entrepreneur, I have been very fortunate to start a number of different companies over the course of my lifetime. I started my first company, Reflections Video, at the age of ten. Reflections Video, known today as Daniels Production Company LLC, started out as a childhood hobby and quickly evolved into a business model. As a child, I was always fascinated with cameras and wanted to pursue a career in film and television production. Utilizing a family video camera that was purchased for Christmas, I started recording everything that I could possibly record, from special family moments and sporting events, to weddings and fashion shows. While having fun as a child, this hobby turned into a business plan by quickly capturing clients within my hometown community.

My second business venture, Daniels Creative Consulting LLC, was initially created as the result of another immediate need within my community. As a child, I was attracted to computer technology. I was afforded the opportunity to design a computer lab for the local

Boys & Girls Club, and this gave me insight in how to build computers from scratch and how to design networks. This further sparked my interest in computer technology and gave me the experience to land a job at IBM while attending college. As an employee at IBM, I had access to the top technicians and equipment in the world. I quickly learned there was a strong need in the workforce for project managers and IT consultants. During my college career, a local bank in my hometown received a startup grant for computer consulting, IT management, and Microsoft training; all skill sets I mastered through hands-on experience as a child and while working at IBM. As a minority within my local community with the skill sets and certifications needed, I was the perfect candidate for the job, with the exception that I didn't have an established company. As a result, I established Daniels Creative Consulting LLC. Since its inception, I learned that project management and consulting is very broad and can be leveraged through partnerships across virtually any industry.

My third company, Daniels Tours LLC, stemmed from a family business in tourism, specifically motor coach and ground transportation. This business was created to partner with my parents who owned a similar company in a different market. Working with my parents for a number of years allowed me to gain the skills needed to create this company. They taught me basically everything I needed to know about the industry. As a motor coach operator, the key is setting up your company correctly, and establishing networks to partner with as you continue to grow your business.

What have been the key factors to your success and why?

The most critical factors that have contributed to my success regardless of the industries that I've pursued have been prayer, hard work, and dedication.

First, prayer. This is the most important of the three. There are simply some things in life that knowledge, experience, and wisdom cannot fix. My faith has taught me that regardless of your path, you will face obstacles that are beyond your control. Whenever you've done all that you know to do and things still do not go as planned, prayer is the ultimate resolution.

Second, hard work. Oftentimes I find myself working until the job is done, regardless of how long it takes. As a business owner, you are often the first person to show up on the job and the last person to leave.

Finally, dedication. As a business owner, you should strive to be the most dedicated person in completing a goal. Players change, the plans change, and in some cases, the ultimate goal may change. As a business owner, however, your dedication, commitment, and persistence to a successful product should never change.

What has been your worst decision and how did you bounce back and still get to where you are today? How did this failure prepare you for your current success?

Perhaps the worst business decision I have made was not fully leveraging all of the resources I had access to while researching something prior to starting. As a result, I found myself running into problems that could have easily been avoided had I done the initial research. In many cases, I lost a lot of money, time, and energy. In addition, I have attempted to resolve many issues without gaining advice from others who may have experienced similar situations. As a result, I learned to surround myself with people who can advise me whenever I need assistance. Your journey becomes easier if you choose to surround yourself with positive people who can advise you whenever you need it.

What has been your best decision and why?

Perhaps the best decision I ever made as an entrepreneur was to start young. Because I started my first company at a young age (ten-years-old), everyone was willing to share information to help me along my way. I was able to get into many doors that I would not have ordinarily been able to get into if I were an adult, from television studios to film studios. Even my competitors opened their doors freely and showed me how to do many things that I would otherwise not have known how to do. They also explained many of their challenges as well as their success stories. I believe if they felt I was a true threat to them in any way possible, they would not have been as receptive to sharing knowledge with me. I would encourage any young person to pursue their passion early in life through mentorships, internships, and relationships. Perhaps even start a business. It's free access to wisdom that may not be available later in life. As a child, no one views you as a threat.

What is an unusual habit you have as an entrepreneur that helps you succeed?

I believe the most unusual habit I have as an entrepreneur is the desire to go over and beyond with every situation. It is my desire to exceed the expectations of every customer where possible. As a child, I was always taught that I needed to work harder and strive to over-achieve in every aspect of my life. I believe this has been one key factor that has helped me to succeed in all of my business endeavors.

With the knowledge and experience you have now, what would you have done differently if you were to start your entrepreneurial journey again?

Throughout my career, I have elected to pursue many different passions for one simple reason - to have a fall-back plan. My goal was to always have a Plan B in the event that Plan A failed. With the knowledge and experience I have now, if I were to start my entrepreneurial journey again, I would invest more time in fewer career paths. There are advantages and disadvantages to both, however, when projects overlap, a business owner can sometimes have too many commitments and not be able to provide services at the highest desired level. The advantages to having multiple avenues are that if one fails, there is always another one to pursue. I often wonder what my life would be like if I had dedicated all of my energy into one passion.

What do you do when you feel demotivated and overwhelmed?

Oftentimes when there is a very large project approaching, or projects begin to overlap, it is normal to feel overwhelmed and in some cases demotivated depending on the circumstances. In both cases, I often find myself reverting back to a simple task that I learned early in life: a checklist. Having a checklist serves many purposes. It allows you to quickly prioritize your tasks, highlight your accomplishments, and quickly identify where you may need to delegate and/or get assistance to complete unfinished assignments. A lack of organization can often lead to unnecessary stress. A simple checklist can help organize thoughts and tasks. Organization is essential when managing multiple projects.

Discuss a crisis situation (2008 depression, 9/11, COVID) that you/your company were in and how you overcame it.

One of the biggest challenges in owning a business is being able to manage the unknowns. In the event of a worldwide crisis every business, regardless of the industry, will be impacted. Some positively, however in most cases negatively. There are several things you can do to reduce the impact to your business from any crisis. First, ensure client diversification. Based on your business model, if more than thirty percent of your income is from one source, it could be problematic if that source of income is ever compromised. Secondly, be willing to adapt to change quickly. Many businesses fail in the event of a crisis simply because they cannot adapt to the "new norm." Finally, and perhaps more important, stay connected to associations such as national organizations in your profession as helpful resources for information and guidance.

The biggest crisis that I have dealt with thus far has been COVID-19. The pandemic has had an effect on every business worldwide regardless of location and size. All of my businesses were impacted; my ground transportation company was impacted the most. Within a few days, virtually all ground transportation companies in the nation came to a sudden stop. Trips were cancelled, and millions of dollars were lost across the industry.

I went through a similar crisis in 2008 during the national recession and transitioned several aspects of my transportation company as a result of that event. Those transitions allowed me to be in a better position to deal with COVID-19. After going through the 2008 recession, I diversified my client base by offering services in different locations accommodating various needs. The lesson that I learned from the 2008 crisis was that some areas of transportation were never affected while others were. The same was the case with COVID-19. Although the worldwide impact to COVID-19 was much more severe, having the diversification in place reduced the impact to my transportation company by nearly twenty-five percent.

One of the most frustrating aspects of the 2008 crisis was receiving critical information in a timely manner. During that time, I felt I was always the last to receive key information. After researching this issue, I quickly learned that information was being distributed through national associations and other business affiliations such as local Chamber of Commerce organizations. As a result, I later became a member of virtually every national organization within my industry as well as every chamber organization in my area. As a result, during COVID-19, I found myself in a better position to quickly receive accurate information. The business relationships I had established over the years helped me obtain key information on grants, supplies, and other resources that were helpful with maneuvering through COVID-19. Knowledge is power, however often it's not what you know, it's *who* you know!

What is that one secret to your business success that would be helpful to current and aspiring entrepreneurs?

Perhaps the most valuable secret I have learned is to connect with people who have already done what you are trying to do. In most cases, you will walk away with wisdom and knowledge which you are unable to gain through any classroom experience. Having a simple conversation over breakfast or lunch could save you years of frustration and possibly thousands of dollars. Starting a business is challenging within itself, not to mention the unknowns you will encounter as you start your journey. What better way to jump-start your business plan than to leverage the wisdom of someone who is willing to give you their blueprint for success and failures. Priceless!

What's your advice for entrepreneurs who are still struggling?

Starting a new business can be difficult at times. It is often stated that the first three years of starting any business are the most difficult; however, business owners may face many challenging times over the course of their journeys. Although it is very common to blame yourself at first, it is unlikely that you are the first person to experience any situation. Connect with other business owners who may have already experienced a similar situation to gain advice and guidance on how they were able to resolve the issue. Don't be afraid to ask questions. Every challenging moment is meant to be a lesson. Learning from the challenge is essential for growth.

What is the best investment you've made and why? (Can be an investment of money, time, or energy.)

The best investments I have made throughout my career have been getting a good education and surrounding myself with individuals and organizations who have given me positive advice and the necessary tools to succeed. Identifying the right people and organizations was not easy. It took a lot of time and energy, from researching to attending networking events and conferences. I have often been told that if I am the strongest link in my circular network, I have no room for growth. However, if I surround myself with smarter individuals, the possibilities are endless. Knowledge is power, wisdom is essential!

Imperfect Knowledge: The Trap Door between Humility and Arrogance

Lawrence M. Drake II, Ph.D.

Lawrence M. Drake II, Ph.D., is the cofounder and CEO of HOPE 360, Inc. The company partners with industry, universities, non-profits, and government agencies to provide expertise and support on how to manage successfully through change transition, growth reorganizations, downsizing, and cultural integration or transformation that occurs as a result of a merger, acquisition, or other environmental circumstances. HOPE 360, Inc. is based in Atlanta, Georgia, and information can be found online at www.hope360inc.com.

Tell us about you as the owner/founder. What's your story that made you the entrepreneur you are today?

I spent over forty years as a corporate executive, moving twenty times and living and working around the world. I now tend to think entrepreneurially about EVERYTHING. During my lifetime I've cofounded or co-led several ventures across numerous industries with a modicum of success, and I am constantly asking myself, what could I have done better? In fact, posing that very question to myself propels my fundamental belief that I haven't done my best work. In fact, I'm not sure I ever will. But I want to keep working toward that goal every day!

What have been the key factors to your success and why?

1. Perseverance: I refuse to give up when I believe in the importance of staying the course. I was homeless at times as a teen, yet I paid for my education including a bachelor's degree, an MBA, another master's degree, and a doctorate in my mid-fifties. I would be the last one to say it was easy, quite the contrary, at times I felt like I wouldn't make it. But I did!

2. Possibility thinking: I am always asking, "why not?" rather than saying, "we can't."

3. Bet on myself: While I can't honestly say that I haven't been completely risk averse, I am willing to try things that others might not.

4. Lifelong learner: I realize each and every day that my knowledge is incomplete. No matter how much I think I know, I am clear that there are so many things that I don't know and must remain on this quest to learn, unlearn, and re-learn. Realizing my own limitations and that others often know more than I do. When I talk about the trap door of arrogance

vs. confidence, I'm referring to situations when you as the founder/CEO are so committed to being the smartest person in the room that even when it's not necessary the outcomes can be disastrous. In instances such as these, your strengths can become your weaknesses and you need to admit to your team and even sometimes your investment partners that you need help. In other words, you will fail if you do not learn how to ask for help. It takes strength to be humble. Conversely, it doesn't take any special skill to be arrogant.

What has been your worst decision and how did you bounce back and still get to where you are today? How did this failure prepare you for your current success?

I have made a great many bad decisions, but one of the worst had to do with holding on to someone in my leadership longer than I should have. This executive was afraid to fly which was problematic since our business unit was based in Cleveland and our corporate offices were located in Long Island, New York. As the CFO, he was integral in helping me to articulate and demonstrate our progress on returning the investment of over $500M to our investor group. I gave too much empathy to his fear of flying which often made him tardy to our review sessions and compromised our ability to pivot to key messages during presentations to the group that would have possibly given our investor group more confidence in us. This proved problematic almost every quarter despite him often leaving early in order to arrive at our sessions on time. Invariably, something would happen, and he would arrive late. My lesson from that experience is you have to be decisive particularly when your feelings hinder your better judgment. I should have demoted or re-assigned him long before things unraveled, but I liked him and his wife was pregnant at the time and he knew the industry benchmarks better than I did. However, I should have let him go.

What has been your best decision and why?

I co-invested in a very successful mid-stage venture whose main product provided a technology-based alternative to the record of a trial proceeding using the standard court reporter. It allowed me to learn how to run a business as an entrepreneur including raising the capital and assuming the risk. The founder of the company was an industry veteran and was already enjoying success. She and I joined forces and we doubled our revenue, margin mix and profitability within two years.

What is an unusual habit you have as an entrepreneur that helps you succeed?

I wouldn't say it's unusual, but I am constantly and consistently curious about everything, so I ask lots of questions. Sometimes it catches people off guard but it's the only way I can sometimes see new possibilities.

With the knowledge and experience you have now, what would you have done differently if you were to start your entrepreneurial journey again?

I would have ventured out sooner (before college) and started my own firm long before I did. I learned so much about myself and about how to think entrepreneurially.

What do you do when you feel demotivated and overwhelmed?

I would characterize my reaction to these two in very different ways. I almost never feel demotivated, rather I sometimes just run out of steam. I am generally working on a number of ideas, concepts, or projects at once and need to just stop and do a self-check. When it comes to feeling overwhelmed, I often need to reflect on my priorities and make sure I am staying true to getting to the outcomes I planned.

Discuss a crisis situation (2008 depression, 9/11, COVID-19) that you/your company were in and how you overcame it.

In 2008 I was the CEO of one of my investment partner's portfolio firms. The company's mission was to singularly focus on enhancing and extending the brand of 'legacy' recording artists of all genres combining the advantages of a traditional recording label with many direct-to-consumer benefits found in web-based companies for both the consumer and business market. Anchored by an interactive peer-to-peer digital network for artists, fans and corporate partners alike, this company was to be the choice destination where music, entertainment, and information connect. Included in the offerings of this firm was a complete range of services including music platform consulting, custom music production, music licensing, virtual and live performance production, social networking, and much more.

The crisis occurred primarily as a result of a significant slowdown in ad spending on our artists and the program offerings. The costs of retaining our artist roster, studio production, and technology platform development were increasing faster than topline revenue. This meant that our burn rate was greater than we anticipated. We were faced with only three months cash (ninety days) and needed to raise additional funds. Due to the market recession many of our investors had lost considerable amounts of cash and were less able to fund our continued progress. After getting down to less than twenty days of cash on hand, we found two Angel investors who were willing to invest $500K which kept us in business for another three months. We were unable to raise a third round of funding and the company folded in late 2009.

We had a terrific concept but were unaware of the depth of the downturn in the market. All investors, including me, lost our investment. The lesson learned is not all ideas are winners.

What is that one secret to your business success that would be helpful to current and aspiring entrepreneurs?

Knowing what you don't know and not underestimating the value of surrounding yourself with people who are smarter than you. Otherwise, we will fall through that trap door between "Humility and Arrogance."

Did you ever experience a time you could not pay payroll costs?

There is no better moment as an entrepreneur than when you realize you will NOT be receiving a paycheck and your staff will. This means you are not only in the game, but you ARE the game! Everyone in the company is relying on you to take care of them and their families. The next big moment happens when you can't pay yourself or anyone else. I've had that happen several times, but as loyal as people may be to you and the company's mission, purpose, and product, they want to be paid and preferably on time!

#getapassportandgo

Rachel Dunbar, Ph.D.

Rachel Dunbar, Ph.D., is the founder and CEO of ReDirect Consulting, Inc. (RDC, Inc.). RDC, Inc. is a small, minority- and woman-owned educational consulting firm specializing in industry assessment and program restructuring in order to help clients realize academic and professional excellence. RDC, Inc. offers practical tools and innovative strategies to enhance the performance and productivity of companies and organizations. Training sessions offered by the company help employees walk away with a deeper understanding of how to capitalize upon their talents to increase efficiency in the workplace. RDC, Inc. is committed to *"Pointing You in the Right Direction."* The company is based in Huntsville, Alabama, and information can be found at www.redirectconsultinginc.com.

Tell us about you as the owner/founder. What's your story that made you the entrepreneur you are today?

I began my career as an educator teaching at the elementary school level and then transitioned into higher education. My job has always been to train teachers on how to give strong instruction. As I watched teachers in the field, I saw that they needed additional training on a regular basis. I also felt that individuals in the business sector needed guidance on how to work with groups from diverse backgrounds. They were not necessarily going down the correct path and needed to be redirected, which is what led me to open my consulting firm so that I could "point them in the right direction." I chuckle a bit at this now because I had so much confidence in how I could help others – even when there were times that I was not confident in myself. Despite the reservations that I had personally, I strongly believed that my skill set would be beneficial to others.

I have a strong interest in international travel and making sure that students learn as much as possible about the world around them. The only way they can do that is through travel. That is why, as part of my consulting, I coined the phrase #getapassportandgo. The purpose was to work with individuals of color, particularly first-generation college students, to obtain their passports to increase their global exposure. This was my way of opening doors to others that they thought otherwise might have been closed to them culturally. In everything that I do, I try to integrate diversity and culture in order to change people's perspective.

What have been the key factors to your success and why?

My success can be attributed to the encouragement that I received from my parents. They were relentless in the way that they taught my sister and I to not only set goals, but to strive to achieve them. My parents celebrated every single accomplishment that my sister and I made, no matter how large or small. They made every moment big so that we always felt supported. My sister was also a big influence, though she did not know it. She was leaps and bounds ahead of me with her success as an entrepreneur. Watching her climb the ladder by making her own rules and charting her own path, I saw that I could possibly do the same thing as a woman of color. That is huge in a male-dominated world where woman have traditionally not been viewed as viable competitors and where women of color have certainly been considered subordinates.

Another key to my success is that I have made it a point to surround myself with really supportive friends. My friends actually live to see me do well! You cannot put a price on the value of true friendship where your loved ones genuinely consider your accomplishments to be theirs as well. When I travelled to different countries to teach and give presentations, not once did my friends ever show signs of envy. Rather, they always sent me away with prayers of safety and then anxiously awaited my return so I could share photos and stories with them. I never felt that any of my close friends were jealous of me or would use their jealously as their fuel to try to sabotage me. I saw them celebrate each success I had as if it were their own. That type of support is golden and rare. When you find a set of friends who build you up instead of tear you down, you should hold on to them.

I would say that an additional key to my success, especially with regard to travel, has been facing my fears. Now, do not get me wrong; I get nervous quite often. However, that has not stopped me from venturing out on my own to try new things and have new adventures. As I conceptualized #getapassportandgo, I reflected on how I have gone scuba diving in deep waters, stayed in a rainforest, visited historic cathedrals, zip lined through trees, climbed a massive wall that spans thousands of miles, participated in a ceremony to receive my African name, and spent time "living like a local." Facing my fears so I could make memories to last a lifetime and also learn about different cultures has been an incredible part of my success. Those experiences undergird the messages I convey when I conduct workshops for big business to help them work on personal biases related to diversity. This is huge when it comes to launching your own business because you are away from what is familiar and comfortable. If you do not face your fears, then it is likely you will never have the courage to do the "big" thing for your life and your business.

What has been your worst decision and how did you bounce back and still get to where you are today?

My worst decision was to let one person convince me that I was not good enough. I was told that I was intelligent, but that I did not have common sense. I was made to believe that what I said conveyed my ignorance, so I had to be careful about everything that came out of my mouth. It would seem to me that a person who has visited five out of seven continents has to be pretty smart in some way. Yet, I allowed someone else to dictate what I thought about myself and how far I could climb on the ladder of entrepreneurial success. That was a terrible decision! You should never let someone make a decision for you when that person does not have your best interest at heart. As a matter of fact, you should not let someone make decisions for you at all! You are the only one who can decide what is best for you. If you happen to fail miserably with the decision you made, at least you will know that it was all by your own accord, not based upon what someone else said. Even though I made the very unwise decision to allow another person to speak for me, I eventually bounced back and regained confidence. My family rallied around to remind me who I was and *whose* I was. I cannot forget that!

How did this failure prepare you for your current success?

That aforementioned setback prepared me by causing me to suffer loss. I essentially lost everything, which included my friends, my finances, my self-esteem, my confidence, and my identity. I had to lose it all just so I could build up the strength to get it back again. This took place over the course of about ten years, which seemed so much longer while I was in the middle of it all. This actually motivated me to push myself harder than before. Mustering up the strength to do so was pretty difficult as well and it was not easy to be motivated in the midst of the whirlwind. Once I got back on track, I set my personal and professional train in motion to go full speed ahead down the path of success. That train only travels in one direction, it does not run out of gas, and it does not allow for stowaways. My current success is in part due to my previous failure; I had to re-learn who I was.

What has been your best decision and why?

My best decision was to leave home when I was in college and study abroad on my own. That was really stepping out on faith! I had to get out of my comfort zone where things were familiar and I felt protected. Leaving the United States to live and study in another country opened my eyes to the fact that there is an entire world spinning on its axis while I was back home being mediocre. I look at myself now and can honestly say there is nothing mediocre about me! Once I got a taste of travelling, it sparked an interest that grew into a passion. If I had not taken a chance on myself to get on a plane and travel thousands of miles away from what I had been exposed to my whole life, I would still be in the same place I was back then. Fortunately, that is not the case. I have seen what it is like in other countries and it makes me appreciate the beauty of diversity even more than before. Using #getapassportandgo as a platform to educate others has been amazing. It is more than just a phrase; it is an outward form of an inner passion. I have witnessed students take what I shared with them through this platform and travel to countries all over the world. I often tease them that I am so jealous that they have more stamps in their passports than I do! In return, they tell me if they had not gained the courage to travel, they never would have seen and done so many things in such a short period of time. What I try to teach them in a domestic setting will never compare to the lessons that they learn while they are abroad. I know that my decision to venture out on my own was life-changing, as it shaped how I viewed everything thereafter. This insight has fueled my mission to make sure that others travel as well.

When I think about how this translates into entrepreneurship, it falls in line with the overall concept of walking out on a limb. There are so many people who have an idea in their minds, but are afraid to branch out because the "limb" is too shaky or it might be too narrow or it could be part of a tree with rotten roots. Whatever the case may be, you have to decide how long you will teeter totter on the branch before you actually walk all the way across it to get to the other side where the fruit is ripe for the taking. You can stay where you are and allow your fears to keep you there or you can make a bold move and have your confidence take you places with your business that you never imagined.

What is an unusual habit you have as an entrepreneur that helps you succeed?

I would not say this habit is unusual, but I pray about what I do and ask God for guidance. He will typically answer in His "still small voice." There have been many times that I have been unsure of what I should do in particular situations. My parents have always told me (and my father continues to tell me) that I have to consult God about each and every little thing that I do. There will never be anything God will not guide us in doing and it will be so clear that there is no way to mistake the answer He has given us.

With the knowledge and experience you have now, what would you have done differently if you were to start your entrepreneurial journey again?

With the experience I now have as a business owner and if I had to start over again, I would advertise differently. I was very timid when I first founded my business. It was not that I did not believe I had a good product to offer; it is just that I hoped business would come to me rather than having to go out and find it myself. For some reason, I expected clients to just fall into my lap without doing the maximum amount of footwork. That was definitely not the best strategy at all! It was as if I had confidence in certain areas, but not in the one that would help me grow as the owner of a new company. Yes, I had business cards that I passed out at conferences and I collected cards from colleagues. Yet, I did not follow up with them as I should have within two weeks. Yes, I had a website, but I did not invest real money to have it look top notch – it was mediocre at best. Yes, I had a slogan that I thought sounded great for my company. However, I did not beat the pavement. I should have marketed myself as a consultant with multiple years of experience in my field or with a wide range of exposure both in the United States and abroad. If nothing else, my time in Asia, Europe, and Australia should have been a selling point for my unique international perspective. What I failed to see is that it was not enough to simply have it in my mind or even have it written on paper. As a business owner, it does not matter how much you have done before if you do not allow other people to see what those things are in real time. I did not advertise and that was a huge mistake!

The best way to build a client base is to put yourself out there so people will know who you are. You cannot expect clients to just come to you out of the blue; they have to know who you are, where you are, what you do, and how you do it. That has been a bit difficult for me as a single mom because I have always put my son first. I have often put my professional and business goals aside in order to give all of my attention to him. Some may say that you can do both: be a mom and build your business. Well, yes, you can, but when you are in the beginning stages of your company, that will not always be as easy as one might think. In order to advertise on a broad level, you may have to travel to make yourself more visible. With that, you have to consider what accommodations to make for your child while you are away from home, especially if it is not convenient for your child to travel with you. That was one of my struggles when I first started: I had to juggle being a parent along with being an entrepreneur and I just did not know the best way to be both. It is easy to be envious of others who appear to have it all together and I did that quite often. I would look at someone who appeared to have the ideal lifestyle with work and home perfectly balanced, but I did not really know what they might have had to sacrifice to make themselves appear as they did. It is truly a sign of personal strength to make it all work and do so with grace. I believe if I had found a more efficient way to market my skills at the onset, it would have made a greater impact on the success of my company in its early stages.

What do you do when you feel demotivated and overwhelmed?

We all feel like the world is just too much and we want it to stop so we can get off rather than keep riding the roller-coaster called life! It comes with the territory of being entrepreneurs and wanting to do multiple things at once. When I feel demotivated and overwhelmed, I drink green tea and sit outside on my back patio. It seems simple, right? It is almost too simple to really be a viable solution. However, what works for me is simply what works. My mother would drink tea and read her Bible every morning. I remember clearly that she specifically wanted a screened-in patio so she could see nature. We had that porch at our house for a while and it was so peaceful for her to sit out there each morning without interruptions, taking time to be silent so she could hear God's voice as she communed with him. My father later renovated the patio to convert it into an office for my mother. He built it with huge floor-to-ceiling windows on three walls so that the maximum amount of sunlight could enter the room. My mother would open the blinds to let in natural light because she rarely turned on lights in her office. She loved the sun. Doing the things that I know my mother once did actually calms my entire soul.

When running our businesses, we have to remember that work is hard enough and it can consume us. We have to find ways that will help us sooth our souls and bring personal peace. Will I always want to get up and work? No, I will not because my bed is very comfortable and the warmth of it makes me want to stay under my comforter. Will I always want to respond to emails in a calm manner? No, because sometimes I may want to snap back at a person the same way they did at me via email. Will I always leave room on my plate so that I will not be frazzled? Of course not, because I am like many other people: I often bite off more than I can chew. More often than not, I say yes when I should say no. I pile on too much and it overwhelms me. However, that is by my own permission. So when I am not motivated to do my best or I feel the weight of the world on my shoulders, I have to pause for a moment with my tea and take in the calmness of nature as my mother did. The stress of the world will still be there after I finish the last sip of my tea.

Discuss a crisis situation (2008 depression, 9/11, COVID) that you/your company were in and how you overcame it.

My crisis has not necessarily been one on a global level, but rather one that is more personal. I had to figure out how to get my business to survive while maintaining another full-time job. I needed to bring in income while I waited for my company to grow. My business has often had to go on hold. That can be discouraging when you want to see growth in your business, but it has to be placed on the backburner in order for you to prioritize other things. There have been many times when I have told myself that I should just dissolve my company and place my focus elsewhere. This has especially been at the forefront of my mind during tax seasons when I cannot show income. We want to have money coming in, not see it going out! I have tried to maintain my focus when it comes to RDC, Inc, because I know what my initial purpose was when I established it. So, yes, my crisis is every year when I have to file taxes, and am reminded that I might not have brought in the income that I wanted; however, it is a perfect time for me to refresh my revenue and profit goals and put together a plan. Currently, we have experienced our best year yet.

A major factor during this pandemic is that #getapassportandgo is centered on international travel. Even though my passion is to explore the world and encourage others to do the same, I have had to be mindful of the fear of traveling many people have with the global health crisis at this time. They really do not want to hear about leaving home, especially when it potentially places them and their loved ones in jeopardy. Most people try to be cautious overall and I do not want to exacerbate their fears or further encourage them to be reluctant to travel. Therefore, I have tried to get people to concentrate on the positive aspects of what they can learn if they have a global perspective, rather than the negative aspects of what has happened with COVID-19. When the world recalibrates, there will still be much for us to see and do! From a business standpoint, I believe that it is important for me to find a way to position myself in order to be ready and available when that time comes so that I can be of valuable service.

What is that one secret to your business success that would be helpful to current and aspiring entrepreneurs?

This is not a secret, it is just good common sense: GET A MENTOR! Find someone who is successful and follow what they do. If it is someone who you cannot reach, simply follow them from a distance on their social media platforms and study their business. It is okay for that person to be your "virtual mentor." If it is someone you know personally, reach out to him or her and ask if they will guide you on what to do as you try to grow your own business. Those who are committed to being true mentors are confident enough in themselves not to think you will steal their shine. They will know that helping you grow and learn actually makes them better at what they do. One of the problems that I've seen as an owner is that too many people want to hide their success. By that, I mean that there are people who would prefer to see others struggle to find answers rather than just offer their help. Those are not the people that you want to follow, no matter how successful they may appear to be. Their true nature on the inside is that they are selfish. Steer clear of them! Instead, align yourself with someone who has positive energy and is an open book in your industry. That is the person that you want to be your mentor. The reality is that there is enough wealth to go around for everyone. How does it take away from my livelihood to be a mentor to someone who seeks to follow a path similar to mine? My success is not contingent upon how well they do, but their growth could easily be stifled by my selfishness. Therefore, it is important for me to present myself as a person that another would aspire to be. You have to thoughtfully select a mentor who sees the growth and potential that you have and who is willing to help you reach all of your goals. The other thing to remember is that if the first mentor does not work out for you, it is fine to find a new mentor. To some extent, mentorship takes a bit of trial and error. Someone who does not work well the first time can still help you learn a lesson. The second time may not work out either. However, the third time might be a charm. Once you find the mentor who is a right match for you, then you get under his or her wing and let that person guide you to the place you need to be as an entrepreneur.

What's your advice for entrepreneurs who are still struggling?

I think that many entrepreneurs struggle because of their fear in venturing out again once they see that things did not necessarily happen the way they wanted the first time. If they face multiple disappointing moments, then it is natural for them to become discouraged. That feeling of failure is often what keeps a new business owner from moving forward with their vision. Yet, disappointment is a fact of life and it cannot be avoided. If everything worked out perfectly every time, then we would never appreciate what we have. The same philosophy applies to starting and maintaining a business. If we always have it easy then we will never know the joy that comes from truly grinding to be successful. If you strongly believe in what you do and it is your passion, stick with it. It may take a long time, but you will eventually get to where you want to be. That "long time" may be years, not months. In those years, consider why you started. Why did you venture out on your own? What is it that you hoped to accomplish when you first started? What were you trying to prove? How many things have you checked off of the list you created years ago when you first dreamt this dream? Who is rooting for you and wants to see you succeed? That last question might be the most powerful because it means you have to take a moment to think about who may be counting on you to knock this thing out of the park! Let that motivate you to continue even if you are struggling now. The struggle will all be worth it in the end.

What is the best investment you've made and why? (Can be an investment of money, time, or energy.)

Allow others to see who you are and what you are capable of doing. When it comes to growing your business, it is critical that you make investments that will be beneficial to you long term, rather than just for a temporary gain. One of my best investments has been a retractable banner. It is light and compact, which makes it easy to take with me wherever I go. Once purchased, it has been a great way to consistently advertise in a "big" way.

All Before the 7th Grade

Julian Frederick

Julian Frederick is the cofounder and CEO of the Step Stool Chef, a business that sells products and solutions that make learning how to cook empowering for kids and easier for parents. The Step Stool Chef believes that cooking is a safe space for kids to learn important life and leadership skills such as decision-making and problem-solving. The company sells products throughout the United States made for kids, by kids, including a cookbook for kids, a line of cooking kits for kids, along with cooking tools and apparel. Julian recently partnered with a global food tech company to launch on-demand cooking classes called The Step Stool Chef Cooking School for Kids which is now featured on a mobile app. The company is based in Dallas, Texas, and information about The Step Stool Chef can be found online at www. stepstoolchef.com. You can learn more about Julian on his personal website, www.meetjulianfrederick.com.

Tell us about you as the owner/founder. What's your story that made you the entrepreneur you are today?

I'm a twelve-year-old award-winning CEO and the co-founder of The Step Stool Chef. I built a successful business developing and selling innovative cooking products for kids as well as signed international licensing deals **all before the 7th grade!**

I'm a cookbook author and a winner of Kid Business Competitions and Youth Entrepreneurship awards. I have been sought out for media and speaking appearances and have been featured on all major TV networks. I have spoken at several conferences, festivals, and culinary events and have had the pleasure of partnering with amazing companies, top organizations, and restaurants.

The story of Step Stool Chef started on my third birthday when I was snowed in. Where I live, it doesn't snow often, and we were stuck at home for almost a week. I had to cancel all my party plans but something in me wouldn't give up. I told my mom that I wanted to make my own birthday cake. Luckily, we had all the ingredients we needed to make a vanilla Bundt cake. Surprisingly, my mom agreed. So, I put on a chef hat and got on my step stool, hence the name of the business, and got started. My cake turned out amazing and I was so inspired because I made a recipe all by myself. Then as I got older, I decided to share that experience of independence with other kids. That's how the Step Stool Chef was born.

What have been the key factors to your success and why?

There are two key factors to my success. The first is the support I have from my family and my community. I found that having a business is hard work especially as a kid and there were times when I wanted to give up. However, my mom, dad, and sister have always had my back, so I persevered. Running the Step Stool Chef takes a lot of time and effort. Thankfully, I don't have to handle this alone. With their support, I've learned not to carry all the weight on my shoulders, and it makes the experience less stressful.

The second factor to success is focusing on a problem and not stopping until you accomplish that goal. This has helped me develop a certain tenacity that won't allow me to give up. Don't get me wrong, I may get frustrated and upset because some tasks may be harder than they seem. But I just take a few moments to rest, gather my thoughts, and come back to it. I use this strategy not only in business but also while doing homework, sports, and in just everyday life.

What has been your worst decision and how did you bounce back and still get to where you are today? How did this failure prepare you for your current success?

I think my worst decision has been trying a new sales strategy during the onset of a global pandemic. Typically, I would sell products online with the occasional in-person event. In 2020, we were planning to make two big changes: we were going to start targeting the educational space by focusing on after-school programs and the homeschooled community, and we were going to start our first attempt at in-person trade shows and convention sales. To begin this new sales strategy, we found a great opportunity to sell our products at a major homeschool convention held in March. The convention was three days and it was a perfect way to sell our cooking products to our new target market. We prepared for it for over six months and spent a lot of time, effort, and money making sure it was perfect.

When March came and the Coronavirus was spreading throughout the United States, we were debating whether to risk going to the convention. It was a tough decision because we had invested so much time and money in inventory that we didn't want it to go to waste. Ultimately, we decided to go for the first day and then use that experience to decide if we wanted to stay for the other two days. The first day went smoothly therefore we decided to stay. However, the next day our county placed a stay-at-home order requiring everyone to stay safe in their houses and we knew we couldn't continue on for the next two days. We had to shut down our booth and later had to give back the money we made on the first day because we didn't have enough demand to fulfill some of the orders we received.

Over the summer, we struggled to find ways to make money while staying at home. While we found creative ways to pivot, we never fully recouped our losses. While switching up sales strategy was a good idea, trying to make such a major change without fully weighing the risk was not. This whole experience taught me how to compare options when making a decision. I now know the importance of constantly weighing the amount of risk and variables in an option every time I make an executive decision and, as a result, I can better anticipate the future because of it.

What has been your best decision and why?

The best decision I've made was deciding to turn the Step Stool Chef from a blog into a business. When we originally started, it was just a blog that shared fun kid-friendly recipes and cooking tips. For me, it was a special way my mom and I would spend time together. I would cook different meals, and then she would take pictures of our cooking experience and post them on our website. It was fun and as the word got out I was invited to give cooking demos and make media appearances. I even got a chance to cook with Guy Fieri and some other great chefs. However, when we would tell people about what we do, parents were always asking if I taught cooking classes. And every time, we would respond, "Not at the moment." Even at school, people would ask me how much money I was making. At that point, I realized how valuable my knowledge was and how others could benefit from it.

When I was eight years old, I went up to my mom and told her that I wanted to make money. A few days later, we had our first business meeting to discuss what kinds of products to sell. After a very long discussion, we decided to finally give people what they were asking for – a cooking class for kids! But for ease of access, we decided to make it online. About a year later our first product, The Step Stool Chef Academy Online Cooking School for Kids, was released. This paved the way for other cooking products and helped make me the entrepreneur I am today. Now, our Step Stool Chef Cooking School can be found on a mobile app along with other smart device platforms.

What is an unusual habit you have as an entrepreneur that helps you succeed?

Visualization is one habit I have adopted that helps me succeed. Before any big speaking engagement or media appearance, I close my eyes and imagine going out there and being super successful and having a great time. And you know what, it works every time! Every time I visualize doing great, it always comes true.

Another habit I have is saying positive affirmations. Whenever I get nervous, I look at myself in the mirror and say phrases such as: "I am charming" or "I got this" or "I am going to have a great time." Just saying these phrases inspires confidence in me and I carry it on to my performance.

Visualization and affirmations are both techniques my mom taught me, and they have helped me through all my successes. It may not be an unusual habit for some adults but this is a skill not many kids have learned. Whether you are a kid or an adult, I highly recommend it.

With the knowledge and experience you have now, what would you have done differently if you were to start your entrepreneurial journey again?

If I started my journey again, I would start my entre-preneurial path sooner. I know I'm still a kid, but for my business, I kind of have a time limit. The fact is I'm not going to be a kid much longer. My youth has been a valuable asset because seeing a young kid cooking has been inspiring to other kids. As I grow older, my youthful shine and energy become less obvious. If we had started selling products sooner, perhaps we would have been further on our path. Although I will never know for sure what would have been different, I am still grateful for my journey thus far.

What do you do when you feel demotivated and overwhelmed?

Whenever I feel overwhelmed by a problem, I pause, take a few minutes for a break, then go back to it. This is something I started doing when I was eight. If I get frustrated by something, taking a moment to pause always helps me regain my focus.

Another thing I do is take some time off to do something I enjoy like reading or riding my bike. I have found that not thinking about the stress of a situation helps calm me down and allows me to focus on something positive.

Another trick I use when a task seems overwhelming is to break it up into portions. Trying to handle a big task all at once can be really tough. When it's broken up, it's easier to see all the necessary actions. I use this skill all the time when I'm working on anything from solving a business problem to just cleaning my room. I even used it while writing this book chapter. I realize that a problem is only as difficult as you make it.

These strategies help me when I'm stressed out about an upcoming situation, or when I'm stumped by a problem.

Discuss a crisis situation (2008 depression, 9/11, COVID-19) that you/your company were in and how you overcame it.

This is a tough question because I haven't lived through a lot of major national or global crises. I was a newborn during the 2008 depression, and I wasn't around for 9/11. While COVID-19 is still a major hurdle I'm currently going through, it actually hasn't been the biggest crisis for my business.

In fact, my website being hacked in 2019 has been the biggest crisis situation the Step Stool Chef has gone through. It was early November and we were just about to release a major holiday promotion for Black Friday. I was returning from a speaking engagement when we got a call from our social media manager saying that the Step Stool Chef website was "acting weird." After checking it out for myself, I found that the site would redirect you to some random, crazy website. The worst part was all of the recipes on the site had been erased. This was particularly tough because our site had become a memory scrapbook of sorts, capturing all of our mother/son bonding moments. You see, the Step Stool Chef is more than a business. It's been a big part of my childhood. Even though company websites get hacked all the time, this felt more personal and violating because it felt as though it was erasing so many great childhood memories.

Eventually, we came up with a workaround solution – an external landing page that would allow people to see our products. It wasn't quite the same, but people could still find out about what we do, learn about our products and connect with us. It was a scary time for us because we felt very vulnerable and, despite our efforts, we couldn't find a way to restore our website. Even though our files were backed up, the backed up files became corrupted. We tried hiring professional programmers but that didn't work either.

Sometimes it's in your darkest hour when you can best see the light. After months of failed efforts to fix the old site, we had a great epiphany. Thankfully, we realized that due to a past partnership with a company named SideChef, many of our recipes and memories were still captured on their app. SideChef is a digital platform that enables people to access many recipes and learn to cook with step-by-step instructions using photos, videos, and tools. This realization inspired us to reach out to SideChef about expanding our partnership as our goals and values were so well aligned. This eventually led to an upgraded licensing agreement that launched the Step Stool Chef Cooking for Kids on the SideChef premium platform.

Even though getting hacked was a scary time that felt like the end of the road for our company, it led to an amazing opportunity with endless possibilities.

What is that one secret to your business success that would be helpful to current and aspiring entrepreneurs?

The secret to my success is that, as I went through my journey, I always knew the big picture of what I wanted for my business and what success looked like to me. Whenever a new opportunity came to me, the first thing I would do is visualize what I wanted to come out of it. Always knowing where you want to go is a very important skill because seeing what you want always makes it easier to see the steps it will take to reach that goal. My parents always instilled that you can be what you can see. When people want to have a business, but don't know what they want out of it, they may not know where or how to start. Once you find your vision of success, you can start planning how to move forward.

How would you describe the culture of your company? Did you develop your company consciously or did it just happen?

The Step Stool Chef is a family-run business so the culture is that everyone pitches in and helps.

One of our key values is the concept that a kid's voice is just as important as an adult's voice. I feel that a kid can be just as helpful as an adult because they can shed a new perspective on a problem. Often, adults can have a one-sided point of view when it comes to solving problems. Kids can find new solutions because their minds are open to more creative ideas. That is why I built a kid advisory board when we were first brainstorming the idea of our cooking kits. The world is constantly changing and we need more outside-of-the-box thinking to help resolve problems.

When you started your business did you have support? How did you handle the naysayers?

We received a lot of support from families and friends when the Step Stool Chef first started off. When we told people about our business, a lot of people were telling me how proud they were and how cool it was for a kid to have a business. People with strong media connections went out of their way to help us get on news segments or cooking demonstrations. Our connections with these people became very important because they helped us thrive both then and now.

Although we've had a lot of support, there have been some naysayers as well. Most have just been people underestimating the power of a kid business. We have been overlooked by investors because they fail to take kid businesses seriously. A lot of people think that kid businesses are only the kinds that sell lemonade or homemade slime. And while there are businesses like that out there, not all kid businesses are like that. There are kids out there with more business smarts and financial literacy than most adults. I'm a kid and I've already begun working on a second business; I'll be consulting to help other kids create their own businesses. And again, this has all happened before the 7th grade!

Unfortunately, some people only see the fact that we are younger. Remember, the concept for the Step Stool Chef came about because my parents actually listened to their three-year-old kid! So, next time you see a kid with a business, don't think of them as just cute or adorable. Think of them as a serious entrepreneur and a potential millionaire.

Concentrated Doses of Knowledge to Achieve Effective Results

Jennice Gist, DNP, CRNA

Jennice Gist, DNP, CRNA, is the founder of Dream Team Anesthesia Associates, Inc. (DTA), a small business that assists with staffing anesthesia providers, such as certified registered nurse anesthetists, for surgical and procedural needs. Unexpected staffing issues can lead to various constraints to surgery center logistics and DTA prides itself on facilitating any unforeseen increases in scheduled cases or gaps in human resources. The company is based in McDonough, Georgia, and information can be found online at jennicegist.com.

Tell us about you as the owner/founder. What's your story that made you the entrepreneur you are today?

I hail from very humble beginnings. My mother, an elementary teacher and early childhood educator, was a major influence in my career endeavors. She often reminded me that she was pregnant with me while earning her Master of Education degree which, I believe, instilled in me a very personal passion for education that feels almost ingrained in my DNA, passed to me from my mother in the womb. To this day, I thrive on learning and advancing my knowledge base and recently graduated with my Doctor of Nursing Practice degree.

I have known I wanted to be a nurse since my fourth grade career day. Admiring the visiting nurse's command of her sleek, shiny stethoscope and her eye-catching colorful scrubs, I was convinced that nursing must be the most exciting job in the world. My reasons for choosing nursing became slightly less superficial as I got older - I am a caring, hands-on person, a hugger, and have been told I have a great bedside manner. Nursing was a clear calling for me, but that fateful day in fourth grade charted my course toward my future career.

My sister began dating her husband in the eighth grade, and her now mother-in-law helped set my path to nursing in a more specific direction. A nurse herself, she enthusiastically campaigned for a career in nursing for me. From a young age, she would take me to meetings of nurse anesthetists and insist that this would be my future specialty. I was grateful for the exposure to the world of nursing, and her advice stuck with me.

In 1997, I achieved my childhood dream and became a nurse. Working in intensive care, the career was incredibly taxing but equally rewarding. By 2001, I was ready to pursue a position that carried more rank and esteem. My prior grooming took hold, and I went back to school and earned my master's degree to become a nurse anesthetist. The nurse anesthetist position certainly did earn me more status, but it was also taxing in its own respect. After working as a nurse anesthetist for some time, I was ready to start a family with my husband of six years and knew I needed to alleviate some of the intense demands of my advanced practice nursing career. Several of my friends and colleagues had gone out on their own, a few of them starting staffing companies. I felt inspired by the prospect of a new venture that would afford me more independence while keeping me entrenched in the nursing career I loved. In 2006, Dream Team Anesthesia Associates was born.

I stepped into my new role as entrepreneur slowly, only providing services on an as-needed basis. But by 2017, the business had blossomed to such an extent that I was managing it full-time and had brought my husband on board to help support the workload. Today, the company is thriving and I am grateful every day to be doing what I love in a way that best fits my life.

What have been the key factors to your success and why?

Determination and perseverance, even in the face of adversity, have assisted me in achieving all that I have accomplished. Though I never felt as though it held me back in any substantial way, the lack of diversity in the nurse anesthesia field did create a few challenging moments for me. I was the only African-American person in my matriculating class of ten studying to become nurse anesthetists. In every challenge I have faced, I have learned that to be successful, you must resist being consumed by the negativity and remain focused on and motivated by your goals. Challenges are a commonality of the human experience, be they financial, physical, emotional, or relational, so it is important to train oneself to stay the course and persevere.

What has been your worst decision and how did you bounce back and still get to where you are today? How did this failure prepare you for your current success?

One of my biggest mistakes in my career was not being mindful of my mental state and not allowing myself enough opportunities for rest. Nurse anesthesia can be an incredibly grueling career field, and because I wasn't intentional about taking time away from work, I ultimately got to a state of full-on burnout. I avoided returning to work after the birth of my first child, extending my maternity leave for nearly six months.

Ultimately, I found a way to channel the burnout into a renewed sense of purpose by breaking out on my own and starting DTA. My experience, however, is a powerful warning to other entrepreneurs and professionals. Maintaining balance is critically important – if you work yourself to the point of complete exhaustion, eventually you may render yourself unable to give what is needed for your business, your career, or your family to thrive.

What has been your best decision and why?

The best decision I ever made was to seek advanced degrees in my career. After four years in nursing, I went back to school to pursue my master's degree to become a nurse anesthetist and, twenty-eight months later, I had my first advanced degree. In 2017, I returned to school again and enrolled in an extremely rigorous doctoral program from which I graduated in May of 2020 with my Doctor of Nursing Practice degree.

Advanced education did not come easy and, with a husband and two kids ages ten and twelve in need of my attention required a lot of sacrifice. There were many late nights and it seemed as though I was constantly burning the candle at both ends. My kids, occasionally to their chagrin, had to learn to adapt and do more on their own. But with the help of the support system provided by my husband and mom, and the motivation and enthusiasm provided by my kids, my family was able to push through and I was able to reach the pinnacle of my education.

Furthering my education has been an immensely enriching experience and has opened many doors to me professionally. Beyond the obvious potential for higher income, my degrees have given me access to opportunities to pursue new goals, branch out into unexpected endeavors, and ultimately become a more well-rounded professional and entrepreneur. Though it is still too soon to know exactly how my doctorate degree will shape my future, I am working on getting my doctoral project published and will likely be invited to speaking engagements as a result of that publication. I have already received invites to do a podcast and collaborate on this book! Most important, the doctorate will allow me to pursue my ultimate goal of teaching the next generation of nurse anesthetists.

I believe education is extremely valuable to any ambitious professional because each new phase of learning elevates your thinking and your desire for greater success. Whether pursuing higher education or greater depths of self-education, the effort involved affords you the opportunity to see hard work come full circle.

What is an unusual habit you have as an entrepreneur that helps you succeed?

My husband often tells me he wishes I would "just relax" because I have a tendency to stay busy and keep my to-do list filled. Though many may find this approach stressful, I am highly motivated by activity and achievement and feel that life's smaller accomplishments give you momentum toward reaching your biggest goals. Executing an activity and marking it as completed is very fulfilling and motivating!

My ultimate goal professionally is to become faculty at a college or university where I can train aspiring nurse anesthetists. To help me in this endeavor, I have begun exploring the CVs of faculty members of various institutions and have been awestruck by the depth and breadth of their experiences and associations. Compared to their seven page tomes, my two or three page resume will need some enhancement if I want to reach faculty status, so I am always in search of new endeavors that will build my brand and help me become a well-rounded professional.

With the knowledge and experience you have now, what would you have done differently if you were to start your entrepreneurial journey again?

If I were to start my entrepreneurial journey over again, I would focus a bit more heavily in the early days on growth and marketing my business to larger potential clients. My business is currently very small and I acquire most of my clients by word of mouth. Though I am relatively content with the size of the business at the moment, I would like the potential to become a bigger player. Unfortunately, growth is extremely challenging as we are in a fairly saturated market in which it is difficult to secure contracts. Being in a space as niche as anesthesia staffing, you tend to get stalled in your established circle of contacts and have difficulty branching out. I feel that we would have had greater success if DTA had made growth a priority at the start of the business, before our workload was such that the day to day needs of our clients were demanding all of our attention.

What do you do when you feel demotivated and overwhelmed?

When my motivation wanes, I try to remind myself that these feelings are only a phase, a completely normal and healthy part of the human experience. Much in the same way that hunger tells us that our physical body needs nourishment, demotivation is a signal from our psyches that we need rest. As a healthcare provider, I understand the importance of listening to these prompts from our minds and bodies and know from my own experience that, if ignored, feelings of demotivation or stress can lead to actual physical illness or complete burnout. To combat demotivation and restore my energy, I am very intentional about building opportunities for rest into my life, be they vacations, short staycations, or just a day or two off of work to reset.

On the other hand, feeling overwhelmed is, in my opinion, usually self-imposed and can be avoided by staying organized, establishing a schedule, and practicing good discipline.

Discuss a crisis situation (2008 depression, 9/11, COVID-19) that you/your company were in and how you overcame it.

Being in the healthcare space, the COVID-19 pandemic had a substantial impact on our business and our clients. Local and national governments encouraged outpatient surgical and health services to cease or reduce services in an effort to reserve personal protective equipment for more critical healthcare settings, and as a result anesthesia staffing needs lagged significantly. This put a strain on our business as most of our clients were forced to tightly limit their operations.

Fortunately, one of our clients, an urgent care provider, was approved to remain open and we were able to stay afloat on its business alone. I was grateful for our lean operation in this situation as it allowed us to sustain the business despite a significant decrease in revenue. Our small, tight circle of contacts and associates was also beneficial during this time as it created almost a sense of comradery as we all struggled through the experience together. Things have ramped up very quickly since re-opening began, and our company is thriving again and, I believe, stronger for the experience.

What is that one secret to your business success that would be helpful to current and aspiring entrepreneurs?

One secret to my success has been my understanding that success cannot be attained without focused, de-liberate effort and a clear plan. In today's world, al-most everything one could want or need is literally at our fingertips. This can potentially deceive young en-trepreneurs into assuming that success is just as easily accessible and attainable at the metaphorical push of a button. Unfortunately, Alexa and Siri cannot deliv-er to you a profitable business. Business success must be hard-earned through intentional planning, sacrifice, discipline, and an unrelenting work ethic.

How would you describe the culture of your company? Did you develop your company consciously or did it just happen?

DTA's culture is one of integrity through exceptional care and attention to detail. We are guided in everything we do by the proverb that instructs us to treat others as we would wish to be treated. Not only does our company convey this in how we serve our clients and staff, but our culture is also imbued in the care provided through our service as anesthesia providers. In healthcare, we like to promise our patients the same level of care that we would provide our own mothers, and we embrace that same level of integrity at DTA.

What's your advice for entrepreneurs who are still struggling?

My advice for entrepreneurs who are challenged by the process of starting a business is just that – start! The only way to learn and move forward is to start. Don't let fear of failure or rejection hold you back. Failure and rejection are inevitable in entrepreneurship, but if you have the gumption to try and the drive to keep going, you can succeed.

The Habits That Elevated My Hustle

David Greene III, SMP, CPF, CPCC

David Greene III is a strategist, executive coach, and leadership behaviorist and development expert. He is the founder of The EverGreene Method Leadership Consultancy, the leadership coaching arm of Urbanomics Consulting Group – a Washington-D.C. based management consulting firm. The EverGreene Method Leadership Consultancy supports organizations with coaching, leadership development, learning and development, talent management, and diversity and inclusion strategies. For over a decade, the firm has worked alongside the leadership of large global organizations, top universities, and associations to develop diverse talent for leadership roles and responsibilities. The company is based in Washington, D.C., and information can be found online at theevergreenemethod.com.

Tell us about you as the owner/founder. What's your story that made you the entrepreneur you are today?

My earliest thoughts of entrepreneurship are memories of my father, who owned an auto repair business in

Brooklyn. I remember realizing my father and mother did very different things for work. My mother left for work and returned home around the same time during the weekdays. As an entrepreneur my father's schedule was very different and, as a result, he had more freedom, flexibility, and more fun. My earliest sense of what I now call a fulfillment formula seemed very different for my parents. I remember going to my mother's job on Take Your Child to Work Day and seeing her in the office environment interacting with dozens of different people who were her colleagues. It was clear to me that my mother was important and happy in her work as a bookkeeper, and she felt fulfilled. I was at my father's business more often than my mom's, and there were only two other mechanics. It was clear to me that my father enjoyed his work. However, I remember having a sense that my father had importance in our neighborhood and community. Everyone knew him. My father's business represented his service and support of families in our neighborhood and his contribution to our community's collective well-being. It is in reflection that I realized that my father's identity as an entrepreneur somehow seemed bigger than a career. It was his purpose. In many ways, this still informs my perspective of entrepreneurship: purpose beyond profit. In my early twenties, to attend college, I had to pay what grants and loans did not. I cut hair, made hats, and produced events. I discovered an enterprising mindset and passion and ability to turn ideas into steady streams of sustainable business income. I am successful as an entrepreneur and business owner because I practice what I call the successful entrepreneur's credo: Reliability, Responsiveness, and being Results-Driven. These habits elevated my hustle to an entrepreneurial edge that resulted in a business reputation for getting big things done for clients.

What have been the key factors to your success and why?

The factors that I attribute to my entrepreneurial success are a commitment to the set of values previously mentioned that also represent behaviors that continue to get high marks from clients: Reliability, Responsiveness, and being Results-Driven. Combined, they have helped create a reputation that gives all with whom we work a great deal of trust in me/us.

What has been your worst decision and how did you bounce back and still get to where you are today? How did this failure prepare you for your current success?

I agreed to have a good friend buy into the business as a partner as a strategy to help grow the business in a down economy. Instead of generating opportunities and income, she generated debt. I learned to make tough decisions so that I could be successful despite what looked like a streak of bad decisions and bad luck.

What has been your best decision and why?

I believe that if you stand by people (when you can), it is the gift that keeps on giving. I have given many young, talented people opportunities to work when others would not. Those gestures, born out of a promise to treat others as I would want to be treated, have rewarded me with many enduring friendships and opportunities I might otherwise not have.

What is an unusual habit you have as an entrepreneur that helps you succeed?

I have an intentional reinvention habit that I apply approximately every eighteen months that addresses four areas of my career and business: 1) experimentation with a future skill or capability; 2) an in-depth dive to assess gaps related to that skill and its overall applicability and fit with the business model; 3) inventory relationships and networks associated with that future skills, and 4) adoption of language and behaviors related to that skill or capability. This habit is not only a practice to make sense of markets but it is also an early warning system (EWS) for me now.

With the knowledge and experience you have now, what would you have done differently if you were to start your entrepreneurial journey again?

I would spend more time raising capital. I am confident that I would have been even more successful if I hadn't taken the bootstrapping approach. I was rich with capabilities but limited in capacity to deliver on multiple long-term engagements of scale.

What do you do when you feel demotivated and overwhelmed?

Another invaluable habit that I have relied on for over two decades is the three R's: Retreat, Revisit, and Reflect. *Retreat* is a reminder to step back from the situation to discover a fresh perspective. *Revisit* is a reminder to review personal and professional plans for relevance, and *Reflect* is a reminder to reflect upon your "why" for the bigger picture.

Discuss a crisis situation (2008 depression, 9/11, COVID-19) that you/your company were in and how you overcame it.

During the 2008 economic downturn, I was overly confident in my ability while underestimating its severity. I chose to maintain staffing at the same level instead of laying off staff for what was the main consulting practice. As a result, I had to leverage much of my personal assets to keep the doors open. For the business to survive, I redesigned our services by paring back from change management to exclusively strategy facilitation and organizational development. I then focused largely on the philanthropic grant makers and redoubled efforts to win business from private foundations and their grantees. They faced challenges from the downturn but were not as agile and would make ideal customers.

What is that one secret to your business success that would be helpful to current and aspiring entrepreneurs?

My business success is built on a personal code of conduct that has become a part of the operational culture. Personal and client relationships benefit from Reliability, Responsiveness, and being Results-Driven.

When you started your business did you have support? How did you handle the naysayers?

When I started my business, I did not have support. I was told the idea of a management consulting firm serving nonprofits and philanthropy and specializing in strategies for engaging people and communities of color in underrepresented markets was a losing value proposition. I tried selling the idea for two years before landing the first big contract. The naysayers fueled my determination and ultimately motivated me to work even harder. For every no, I asked what would need to happen for them to say yes.

Did you have capital limitations and how did you finance your business?

I did have capital limitations. I launched my business while working for another firm. After a few failed attempts to get them to start a practice area that would allow me to leverage my experience and relationships and grow my income, I decided it was time to stop splitting my energy and leave. I used the little savings I had and a credit card to finance my business. Two months after leaving the firm, I signed my first client to a two-year contract.

Eyes in the Boat!

Karen Marieke Heine

Karen Marieke Heine is the founder and CEO of Marieke Consulting, Inc. She started the company in 2003 with the mission of providing services to the Federal Aviation Administration (FAA) as a business systems analyst. Today, Marieke Consulting is a woman-owned, veteran-owned company that continues to support the FAA in the areas of software development, system and data integration, financial analysis and forecasting, business process reengineering, and data analytics. The company's namesake comes from her middle name – Marieke – which derives from the song of the same name by Jacques Brel. She often says that she strives to bring as much passion, energy, and joie de vivre to the company and its customers as Mr. Brel brought to the song. The company is based in Washington, D.C., and information can be found online at www.mariekeconsulting.com.

Tell us about you as the owner/founder. What's your story that made you the entrepreneur you are today?

For as long as I can remember, I have been engineering-minded, enjoying and excelling in the math and science classes that my classmates loathed. Combine this with my mom's insistence from about the age of six that I would attend the United States Naval Academy (USNA), and it was all but certain from the early years of my childhood that I would begin my career in the military. In 1990, at the age of seventeen, I began my four years at the USNA and decided to major in systems engineering. Though I had no idea what I was walking into on my first day at the USNA (wait, the Navy has airplanes?!), I understood that it was an exceptional school for engineering and represented a great opportunity for me. With no college fund set aside, I recognized that the USNA was my best route to an excellent education.

After graduating in 1994, I spent a few years on active duty service in the U.S. Navy and a few more years working in corporate America. The impetus for my venture into entrepreneurship came in 2002 with the birth of my daughter. Almost immediately after returning to work from maternity leave in early 2003, I was convinced I was ready to strike out on my own. Corporate restructuring, inequitable pay, and my general desire for more autonomy convinced me I didn't need, or want, the corporate infrastructure any longer. At only thirty years old, my substantial leadership experience and technical skills were undervalued to the extent that older team members who worked under me were being paid more than me. In short, I wasn't being paid commensurate to the title of program manager and it became clear to me that the leadership experience I gained in the military, including leading a naval division of about forty people, just wasn't going to translate to respect or stature in a corporate organization dominated by men without military experience.

In forming Marieke Consulting, it was my intent to continue supporting the FAA. Government work is all about finding a contract vehicle, a partner that already has an established relationship with the client and is working with them as the prime contractor. I quickly found such a partner, an established prime contractor for the FAA, that was happy to take me on as a subcontractor given my past experience and client relationships. Though I founded Marieke in 2003, I began building a relationship with the FAA years before I took the step to break out on my own. From 1998 to 2003, I supported the FAA as a program manager and senior systems analyst for Titan Corporation, providing advice and guidance in strategic planning, system management, process improvement, and best practices. Over the next seventeen years, our growth with the FAA continued steadily and deliberately and many of our employees became known as Subject Matter Experts (SMEs) on multiple financial and project management software applications.

In terms of my day job, supporting the FAA under my own business was much the same as supporting them as a corporate employee. My nights and weekends, however, changed dramatically. I was wading through the endless paperwork that is prerequisite to becoming a government contractor. I was running my own books and payroll, teaching myself QuickBooks and the ins and outs of bookkeeping along the way. I had no mentors or advisors to help me navigate the tempestuous waters of business ownership. Add to this a second child, a son, who was born in 2004, and one could safely say that my life had become markedly more hectic.

I feel that this fledgling period of my business was made considerably more challenging due to my lack of mentorship, which is why today I strongly recommend that new entrepreneurs seek out opportunities to glean wisdom from more seasoned business owners. If, like me, you are lacking in mentorship opportunities, organization is key. In the early days of my business, I compiled what I came to call my "magic checklist," essentially a list of critical checkpoints for starting a business such as establishing a bank account, creating a website, and submitting required paperwork. Eventually, I expanded the checklist to include tasks that must be completed every month, quarter, year, etc. Today, I share the magic checklist with every new entrepreneur who comes to me for advice on establishing their business. The checklist is purely pragmatic and the items on it may seem to be common sense, but when you are attempting to nurture a business in its infancy, often amidst chaos and sleep deprivation, it is extremely beneficial to have the obvious but critical tasks all laid out before you.

What have been the key factors to your success and why?

The key factors to my success have been much what you would expect - hard work, long hours, attention to detail, patience, persistence, and curating an amazing team of employees. The *most* important factor, however, has been my dedication to remaining focused on success. In my business and in all of my endeavors, I am committed to keeping my "eyes in the boat!" This phrase is a mantra borrowed from my years in the Navy that is meant to inspire focus in the face of rejection, disappointment, setbacks, distractions, and other deterrents from success. At the USNA, this refrain was screamed at us thousands of times throughout plebe year, reminding us to stand in formation with eyes forward and not get distracted by the poor classmate doing pushups four people down. The phrase proved invaluable during the two years I served on a ship out of Japan, where a lack of vigilance made it all too easy for other ships and boats to sneak up on you.

In business, keeping your "eyes in the boat" can be equally critical. It is important to define what success means to you, set a plan to achieve it, and stay focused on that plan. When facing proposal rejections, disappointments with colleagues, contractual setbacks, and distractions in both your professional and personal life, the success of your business depends on your persistence and a laser focus on your goals and objectives.

What has been your worst decision and how did you bounce back and still get to where you are today? How did this failure prepare you for your current success?

My worst business decision was hiring a business development manager who delivered nothing to the business in nearly a year. He was a friend of a friend and a former colleague who needed a favor, and while he had been successful at other companies, in the end his high salary and lack of performance became a drain on my company. Though we had multiple irons in the fire in terms of proposals and leads, none of these prospects came to fruition and it became apparent that I would have to let him go.

Though the seemingly obvious lesson from this experience is the age-old "never hire friends or family," I feel that the more significant piece of wisdom I gained was to stick to my instincts when it comes to business development. My primary focus has always been my work product, and as such I have maintained a slow and steady pace for business growth in order to avoid overextending myself and my team and to ensure consistent high-quality work. When I bought into the conventional notion that entrepreneurs should always be hyper-focused on growth and that every business requires constant "business development," I ended up paying dearly to chase down growth opportunities that I didn't even truly want or feel the business needed. In reality, there is more than one approach to growing a business. Listen to your instincts and choose a pace that feels comfortable and manageable for you and your team.

What has been your best decision and why?

My best decision has been to focus on a narrow set of services, specifically financial systems for the FAA, and to become an expert in those key areas. By establishing a niche and building a reputation as reliable experts within that niche, we have been able to convince the

FAA that the services Marieke provides are invaluable to their organization.

Maintaining a narrow focus in my service offerings has enabled me to differentiate Marieke from our competitors. By dedicating all of my years of experience to an incredibly specific set of services instead of stretching my attention across an expansive service offering, I have acquired a level of expertise that is unmatched by most of my peers. As a result, we are the FAA's go-to resource for financial systems projects.

What is an unusual habit you have as an entrepreneur that helps you succeed?

Before I even leave my bed each morning, I start my day by doing some sort of puzzle such as crosswords, anagrams, or Sudoku. I have had an affinity for puzzles for most of my life, to the extent that as a child I subscribed to a puzzles and word games magazine. Though puzzles just represented a fun diversion when I was a kid, today I feel that the mental exercise of solving puzzles primes my brain to tackle the various issues or conundrums that I may encounter throughout the day.

With the knowledge and experience you have now, what would you have done differently if you were to start your entrepreneurial journey again?

In a sense, I recently gave myself the opportunity to start over by taking on a business partner. I had al-ways had my eye on attaining service-disabled veteran-owned small business (SDVOSB) certification from the VA. My new partner is a service-disabled veteran and from the earliest days of our acquaintance I proposed the idea of going into business together. When she completed her military service in 2016, we formed a new LLC and began the process of attaining our SDVOSB designation. The application process was a grueling rigmarole that included several rounds of unjustified rejections and took more than two years to complete, but ultimately we earned our SDVOSB status, thanks in large part to our persistence and "eyes in the boat" approach.

Though taking on a partner was a largely strategic decision in that our SDVOSB certification gives us a leg up in winning government contracts, business partnership has proven enormously enriching and beneficial to my company in ways I would never have anticipated. She presents the enormously valuable opportunity to see our business through a fresh set of eyes and, with the help of her unsullied perspective, I am suddenly able to identify opportunities for improvement and growth that had previously escaped my notice. Even better, joining up with a younger, more idealistic entrepreneur has given me the opportunity to channel some of her enthusiasm and eagerness for growth, injecting a renewed energy into the company that was probably needed after more than fifteen years in business. This, I think, is the key to selecting an exceptionally beneficial business partner: find someone who not only brings a coveted set of skills or experiences to the table, but who also complements your business approach and perspectives.

What do you do when you feel demotivated and overwhelmed

A few years ago, I was extremely stressed at work, was not making any time for myself, and was generally failing to strike a healthy work-life balance. I was the lead on a major software modernization project, working around sixteen hours per day, seven days per week. I was fighting depression and had taken on a generally curt attitude with my loved ones and clients. One morning, I woke up on the verge of a nervous breakdown and realized that something had to change. That day, I resolved to set aside some time to completely disconnect and take a walk. After my walk, I found that my mood was immediately improved and I had regained the mental calm I needed to finish out my day.

To this day, I continue to make time each day, rain or shine, to go on a couple of walks and disconnect from all devices. The healthy release provided by these daily walks has improved my overall health and attitude. When I avoided an emotional collapse on that stressful day years ago, I learned that we cannot possibly care for anything – our business, our families, our friends – if we do not also take care of ourselves. As entrepreneurs, I think we often struggle to recognize and address our own needs because it is in our nature to pour 110% of our energy into our businesses. But if we run ourselves into a state of total depletion, we will have nothing left to pour into our businesses.

Discuss a crisis situation (2008 depression, 9/11, COVID-19) that you/your company were in and how you overcame it.

In October of 2013, the FAA underwent a furlough period and all contractors, including Marieke, were placed on a stop work order. My primary goal was to retain my entire staff for the duration of the furlough. This was a tall order, as I still had to make payroll for hours I would never be able to bill. Though the situation seemed dire, I was able to recognize the downtime as an opportunity for my employees to receive additional training. For two weeks, I gave them the option of taking courses that would enhance their skills on topics such as Excel, SQL, Tableau, and MS Project, or taking vacation time or leave without pay. Every one of my employees opted to take the training classes. Not only did morale improve because my employees felt they were being taken care of, but my clients also benefited from the additional skills my team acquired during the furlough period.

What is that one secret to your business success that would be helpful to current and aspiring entrepreneurs?

Keep your "eyes in the boat!" avoid distractions and remain focused and persistent.

What is the best investment you've made and why? (Can be an investment of money, time, or energy.)

My best investment is undoubtedly the time, energy, and money I spend recruiting, training, and retaining my employees. Without them, I would be severely limited in the value I could offer to my clients and I would have no time to grow the business. You cannot do everything for everyone, so it is invaluable to find amazing employees you can trust and who produce work that makes you proud.

Did you have to deal with tough barriers to entry?

Competing in my industry in the government space was made all the more challenging because some in the industry found it difficult to accept a woman in the roles of engineer and business owner. I remember around 2010 being at a small business owner networking event and bringing along my white-haired male colleague. Everyone assumed he was the business owner and I was there to hand out brochures. I took great pleasure in seeing the looks on faces when they read my business card and realized that I was the President and CEO. Even though I have established myself in the government space and built an excellent reputation, it continues to be a challenge to remain "in" and be accepted in that space and in my industry.

Not Your Average CEO: How I Created My Brand by Drawing outside the Lines

Tomeka B. Holyfield

Tomeka B. Holyfield is the founder and CEO of Helpppp Agency Group (HAG). HAG is a group of companies under one umbrella that provides strategic branding, creative marketing, event production, and business solution services. The company is based in the Atlanta Metropolitan Area and information can be found online at www.HelppppAgencyGroup.com.

Tell us about you as the owner/founder. What's your story that made you the entrepreneur you are today?

Helpppping people, simple as that! Helpppp stands for "Helping, Empowering, Loving and Preparing people for their Purpose, Plan and Platform."

I knew at an early age I wanted to make people feel special, because I always felt so special. I began creating family functions at the age of six, yes six. I created the family holiday functions, created the menu and meals that the elders would cook. I decorated the family dinners; I was producing full-fledged family events in junior high school.

I created these amazing stories in my head. I saw myself running my own company long before I really knew what that meant. I have the gift of always wanting to help someone. So, I turned it into a business and began motivational speaking before motivational speakers were even popular. I knew I wanted to work for myself and create opportunities for others. I just never imagined it would turn into three companies and one non-profit organization some thirty years later. HAG was created in my mind long before it was actually created!

What have been the key factors to your success and why?

Two key factors have played a part in my success. Let me share them in hopes of motivating you to your success.

First, I absolutely love what I do! I love creating and turning a concept or idea into reality. Helping individuals, companies, corporations, and foundations brand their image and concepts are unexplainable joys. Creating platforms and productions where people leave better than they came brings me the greatest fulfillment. I used to do this for FREE, but now those free days are over! The joy, however, is as exciting today as it was some twenty-five years ago. I believe you should do what you love and love what you do!

Second, my work ethic has been my driving force and the force behind our success as a company. I work until the project is done, no exceptions, no excuses, and no returns. It is something I've practiced since college. While everyone sleeps, I grind. I'm always the first one to arrive and the last one to leave. I am one-hundred percent all in until the final project is done.

What has been your worst decision and how did you bounce back and still get to where you are today? How did this failure prepare you for your current success?

The worst decision I've ever made was trusting people I should not have trusted. Being loyal to people that used me while knowing I was being used. I kept giving second and third and fourth chances to see if the individuals had changed. They had not; the only thing that changed was time.

They would always come back and their old habits would arise. I truly love hard and believe in being loyal, sometimes to my detriment. In business, you must not let emotions cloud your judgment. You must have tough skin, cut your losses, and run in the opposite direction when you know something and someone is not in your best interest.

I had to learn not to take it personal, that someone else's inexcusable characteristic traits were their deficiency. I began to change my perspective on how I viewed the many times I was used for my creativity, ideas, talent, and even something so simple as my bubbly personality. I began to view it as my greatest asset, my weapon of mass destruction. Humbled and honored that my God-given gifts were in high demand by individuals that didn't know how to simply just say, "I need you to help me."

Now, when I run across users, and rest assured they're still out there, I simply smile inwardly and either allow myself to be "used" to help the person out, or I simply walk away without them even knowing I've walked away. A gentle whisper goes a long way!

What has been your best decision and why?

Keeping one-hundred percent ownership of my company, owning my content, my properties, and my overall brand has been by far my best decision. It's important, however, to learn the basics of your industry. You will always be at a disadvantage if you don't understand the basics of what's going on in every aspect of your company at every level.

As an entrepreneur, there are realities we have to face. You can't be a CEO/founder and think investors will pump money into your company and not allow those investors to have any control. An entrepreneur will always lose some control when using venture capital financing. But as an entrepreneur you don't have to give up control if you know what you are doing and if you decide to draw outside the lines. Be creative, utilize your contacts, network, and even lean on family members. This is about your long term-goals, how you want to operate or see yourself in the future.

Owning one-hundred percent of my company was a decision I made for myself. It was based on how I saw myself and my company in my future more so than what my company was at the time of my decision. Sometimes, we must make decisions not according to our current situation but according to the vision we have of our future!

What is an unusual habit you have as an entrepreneur that helps you succeed?

I'm everyone else's biggest cheerleader. Let me explain! I am always excited to celebrate other people's success stories. Whether they are in my field or not, I will celebrate those successes. It's just something about seeing people prosper, grow, and succeed.

I'm the person that will share your success publicly and use my platform to lift others up. I will share events, opportunities, and use my networking resources. I have always believed that someone else's success and opportunities have nothing to do with what God has planned for me and my destiny. This has been a key element to my success and happiness; always being happy for other entrepreneurs has brought me great joy and success professionally.

With the knowledge and experience you have now, what would you have done differently if you were to start your entrepreneurial journey again?

If I knew then what I know now, the number one thing I would do is train a few family members to join me and grow with the team. I've invested an incredible amount of time, money, and energy in employees, volunteers, and interns, with no long-term return on my investment. I could have made that same investment in my family who literally will be by my side in the long run.

Now, there are always exceptions when it comes to family (this is where you laugh)! I'm speaking of family members who are responsible and have a great work ethic. There's a certain comfort in having a few people that you can trust one-hundred percent within your organization. Keeping the business within the family also gives back and provides a legacy to pass down to future generations.

This same concept holds true with close friends; it's just as easy to give close friends an opportunity within the company. Sometimes building your company as an entrepreneur can be a lonely journey. Enjoying the fruits of your labor with loved ones can make the experience more gratifying and memorable while building your wealth and brand simultaneously!

What do you do when you feel demotivated and overwhelmed?

I have created an 80/20 bulletproof concept to stay motivated and not get so overwhelmed about life. Are you ready? Let's get started! I'm sure by now you've heard about the 80/20 relationship rule; well, apply that to your business. Eighty percent of the time, what you've put out you get back. Then, there is the twenty percent when life grabs you by the collar and throws a curve ball at you. It takes the chair from beneath you, and sometimes you feel you can't breathe. Life is full of ups and downs. You are either in a storm, coming out of a storm, recovering from a storm, or preparing for the upcoming storm. The key is how you handle every stage of the storm. Life is a journey more so than a destination. How we handle the journey is our story. If eighty percent of the time life is going well, this is when you build your strength up. Your time in your eighty percent space will prepare you to handle that twenty percent space.

It's all about your perspective on appreciating the time of rest, the smooth sailing that will help you learn how to handle the storms. When you become overwhelmed, remember it's only temporary. It's just your twenty percent. The eighty percent of memories and successful experiences will motivate you back to life when you are experiencing your lowest moments. Remember, they are just that…moments!

Discuss a crisis situation (2008 depression, 9/11, COVID-19) that you/your company were in and how you overcame it.

The COVID-19 pandemic has been the most challenging situation to date for our media production company. At the same time, our branding agency and business solutions companies have flourished.

Our February 2020 NBA All-Star event was our last public event before the world literally shut down. If the government had shut down three weeks earlier, we would have found ourselves refunding thousands of concert goers as well as corporate sponsors. It was a wake-up call and sent our employees into survival mode.

We began to see the entire entertainment community shut down and dismantle. From Hollywood, to Broadway, even the movie theaters. The turning point for us was when the NBA and NFL canceled the start of their season. Shortly thereafter, every other entertainment-related entity shut down and it became very clear we were in trouble. We realized immediately that our line of business was not essential during a pandemic. As a CEO, I had to reassure my employees that we would survive, they would still have a job to put food on the table for their families. As a team, we became creative. We had to restructure and pivot our business blueprint and workflow. We uplifted one another, we couldn't let anxiety and depression take root.

Staying focused and purpose driven was the key to our survival. Remember, when insurmountable circumstances take place in your life, in your workplace, or in your relationships, always focus on the solution rather than the current temporary problem at hand.

What is that one secret to your business success that would be helpful to current and aspiring entrepreneurs?

The secret to my success and the secret to your future success is really simple. Once you begin to operate in a space where you and you alone create the narrative of your life, success starts at that exact moment.

I remember the early stages of building my company. I believed everything everyone promised or committed to me on projects, sponsorships, and contracts. I was running in circles on people's promises, words, and time. After several disappointments and heartaches, I decided to take my life and business back! I changed my perspective and began to set the narrative of my own life. I realized early on that my emergency is not everyone else's emergency. Your timeline is not everyone else's timeline. Your dreams are yours and yours alone. The moment you set the narrative of your own life, the timeframe for your own business goals, and the vision you see for yourself and your company, then and only then does success begin. Always remember, your emergency is not their emergency.

What's your advice for entrepreneurs who are still struggling?

Never ever quit! There is favor in the "AGAIN." Let me say that one more time....there is favor in the AGAIN.

Do it AGAIN. Try it AGAIN. Email them AGAIN. Call them AGAIN. Fill out that loan application AGAIN. Apply for that contract AGAIN. Call the bank back AGAIN. Schedule another meeting AGAIN. Hire another employee when one doesn't work out AGAIN. Trust AGAIN. Take a chance AGAIN.

When I look back at some of my most successful accomplishments, they are the result of never giving up and trying AGAIN and AGAIN. I never gave up despite the many failures I experienced. I kept trying again and again and again. You will only experience success when you do it again. "FAVOR is in the AGAIN". Every entrepreneur struggles: the ones who succeed are the ones who tried AGAIN. Go be great and make all your dreams a reality. You've got this!

What is the best investment you've made and why? (Can be an investment of money, time, or energy.)

In 2016, I made the best investment of my career. I took a year off from my production company to restructure, revamp, and revitalize myself. A mentor suggested that I expand my portfolio and create another arm of my businesses. So, I took classes at Georgia Tech on government contracting. Yes, government contracting.

How to secure some of the same type of work I was already doing, but now restructuring it to meet the needs of other entities. I created a business solution services company as a sister company to our branding and marketing company as well as our production company. They all work hand and hand with one another. Remember earlier when I spoke about how we survived during COVID-19? My other companies kicked into full flourishing mode and my solution services company was a slam dunk!

The moral is to always reevaluate yourself, as well as your assets, and always be willing to learn and excel in something new. Sometimes, you just have to jump into something new, something different, and something outside of your comfort zone. Just jump! It has been the winning ticket for me and my survival. The time invested in myself and the restructuring of my company in 2016 were the glue holding my company together in 2020!

Indigenuity: Indigenous Ingenuity

Dawn M. Houle

D awn M. Houle is the president and CEO of SunSinger Consulting, LLC. Established in 2015, the company is a Native American, Women-Owned Small Business (WOSB) dedicated to the stewardship of strategic partnerships for and with Native American tribes, artists, business owners, and individuals. The company is located in the Washington, D.C., metro area and information can be found online at www. sunsingerconsulting.com.

Tell us about you as the owner/founder. What's your story that made you the entrepreneur you are today?

My name is Dawn M. Houle and my Cree name is Chief Thunderbird Woman. I'm a tribal citizen of the Chippewa Cree Tribe of Montana and proud mother of two children. As indigenous people, we are tied to the land both spiritually and culturally, as well as one another. As such, I have expressed my cultural values by spending my entire professional career working for and with tribes to sustainably manage their natural and cultural resources.

Growing up on the Rocky Boy's Indian reservation in Montana, I was exposed to the power of giving back and the satisfaction of hard work. My mother was a single mother of three daughters who dedicated herself to sustainable long-term impact in our tribal community. I observed firsthand as she co-founded our tribal college, bringing educational opportunities directly to our people and allowing them to thrive and grow. This exposure to goal-oriented community service helped shape the person I am today.

Over the course of my career I saw business opportunities for Native communities or individuals halted due to the common obstacles that plague minority communities such as lack of access to capital, lack of proper business networks, lack of trust, lack of specialists, and other discriminatory burdens. I would advise and encourage my friends and family to start businesses all while asking myself, "Why don't I start a company?" From the manifesting of success around me, SunSinger Consulting, LLC was born.

SunSinger Consulting, LLC is a business development firm that specializes in optimizing business opportunities for Native American tribes and individuals. The name of my business was chosen from my son's Cree name – Chief SunSinger.

Prior to dedicating myself to business development, I spent the majority of my career in the Pacific

Northwest working in forest management with various tribes. As a forester, I was exposed to different tribal cultures and diverse traditional knowledge systems. These indigenous ways of being and knowing were incorporated into my day-to-day work. From this experience, I learned about the urgency of protecting tribal sovereignty and natural resources for current and future needs. The U.S. Constitution recognizes Indian tribes as distinct governments and tribal sovereignty provides them, with a few exceptions, the same powers as federal and state governments to regulate their internal affairs. My efforts supported critical jobs and provided tribal revenue. Yet, most important, I encouraged and supported tribal citizens to obtain natural resource degrees.

Creating tribal businesses is an assertion of tribal sovereignty which builds tribal economies on tribal lands as tribal leaders see fit. My forestry experience helped highlight the challenges that small business owners encounter and the creative ingenuity that it takes to survive. My entrepreneurial spirit grew as my career as a forester developed. As the manager of forestry, I oversaw multiple small individual Indian-owned businesses that created opportunities and overcame business obstacles. Managing a multimillion-dollar forestry program triggered my passion to obtain a Master's in Business Administration (MBA) degree.

While in business school, I spent one summer abroad studying in China and Japan exploring business practices from an Eastern perspective. Walking through cities and towns in Asia with thousands of years of history brought me back to the forgotten and all too often misunderstood history of Native Americans. This reflection further sparked my desire to use business as a tool to educate and create revenue in tribal communities. I have been an avid admirer of Native American art and used my time in business school to create a business plan for my Native American artist friends with the goal of establishing a marketing and sales platform for their beautiful handicrafts. Business startup is always a risky venture and commissioned art is even more so, making my efforts to help that much more worthwhile. Several of these artists used my plan to establish an artist following, collaborate with local art markets, and find time to focus more on making art and not on the aspects of marketing.

After graduating with my MBA, and after a few exciting years creating and serving as the executive director of a tribal non-profit, I moved to Washington, D.C., to serve as a policy advisor to the Assistant Secretary of Indian Affairs under the Obama administration. I then made another career change to become the chief of staff for the National Indian Gaming Commission. My former network of executives convinced me to make this move to the East Coast plus assisted me with the complex federal hiring process which led to each of my jobs in D.C. My career goal at that time was to learn the internal processes of the federal government and gain insight into how I could best help tribes navigate federal processes more efficiently. While building strategic partnerships across federal and state agencies,

I was instrumental in initiating organizational changes for many tribal communities due to policy realignment that actually benefited tribal economic development. Prior to the end of President Obama's second term, I started my consulting business. My Washington, D.C., experience served as the cornerstone to launching my own business.

I started SunSinger Consulting, LLC while maintaining a full-time position ensuring I maintained both health benefits and a steady income as I built my business portfolio. Initially, I worked for the Seminole Tribe of Florida, Inc., a Section 17 federally chartered corporation, and developed a government procurement program. I accepted limited work that did not conflict with my full-time employer and made them fully aware of the type of work that I did accept so there was full transparency. Two years after launching my first business, I launched my second business called Salish Sun Partners, LLC. This company is a forest carbon offset business offering culturally-based modern solutions to tribes while enhancing natural resource sustainability, creating a new revenue stream and jobs, while offering the opportunity to actively participate in greenhouse prevention. Salish Sun Partners, LLC offered me an opportunity to fully utilize my educational background in forestry in conjunction with my MBA. This business creation was the result of being approached by several non-Indian companies to work for them on carbon offset, a new forestry business opportunity for tribes. My research showed that many of these companies had insincere interests in the success of tribal communities. As a Native person, I feel it is my obligation to have the tribe's best interest at heart and by creating my new business I again was afforded the opportunity to both live my values in protecting natural resources and drive tribal sovereignty.

What have been the key factors to your success and why?

Success is a very individual evaluator. Graduating from college is a success for some, while starting a business is a success for others. I find that creating clear plans with specific, tactical, and actionable items that generate measurable results is a true key factor not only for entrepreneurs but for life. When I plan, I like to start with the factors that I can control such as the name of my company, signing up for free business sessions, saving money for a business license, etc. Secondarily, I include in my plan backup options for the factors that I cannot control, such as finding capital or the length of time it takes to receive a positive response from a client. The process of outlining and organizing controllable and noncontrollable factors serves as a means to measure progress and outlines areas to seek help.

Other key factors to my business success have been strategic partnerships with individuals who dedicate themselves to improving the lives of others. Expanding my knowledge in new areas has also helped my path to success. For example, I was selected as a Sundial Fellow for the minority business executive development program at the Tuck School of Business at Dartmouth. The experience was not only a networking gem but an opportunity to stop and assess why I am an entrepreneur and determine if my business was heading in the right direction. Other key factors that have guided me are working from the standpoint of what can go wrong then creating solutions based on each obstacle. This strategy has proven to be worthwhile given it approaches a Strength, Weakness, Opportunity and Threat (SWOT) analysis from a position of sustainability. If the solutions don't outweigh the obstacles then this alone is a great indicator of whether or not to proceed with a project.

In addition, I utilize life and/or educational skills to assess situations and communicate strategies that clients can relate to. This is very helpful in business when working with a prospective client to convey in simple terms the opportunity, investment, and outcome. I don't employ big flashy sales pitches. I try to approach prospective clients directly and with honesty just as if we were friends. I do not make recommendations for any of my clients that I would not recommend to myself or my own Tribe. If the prospective work is not a good fit for my company, I have no problem referring them to good reliable associates that I have vetted over the years. Being true to your company's capabilities is another key factor; do good work without sacrificing your integrity and values.

What has been your worst decision and how did you bounce back and still get to where you are today? How did this failure prepare you for your current success?

During one of the many product crazes that are out there, I had an opportunity to start a business with a few friends prior to a new product being introduced to the market. This product, which I will not mention since it is still a sore spot for me, took off fast and went global at a time before we had social media to help. We discussed, we planned, we financed, and we aligned with the right distributor but in the end never got out of the gate. This experience reinforced in me the need for good partners, the ability to assess personal risk, and the importance of taking action even if it hurts. In hindsight, I should have launched the business by myself or with one friend then invited others in after it got started. I'm more hesitant now because of this experience and more aware of the complexities of working with too many people at once. Currently, I still review each client and business deal from the angle of the level of trust I have in the person and project before leaping in. I feel that any decision, even if it is a "no decision," is still a decision that impacts the trajectory of your business. I embrace setbacks for the lessons that they offer combined with discovering internal business inefficiencies and fixing them, hopefully with little expense and simply a bruised ego. I'm not afraid to make mistakes as long as I learn from them.

What has been your best decision and why?

Starting SunSinger Consulting, LLC has been the best decision because it allowed me to fully actualize my talents. Starting a business is a big decision but once I got started, which was slow, I had much more pride in my abilities. It is gratifying to see your efforts being put into action by a client. The best reward from a client is them actually following your advice and implementing it.

What is an unusual habit you have as an entrepreneur that helps you succeed?

I give a lot of my services away for free, especially to those individuals or tribes who need it. Compared to other businesses, this habit may seem unusual but to me it is a way of giving back while establishing credibility, loyalty, and living by my values. I approach business from the standpoint of trying to make a difference and not from a position of how much money I can make. I will admit this is risky, but in almost all cases, the people or tribal communities that I have helped have eventually hired my company and become long-term clients. I find that giving away a little bit of my time and effort gives me a sense of who the client is plus gives me time to assess our future business relationship compatibility without expending a lot of resources on a bad relationship for the sake of money.

With the knowledge and experience you have now, what would you have done differently if you were to start your entrepreneurial journey again?

If I were to start my entrepreneurial journey again, I would start earlier in my life. I fell victim, like many others, to fear of failing, fear of not having enough time, money, and other woes that prevent people from starting a business. This fear was due to my perception that I needed the right credentials, the right degree, the right network, etc. Yes, some of these help but in reality if you have the right product or service, you can jump right in and start. What I would do differently is create a flexible plan with items that I can control with small measurable benchmarks so that I could feel less afraid as I get the business up and running. I believe, in the era of Shark Tank and YouTube, many more people are willing to kick off their ideas which make business startups so much easier.

What do you do when you feel demotivated and overwhelmed?

Making a list helps me juggle the pressures of balancing the feeling of being overwhelmed. I gain more sense of direction if I actually use a pen and paper to create this list. Items that are less critical are listed at the bottom of the sheet, those items that need attention within the next few days go to the top, other items that can be pushed a few weeks out go in the middle. Of course, life doesn't always work out the way we want so I make sure that my list is flexible, and I understand the impact on other items on the list when changes happen. I feel a list helps your brain navigate the pressures and responsibilities that are demanded of us.

Additionally, I utilize my list to identify areas where I may need additional support. I think a setback many starting entrepreneurs face is single-handedly trying to do too many things. Tapping into your network and utilizing your resources is key to managing work backlogs and continuing forward movement.

Discuss a crisis situation (2008 depression, 9/11, COVID-19) that you/your company were in and how you overcame it.

During the current COVID-19 crisis, many of my clients had to refocus on securing the basics thus impacting renewal of my contracts. But what did develop was the launch of new business endeavors by my clients who reached out for business guidance and advice. The reality is helping others regardless of crisis is not only the right thing to do but also deepens a relationship with your network for inclusion in future work. Crisis management should be looked at as "what opportunities exist for me or my clients?" Helping companies pivot into new industries has been SunSinger Consulting's focus this year.

What is that one secret to your business success that would be helpful to current and aspiring entrepreneurs?

Asking for help is the one secret that new or aspiring entrepreneurs should always implement. Be as direct as you can. For example, someone in your network just got a new client or project. After congratulating them, ask if there is any opportunity for collaboration with your company. Or ask someone you admire in business if they would review your product or service for ways to improve. You will be surprised at how many people love to give their opinions! As the saying goes, you never know until you ask!

What's your advice for entrepreneurs who are still struggling?

Research and sign up for free resources like SBDC (Small Business Development Center), talk to friends for advice, and monitor business school websites (even if you did not go there) for advice and potential network leads. Don't let a lack of capital be the barrier that limits your company's vision; determine what you can do regardless of finances.

Evaluate your business offerings based on the current pandemic, how flexible is your business, can it be used in a different way, who do you know that you can collaborate with, etc. This evaluation may or may not help strike a chord within your creative spirit leading to a new way of earning money and helping people. Business is really about finding solutions to a problem. Ask yourself, "What problem are you solving?" Right now, hairdressers are offering YouTube haircut lessons or delivering mini hair coloring kits, all ingenious solutions to people's hair problems. Other advice I would offer, even if you are not struggling, is to assess your partners. Ask how they are supporting your business, can these partnerships be improved, and are they adding net value, subtracting, or preventing business growth.

What is the best investment you've made and why? (Can be an investment of money, time, or energy.)

The best investment I made was in myself. Throughout my career I have pushed myself, first in college as the first women from my Tribe to graduate with a forestry degree, then as the first woman to serve as director of forestry which is typically a field dominated by men. Working hard and advancing my career brought me to D.C. where, after rising to the top as a federal employee, I found myself still feeling unfulfilled. This drove me to bet on myself again and launch SunSinger Consulting,

LLC which allowed me the freedom to work for tribes in a manner that helps them build success in regions that have not typically had opportunities due to a multitude of reasons. As the CEO of my company, I try to expand my knowledge base by growing my circle of friends from diverse backgrounds. I also read books not focused on my industry. A person's circle of influence has the potential for great impact both personally and professionally.

Buying Dirt

Robert Merrill Jefferson

Robert Merrill Jefferson is the owner and founder of Merrill Jefferson Enterprises LLC, a real estate investment and consulting company that invests in multifamily apartments and retail businesses. The company has been operating since 2013 and is based in New York, New York. Information about the company can be found online at facebook.com/merrilljeffersonenterprises.

Tell us about you as the owner/founder. What's your story that made you the entrepreneur you are today?

"Go out there and buy some dirt!!!" Those were the words I heard at the end of my Hampton University graduation ceremony, and those words still remain vivid in my mind today. It was at that moment, with my family sitting in the crowded HU Convocation Center sheltered from the pouring rain, that I knew I would one day become a real estate entrepreneur.

I chose to attend Hampton University because I knew that the supportive environment offered by Historically Black Colleges and Universities (HBCU) would prepare me to be a future business leader. It then took me four years to figure out that real estate ownership is something personally important to me. Real estate is a physical element of wealth and can equate to economic, social, and political power. I grew up in a Brooklyn, NY apartment building and during my childhood I did not see the benefits of homeownership. Back in the 1980's, only a few of my friends had families that owned homes, and those homes were not in the safest neighborhoods. One day I remember going to my friend's house for dinner, and somebody had broken into their home and stolen the meat out of their refrigerator a few days earlier. I figured living in an apartment building was safer. Even if someone robbed an apartment in a 100-unit building, there was only a one percent chance that it would be your apartment being robbed. But the tragedy is I had no idea of the tax benefits, property value appreciation, and equity benefits of real estate until much later in life. Now I have a lot of catching up to do!

What have been the key factors to your success and why?

Education, network and experience. These three key factors to my success are linked together.

Education is a continual process for me and led me to understand how to create value. As a business owner, it is important to understand your industry, to know how your market develops, and how to interpret inherent risks. All this knowledge comes from some sort of formal or informal education. I personally have benefited by observing, reading, and talking to those that have done what I intend to do. When I come across a key concept or learning, I take notes on my cell phone. When I am waiting somewhere, I take out my cell phone and review those key learnings. After reading them dozens of times, they are embedded within me.

I have been fortunate to have a broad network of like-minded, intelligent professionals who I consider my network link. I can go to almost any major city and get linked with those that can guide me and connect me with others. This opportunity will be there for you if you are the type of person that helps to open doors for others. There are individuals that are "one-way networkers" who try to get connections that they can benefit from but never want to bring opportunities to others. I try to stay away from those individuals and strive to always connect with those in my network who have similar goals.

Making the decision to go back to graduate school and obtain my MBA from The University of North Carolina at Chapel Hill (UNC) was definitely a critical milestone that helped me develop a deeper understanding of real estate development. Through my real estate program, I had the opportunity to work on my first real development project in Garner, North Carolina. Additionally, the experience allowed me to build my network within the university. The UNC Tar Heel network is dynamic and resulted in my first partnership with my classmate Tim, who was also from New York. I met him at Chapel Hill and we started "buying dirt" together across the country many years later. The network I developed and formal education at Chapel Hill were both important, but the other key factor to my success was working on "live" deals. You can learn basic concepts from books but there's nothing like working on real projects and solving real problems. A real estate deal is often created by a problem and if you can solve the problem you will create opportunity. *Entrepreneurship is ultimately about creating opportunities!*

What has been your worst decision and how did you bounce back and still get to where you are today? How did this failure prepare you for your current success?

The worst decision I ever made was switching gears and not listening to those that advised me to stick with investing in my core multifamily apartment business model. When my initial apartment deal flow slowed down in 2016 (and, as an investor, at some point it will probably slow down), I started to invest in other types of real estate and followed the lead of someone on my project team that had more experience than I did. I then allowed that team member to control aspects of my investments, despite the doubts I communicated. At the end of the day, I assumed that individual had better insight just because they had more experience. *More experience does not mean having the right experience!* In hindsight, I should have followed my instinct and never diverted from investing according to my original core business plan.

At the end of the day, that shift of investment focus was a learning opportunity and allowed me to then concentrate more on my core business. As an entrepreneur, it can be beneficial to try new low-risk investments. If they fail, you need to change course quickly and limit the exposure that you have.

What has been your best decision and why?

Owning a business did not come as a new concept to me, it actually started back in junior high school. I did not start with a lemonade stand or a newspaper delivery route. During the day I was a normal 7th grade student, but at twelve years old I started a DJ music service called WAKE UP SOUNDS. My business partner DJ BAMN and I were politically minded and that was reflected in the music we listened to (Public Enemy was my favorite group), the movies we watched (Spike Lee's *School Daze* shaped our lives forever) and the political causes we supported (marching through the streets for racial justice in Washington, DC and New York). WAKE UP SOUNDS represented us and allowed us to become twelve-year-old entrepreneurs, which was one of the best decisions I ever made. At the time, we were not nearly the best DJs in New York City; we were pretty much just trying to figure out the business on our own, but that did not matter. We were able to book parties and shows, invest in expensive equipment, and plan the logistics for moving car loads of records and speakers across the city. Many times, this coordination occurred in the middle of the night at about 3 a.m., in not exactly the safest parts of New York City, but we lived to tell about it. As business owners, we found our niche market and followed the demand. That was the business foundation that inspired me throughout my life. DJ BAMN always said that we would form a conglomerate called Mega-Mega Global and now Merrill Jefferson Enterprises LLC is my operating arm of the Mega-Mega vision. Next step is to take it global. *Always consider growth; that is how an entrepreneur thinks!*

What is an unusual habit you have as an entrepreneur that helps you succeed?

My unusual habit as an entrepreneur is virtual strolling. During the night, I may walk down the block in West End, Atlanta, and then minutes later walk through the streets in South Shore, Chicago and then roam down an avenue in Durham, North Carolina. I am able to do this all virtually, from the comfort of my home, using Google Street View. I experience these neighborhoods as if I am actually there.

When I first started my company, I would often find myself on Google Street View closely looking at the screen while reading the street signs as I moved my mouse up and down. I could get a feel of the neighborhood by just looking at the types of cars parked on the street. That information would be helpful later when I made offers to buy properties. Sometimes I would fall asleep at the computer and wake up feeling like I had walked miles. In reality, I never left my office chair.

With the knowledge and experience you have now, what would you have done differently if you were to start your entrepreneurial journey again?

I would have started my real estate investment business sooner, ideally after the dot-com bubble in 2001. Real estate markets operate in cycles and if I had started investing earlier, I could have experienced more growth, realized larger asset values, and now have a bigger business network.

Time is important and the early bird gets the worm. I am trying to instill this concept in younger investors so they start building their assets and knowledge base early in life. The only caveat is that these younger investors should seek guidance and mentorship earlier if they start investing before learning about the inherent risks and pitfalls of investing in a business.

What do you do when you feel demotivated and overwhelmed?

When I start to get demotivated and overwhelmed, I turn from my desk in my swivel chair and l look at "The Wall." "The Wall" is simply a white wall in my office filled with color pictures of all the multifamily apartment properties I have acquired throughout the years. When I look at these framed photographs, I don't just see buildings. When I glance at the images, I think about all the residents who live in the buildings and create the community. I think about the children that are playing in the playground today that I purchased for the property because they were just sitting in an empty parking lot throwing rocks when I first acquired the property.

I also think of my real estate team in those markets, including the property managers, supers, attorneys, brokers and contractors, who all benefited from the acquisitions my company has made. I know that they have bills to pay, families to support, and dreams of also investing. As I look at "The Wall," I am motivated to continue to help them achieve their goals.

Discuss a crisis situation (2008 depression, 9/11, COVID-19) that you/your company were in and how you overcame it.

A national and global crisis often cannot be predicted and are significant risks for most businesses. One reason why I decided to invest in real estate and focus my company in that sector is that it can benefit from market volatility created from economic downturns. I launched my business after the 2008 financial crisis and was able to acquire several properties at price points that were much lower than historical highs. This was a strategic positioning that I was able to professionally benefit from.

The investments that I made after the 2008 recession had a positive impact not just for my investors but also for the residents living in our properties. After national economic downturns, there is much uncertainty and little cash for apartment owners. As a result, many neglected properties become distressed at this time. My company was able to acquire these types of properties, inject capital for physical improvements, and create a better quality of life within the communities.

My company was able to benefit from the 2008 recession, but I caution that it was truly due to timing. If I would have started acquiring properties a few years earlier, I would have had a much different outcome. A more critical situation for my business was a local issue in which one of the largest employers in a Connecticut town decided to relocate its employee base. As workers moved out of the town, vacancy rates increased and it became very difficult to rent an apartment. A national depression helped my company acquire valuable properties but a small local company closing had a significant negative impact on our ability to collect rent or sell the property.

What is that one secret to your business success that would be helpful to current and aspiring entrepreneurs?

Consider your time. As an entrepreneur, your time is very valuable and managing time effectively is important. As a real estate investor, a great opportunity may come and go in a few hours, so you have to be in a position to make offers quickly. I tend to make quick offers and do extensive due diligence after making those offers. I typically work with brokers, attorneys, and sellers to create more time for me to consider the deal. It is important to lock up deals quickly, but take your time to consider them.

What is the best investment you've made and why? (Can be an investment of money, time, or energy.)

The best investment that I made was initially engaging with professional coaches who guided me through the purchase of my second apartment acquisition. I was coached by a husband and wife team who were awesome and acted not only as coaches but were also advisors, connectors, and cheerleaders that encouraged me to take calculated risks.

The benefits that I received from my coaching relationship included the instilled confidence within me to invest in larger apartment buildings, the direct one-on-one coaching and support to analyze deals, and the linkages to a community of other investors to share market information. The investment in coaching was an investment in myself. At the end of the day, your investors are not only investing in your business but are also investing in you. *As an entrepreneur, you should make investments in yourself.*

Did you have to deal with tough barriers to entry?

Investing in apartments has significant barriers to entry that are not easy to overcome. That is one reason, however, why it is a good real estate asset type to invest in as it is not very competitive in smaller markets. The two main barriers are accumulating the capital need-ed for acquisitions and obtaining resources needed to source deals. I attempted to solve the access to capital barrier by investing in smaller lower-cost markets. The issue is that although many smaller markets have low-er purchase price points, they typically also have less inventory. Finding deals can be more challenging in these markets. *As you see, when you take steps to avoid one barrier, you often encounter another barrier.*

Sourcing deals gets a lot easier once you start acquiring properties and can build a reputation with brokers. So, for all the new investors out there, I encourage you to put in the work to get that first deal, but only after doing proper due diligence. Do the diligence and then buy the dirt!

Bringing MARS to Earth

Rashi Arora Khosla

Rashi Arora Khosla is the founder and CEO of MARS Solutions Group (MARS SG), an IT professional service agency that helps clients assess, plan, and execute business and technical projects. The company assembles optimal project teams and crafts customized solutions that exceed client expectations. MARS SG has received numerous awards and accolades, including being recognized as one of America's fastest growing companies on the Inc. 5000 list. The company is based in both Waukesha, WI, and Indore, India, and information on their various offerings can be found online at www.marssg.com, www.getreturnship.com, and www.Giveovation.com.

Tell us about you as the owner/founder. What is your story that made you the entrepreneur whom you are today?

My story is not one that follows the theme of countless hours, sweat, and tears, but instead is one that finds sustained success while balancing my work in favor of my family time. The beginning of my entrepreneurial journey was rooted in a concept that would appear simply outrageous or "out of this world" to most successful entrepreneurs.

I brought MARS to Earth.

I started my business on the side of my successful IT job. I wanted to have more time with my two daughters who were ages four and one at the time. Even though my corporate job offered a lot of flexibility, I still wished to work at my own pace and under my own control. With this naïve desire and no clue as to what the business would do, I incorporated MARS. MARS is an acronym made from the names of my daughters, myself, and my husband: **M**ona-**A**lisha-**R**ashi-**S**apan.

The start of the company was accidental and unplanned, and its success has been an amazing evolution for me as an entrepreneur. The journey, however, has led me to a purpose.

As the business has evolved, I also have evolved as a leader. Most important, the 'why' behind MARS has evolved tremendously. It has shifted from my personal need to have work-life balance into wanting to have a legacy while making an impact for all Martians and the community at large. I feel so fortunate to be at a point in my career and life that I can engage in my passion projects.

Both MARS and I have been supporting various organizations in different capacities. MARS also runs a Returnship program that is an on-ramp for women looking to restart their careers in technology following a gap in employment. We provide on-the-job training, mentorship, and a partnership approach to prepare our cohorts to successfully rejoin the workforce.

To date, with 165 Martians and counting, MARS has stayed true to our culture of family values, work-life balance, and an entrepreneurial mindset.

What have been the key factors to your success and why?

The naivety of the beginning of MARS also meant that very little, if any, market research was done about its service portfolio. MARS focused on the competitive, conventional, and traditional business space of IT staffing. Even in the crowded marketplace, MARS grew consistently and organically year-over-year.

I strongly believe that our success came from our conviction surrounding the concept and a complete detachment to a conventional way of thinking. We found our niche in a delivery model for staffing that is unique and out of this world, again MARS-like.

Since I had no experience with staffing, I devised how the business would work for me rather than modeling it based on what other staffing firms do. The product of doing so was an innovative delivery engine that had high reliance on technology along with a staff of recruiters that came from software and engineering backgrounds, just like I did. I simply had to stay true to my being and tuned into my instincts.

As MARS evolved, I had the privilege to develop a new SaaS product called Ovation which incorporated my three passions: data and artificial intelligence, diversity and inclusion, and entrepreneurship.

I have stayed original by deflecting a lot of conventional wisdom and doing things my way. This has served me well for the most part, but there have also been some consequences that I have accepted as part of the package.

What has been your worst decision and how did you bounce back and still get to where you are today? How did this failure prepare you for your current success?

I am not sure if this is the worst decision that I have made in the history of MARS as I have made my share of them, but this one jumps out at me the most.

In the early days of MARS, when I was still running the business as an absentee owner, I ended up attracting a lot of unwanted, negative attention from a much larger competitor. I hired one of their top salespeople after she had been terminated for causing an accidental loss to them. She sued them for her termination, and I agreed to pay her legal fees. This turned into an increasing burden on MARS as the case went on for an extended period of time, yet we had zero knowledge of the actual details of the case. This was just the beginning of a stressful year.

This salesperson delivered positive results, but her aggressive approach created a very toxic environment leading to four other team members exiting MARS. The same competitor took these people under their wing and proceeded to take frivolous legal action. MARS prevailed, as expected, but the situation distracted me as a leader and slowed my decision-making ability.

This experience forced me to quit my corporate job and focus full time on MARS. That trying year helped me grow as a leader and allowed me to deeply appreciate the value of organizational culture and having the right people. Now I hire for cultural fit over skills every single time. One of my mentors at the time told me that company culture starts with you, and that has stuck with me forever. Since then, I try to lead by exemplifying the culture of MARS.

Above all, this experience made us so much more successful as a staffing supplier. We were able to find the best cultural fit for MARS which translated into how we helped our clients. Our recruiters already had superior technical skills, and we have now ingrained the importance of team and cultural fit into their minds to set us apart from the crowd.

What has been your best decision and why?

MARS is a product made up of a lot of balanced risks and decisions. There have been several notable choices which have kept us moving in the right direction, starting with quitting my corporate job, to hiring and farming amazing Martians, and diversifying ou portfolios. Recently, I was able to convince my husban to become a full-time Martian despite the convention wisdom that says do not work with your spouse. H association with MARS has become the catalyst to tak our growth to the next level.

What is an unusual habit you have as an entrepreneur that helps you succeed?

I am a hobbyist astrologer. At one low point in m personal life, I became involved in astrology. I hav since learned a lot about planetary movements and tr to apply the positive planetary alignments to all aspec of my life. That may sound superstitious, but I vie this hobby more as a science and do not get into th forecasting aspects of horoscopes. Good, bad, or ugly this has become my unusual habit. It helps me wit my mindset and therefore has an indirect impact o MARS' success.

With the knowledge and experience you have now, what would you have done differently if you were to start your entrepreneurial journey again?

I would not change a thing. As a spiritual being, I tak joy in the journey and try hard to detach from th outcome. Failures are there to learn from, and I surel did fail, sometimes needing more than a few tries t eventually succeed.

That being said, if I had known some of the ingredient to a successful business that I know today, I could hav been on a faster track to success. The maturity and experience that I now have as a leader are vital for the new expansions in progress at MARS. It is starting to become an exciting journey. All the painful mistakes I made pushed me to grow as an entrepreneur and as a leader. The journey has been so meaningful with its ups and down, and I have never stopped learning because it is my necessary fuel.

What do you do when you feel demotivated and overwhelmed?

I continuously need variety in my work and life routine. As the primary visionary for MARS, I start coming up with ideas for change even before I have had my cup of coffee in the morning. I am also eternally optimistic and see so much opportunity for MARS each day. However, I get overwhelmed and demotivated when I am not able to execute on my amazing ideas, or the opportunities we receive, due to capacity constraints. I feel like I am constantly scaling the team to keep up, and I struggle when I know I am leaving money on the table and can quantify missed opportunities.

Discuss a crisis situation (2008 depression, 9/11, COVID-19) that you/your company were in and how you overcame it.

MARS faced the 2008 recession in its infancy. I had just launched the business and had no other employees. I was still at my corporate job and in all practicality my journey as an entrepreneur had not even begun.

In a way, there was not much to lose at that time. Most other staffing companies were closing doors, and it obviously was not the best time to start a business, let alone a staffing business. It was not so much about overcoming the recession as it was about developing strategies that helped put us on the map. I hired the top talent available due to the recession and was able to bring in a very strong entrepreneurial salesperson that worked on a high commission model. He prospected companies even though they were not hiring. He worked on our diversity certification and on our sales processes. Two straight years of foundational work helped us reap the benefits in 2011 and onward. A lot of this work was done by him and two other employees who were extremely dedicated and who wore all the hats needed to keep the business running.

Fast forward to COVID-19, which is also the seventh year of my running MARS. We had to act swiftly to ensure we were prepared to meet the challenge head-on. Our teams efficiently adapted to the virtual work atmosphere since most were used to doing so already. Our human resources and marketing teams came up with a solid plan to keep up the engagement level for all employees. Technology was always our good friend, and it became essential during COVID-19.

What is that one secret to your business success that would be helpful to current and aspiring entrepreneurs?

Success is personal. You define your own path and milestones. Stop benchmarking your business against others.

What is your advice for entrepreneurs who are still struggling?

Overnight riches come to very few. Have an agile mindset. We hear a lot about how failures are stepping stones to success, but no one can guarantee that for you. You know your situation the best so make sure you are tuning into your instincts and consciously tuning out the conflicting information you'll receive on the path to success. You already know when to stop, when to pivot, when you are close to your dream, and how much more risk you can bear. Lead from that place of intuition and confidence.

Be pragmatic. Design your sprints of entrepreneurial execution such that you can measure and pivot periodically and, in some cases, stop before it is too late. Learn what you do not know, augment in areas that you are not already an expert, and most important, seek inspiration and joy. If you believe, keep working so others can also believe.

How would you describe the culture of your company? Did you develop your company consciously or did it just happen?

Our culture is built around family values and supports the individual need for work-life balance while promoting an entrepreneurial mindset. This translates into all aspects of our business. All Martians that end up thriving in our environment value these key factors of our culture.

We are very intentional about our culture and passionate to the point that we have built a product to help businesses with baselining and measuring inclusion, a key component of a successful culture.

In the beginning stages of MARS, there was no leadership or intentional culture; I ran the business as an absentee boss. When I became dedicated to leading, I finally instilled my version of company culture. I envisioned and instituted what MARS would stand for and hired people who aligned with those visions.

Lead with Love

Lianne Lami, PE, CEM, CEA

Lianne Lami is the founder, president, and CEO of Bocci Engineering, LLC. The company delivers Solutions That Pay For Themselves™ through best in class turn-key sustainable engineering design and construction services. Since Bocci's inception in 2002, the collaborative team is motivated by strategies to reduce impact on the environment. Through our passion and operations first perspective, we innovate, drive economic value, integrate and optimize. The sustainable solutions focus on infrastructure, utilities, commercial mechanical, electrical, plumbing (MEP), instrumentation, controls, automation, environmental, alternative energy, and renewable technologies. The company is based in Houston, Texas, and information can be found online at www.bocciengineering.com.

Tell us about you as the owner/founder. What's your story that made you the entrepreneur you are today?

I have always been a high energy, driven, curious, and compassionate person who loves math and science. I knew I wanted to be an engineer since the eighth grade when my neighbor showed me what puzzles he could solve. His wife brought me inside to warm me up from raking leaves in their yard on a cold fall day in Pittsburgh. He had all these drawings, scales, books, and a calculator spread out on his dining room table. While sipping hot chocolate, I asked him the first of many questions: "What are you doing?" He loved my curiosity and patiently explained about the plant design he was working on. I was hooked. Thank you, Mrs. and Mr. Witchey!

I graduated in 1988 from Virginia Polytechnic Institute and State University (Virginia Tech) with a Bachelor of Science degree in mechanical engineering. At every given opportunity during my twenty-year corporate career, I consumed and completed years of professional development. I took nearly everything offered to me, even if it meant working overtime. After starting up several new technical businesses and supporting mergers and acquisitions with prior employers, the fall of Enron was the catalyst to form Bocci Engineering in 2002. Due to the energy industry instability caused by the Enron collapse, as well as other financial market repercussions, tests of my business plan and market proved the timing was not yet ready to launch the business. I consulted independently under Bocci until August 2006, mostly in industrial oil and gas markets. I also took a couple of full-time assignments in the energy risk management industry. On the heels of the Energy Policy Act of 2005, which contained significant financial incentives for energy efficiency projects in industrial and commercial infrastructure, I re-launched Bocci Engineering in August 2006. By

2007, I had a sufficient backlog of work to incorporate as Bocci Engineering, LLC and began hiring full-time employees. Bocci grew organically to an award-winning twenty person consultancy just ahead of the American Recovery and Reinvestment Act of 2009 (Recovery Act.) The Recovery Act further incentivized sustainable development, energy efficiency, conservation, and emissions reduction and had available grants for shovel-ready cogeneration and renewable energy projects such as generation power, biomass, and biogas plants.

Since 2009, Bocci has pivoted many times, adapting to local market fluctuations, industry procurement and technology changes, regional and national market hurdles, catastrophic storms such as Ike and Harvey, global economic recessions, and today's pandemic. I have participated in at least two executive MBA-type development programs per year since 2011. These programs have helped me expand my networks, hone executive skills for small business management, form business alliances, and develop a continuous process for innovating solutions, including Bocci's success through current and future challenges.

I see something similar in being an entrepreneur and an equestrian. For me, I just can't have one horse or one business. I live with my fearless first responder fiancée, Denise Hamby. She amazes me every day with her capacity for giving herself, her integrity, and her work ethic. Together, Denise and I own three horses and are boarding ten more, and along with her mother Barbara, we have two goats, four dogs, two cats, nearly thirty chickens, and fifteen fish at Trotting Spirit Ranch, our small sustainable acreage homestead in Cypress, Texas. Barbara, or "Granny" to all she wants to be called, loves to garden, cook and keeps us and the ranch clients stocked with an abundance of fresh eggs and homemade cowgirl cookies. The ranch has hosted several equine-facilitated programs in leadership development, team building, and communications skills training programs.

What have been the key factors to your success and why?

The key factors to my success are tenacity, perseverance, a strong sense of integrity, not being afraid of work, a willingness to fail to improve, asking for help, receiving help, and asking the same questions of many mentors, advisors, and other business owners. Listening, listening more, listening to my heart, and making decisions and proceeding with compassion and empathy are additional factors to my success. I am reminded by the strength and experiences the women in my family have shared, and I am most grateful for my mother, Margie Lami Linton, who taught me to hear my inner voice, to take care of me, and through example and courage be an independent, self-sufficient, and gracious woman.

What has been your worst decision and how did you bounce back and still get to where you are today? How did this failure prepare you for your current success?

During the first slow down experienced by Bocci, I hesitated and took too long to downsize, simply not believing the slow down would last as long as it did. Maintaining employees and a payroll above the ratios and burning through cash reserves was my worst decision.

Today, we maintain a business dashboard with leading indicators of market and financial indices, so executive management behaviors are objective and timely. Furthermore, everyone on Team Bocci is involved in sales efforts and client retention. I operate Bocci with job cost accounting open internally so my employees know their contribution to costs and margin and are able to see where and how they add value.

Bocci is navigating and growing through our current pandemic. We are openly sharing our insights with others on leveraging the gig economy, strategic partnerships, and supporting and mentoring others.

What has been your best decision and why?

My best decision has been not quitting. In the worst times of Bocci's history, many advisors, even a CEO round table leader, tried to convince me there was not enough value in the company worth keeping it going. Nearly everyone said shut it down except for me and one professor of accounting.

While attending Tuck Executive Education at Dartmouth, I scheduled a formal review of Bocci's financials by Phillip Stocken, Professor of Accounting. He has developed a financial analyzer tool which goes way beyond five or six typical bank metrics. I went into the meeting and shared the previously-advised negative thoughts. He said, "Well let's take a look at what you have and let the numbers speak for themselves." In about twenty minutes, Dr. Stocken had run the numbers, added several hand calculations, and six or seven key actions he recommended be taken. He said our company's margin was more than twenty percent better than the mean, and that our debt could be paid off and managed with small changes to our operations. Thank you, Tuck's "Growing the Minority Business to Scale" program, and Dr. Stocken!

What is an unusual habit you have as an entrepreneur that helps you succeed?

The habit that has worked the best for me is creating space for mindfulness. I rejuvenate when outside and especially when grooming or riding my horses. Horses have this amazing ability to be very present, to immediately read my temperament, and draw me in. I'm an early morning person, and I afford myself the time every morning to meditate, have coffee while watching the horses, feed, and ease into work. Practicing mindfulness enables me to not be reactive. I try to make big decisions in the morning when I am most refreshed and have had the opportunity to sleep on things and meditate.

With the knowledge and experience you have now, what would you have done differently if you were to start your entrepreneurial journey again?

I would not be the sole owner in Bocci Engineering and I would utilize investors and board advisors to grow with others who have a stake in the game.

There is a constant challenge managing cash flow when growing. It's not if, it's when the crisis happens and how resilient your business is in pivoting. You must have the ability to ebb and flow. Growth is necessary for a financially successful exit plan, and growth requires more resources than just capital.

What do you do when you feel demotivated and overwhelmed?

I go horseback riding on my heart horse Al Azrak for a three or four hour ride as fast as we can. And yes, normally I am riding solo. Most folks I have ridden with don't like riding that far or that fast. If you ask me what I do to celebrate....you guessed it! Al and I go blazing down the trail.

Discuss a crisis situation (2008 depression, 9/11, COVID-19) that you/your company were in and how you overcame it.

Bocci had a couple of perfect storms fairly close in timing, and just after recovering from the 2008-2009 depression, we had a backlog of over one million dollars in engineering services sold in 2010 and had moved to our custom-built green (sustainable) office space in the energy corridor. Unfortunately, soon after we relocated, we had three contracts stall within a month of each other, and our backlog shrunk by over fifty percent. One was a large commissioning contract with a federal design build contractor. It took over seven months to get authorization to restart the contract without having to go out for rebid. When the contractor restarted, they were asking us to cut our fees and still perform the same amount of work. We chose to walk away from the contract.

I had learned a lesson previously about waiting too long to enact layoffs. In May 2012, I had a company-wide meeting and gave the entire team a three-month notice with pay and offered to assist them with recommendation letters and part-time employment opportunities to continue with Bocci after the three months were up. All of my team found wonderful positions, several went to our clients, and a few went to firms which became new clients. To this day, several of the original team are still Bocci's part-time employees and our best advocates for referral and teaming opportunities. We utilized the gig economic model before "gig" was a common term amongst millennials.

The Bocci green office space was in an owner-occupied building, and the landlord was willing to allow Bocci out of the contract if we agreed to move out within ten days. You ask, how do we move an entire engineering firm in less than 10 days? I asked for help and three angels showed up! Denise Flores, owner of Sunrise Deliveries, helped us move. Cynthia Kelsch, owner of Merlin Services, bought Bocci's furnishings and appliances in exchange for her subcontract fees. Kristin Rickett, part owner in Collaborative Engineering Group, contracted me for a Leadership in Energy and Environmental Design (LEED) highest level Platinum consulting project. My mother was my fourth angel. She kept saying, "Lianne, you define your own success", "This too will change", "Keep your chins up" (yes, she affectionately and purposely used chins plural), "Feel the joy in how you cared for your team and the difference you are making in each other's lives." I am grateful and humbled that leading with love, while doing the right thing during very hard times, could be so impactful in a positive way. Thanks Mom, and my angel sisters, for always believing in me.

Bocci has been one-hundred percent remote since 2012. We moved the entire engineering platform, software, and technology tools into the virtual cloud. We set up our part-time and full-time employees with "offices in a box" to work from home, and provided stipends to cover their home office expenses. When COVID-19 hit, we were ahead of the game. Our resiliency and success are driven by having a low overhead, highly responsive talented team that has worked together for many years.

What is that one secret to your business success that would be helpful to current and aspiring entrepreneurs?

You should authentically and openly follow your passion. Smiling and excitement are contagious and all bumps in the road are just opportunities to expand, learn, and share.

How would you describe the culture of your company? Did you develop your company consciously or did it just happen?

Our culture is our people and we are sustainability pillars. Each Bocci team member feels they have room to grow, are valued, and their individual contributions make a measurable difference to the environment and their community. Team Bocci exemplifies integrity, knowledge sharing, and collaboration, and collectively strives to improve the environment one project at a time. We celebrate successes and empower innovation and inclusion.

The culture was ignited consciously, groomed, improved, and peer-to-peer elevated. When drafting the very first employee manual in 2009, we had to educate our human resource consultant to add language to adapt it from not discriminating regarding sexual orientation. In all company meetings and communications, we use techniques to gain contributions from quieter and marginalized individuals and shut down discriminatory or silencing language. I have coached employees, especially if it's with a peer or a junior engineer of color, female, or other marginalized person, to speak out to stop the silence. I have coached employees to say something positive like "I'm certain that Susan's answer is correct, she is far more knowledgeable about the details of your project and she has tremendous experience in this area. I would trust her recommendations."

What happened naturally in our culture and team was that we hired a very mixed group of women, men, people of color, and LGBTQ+. I believe fully it's part of what makes Bocci so innovative and successful at delivering Solutions That Pay For Themselves™.

Did you have to deal with tough barriers to entry?

It was not common in the 80s for women to be in the mechanical discipline of engineering. I still remember, when we sat for class pictures, there were about twenty women in a class of close to five-hundred at Virginia Tech. When graduation came, you had to sit for the Engineer In Training (EIT) exam if you wanted to be a design engineer. Even during job interviews, many of the recruiters steered women towards sales, and the professors seemed to wave off the need for women to take the EIT exam. Fortunately, I knew I wanted to do design and sat for the exam. Passing this exam, then achieving four years of practical training while working under the supervision of a professional engineer, is required before qualifying to take the licensing exam. Working in design is difficult if you don't already have your license or design experience. I had gained design experience as a co-operative education student, which helped me succeed in getting a design role.

The licensing exam to become a Professional Engineer (PE) is an eight-hour exam, the first half is objective, and the second half is subjective. The first time I took the exam cold turkey, just to see what it was all about and, as expected, didn't pass. You could only take the exam once every six months in a three-year period before having to reapply to qualify again. It took me five attempts to pass and obtain my professional engineering license. The second time I sat for the exam I took a three-month night class to prepare and took a week off before the exam to study and practiced like crazy. I had a strategy plan and I went after my best subjects: thermodynamics, Heating, Ventilation, and Air Conditioning (HVAC), and power. I thought I did great and when I got the scores back, was disappointed that I had failed by only four points. I learned I could get a copy of the exam results with the score grading and use it to learn what I did wrong. What I learned was the graders knew less about HVAC design than I did, so I submitted a written appeal. The response was, "Our policy is such that unless you are within two points or less from passing, we will not change the expert's opinion and score." Well, I chalked it up to "only the toughest make it through" and scheduled and paid for another exam and studied for months. This time after the exam I knew I had passed, hands down. When I got the scores a couple months later – I failed. Again. This time missing by... yep, three points. No reason to appeal. The fourth time I took it, I missed by two points. I appealed again, and got a letter saying I did not sufficiently justify my position and the score would remain at it was, encouraging me to take the exam again. I was burned out. I remember speaking with another female engineer who owned a civil engineering firm in Richmond, Virginia. She encouraged me to keep trying. I missed the next exam, and as I got close to my last chance in the approved three year period I got a call from my mentor. She said "Lianne. You have to take the exam again. I can't give you details, but trust me, you will do fine this time. It's absolutely necessary if you ever want to own your own design firm. Go for it!" I mustered up the energy and sat for the exam. This time I skipped the class and used the materials previously received to study with the week before the exam. I passed!!

What I didn't know was that the first four times I took the test, the State of Virginia had an all-male review team that was purposely failing women. My mentor was involved in a case against the state for discrimination, and my appeals were part of the proof. Heads rolled, and a new review board was assigned. Thank God for mentors and women who support women. None of us can do what we do alone. I would not have Bocci Engineering today if it weren't for obtaining my PE and the encouragement of a mentor who stood up for others.

Chefdivah Is the Female Version of a Kitchen Hustler

Chef LaToya Larkin, MBA, CCE

LaToya Larkin, known as Chefdivah, is the program coordinator of the Culinary Arts Program at Spring High School in Spring, Texas. She received her Master of Business Administration (Nonprofit Management) from Springfield College, a Bachelor of Science degree in Culinary Management from The Art Institute of Atlanta and an Applied Associate Degree in Science with a concentration in Culinary Arts from The Art Institute of Houston. She is the owner and operator of Black Girl Tamales, home of creative fusion tamales where "South of the Border meets Southern Comfort Soul Food." Signature tamale dishes include Collard Green with Smoked Turkey, Oxtail, Smothered Chicken, Smothered Pork Chop, Chicken Fajita, Blood Orange Pork Carnitas, Shrimp Etouffee, Crawfish Etouffee, and Red Beans and Rice. The company is based in Houston, Texas, and information can be found online at www.blackgirltamales.com.

LaToya is also the owner and operator of Not Enough Thyme Personal Chef Services. This company provides in-home meal preparation service and meal prep for clients on the go or who want to step up their dating game by having her create intimate date nights. Information can be found online at www.notenoughthymepcs.com.

With a line of Divah Chef Apparel that has catchy phrases for the kitchen hustler (male or female) at www.divahchefapparel.com, LaToya knows how to outfit her clients for culinary success. She is also the creator of It's Thyme 4a Change Nonprofit, which works with at-risk youth to plant a seed of culinary positivity. Her endeavors demonstrate that people can do positive things with food and make a great honest living because regardless of anything in life, people love good food! Information can be found online at www. thyme4achange.org.

Tell us about you as the owner/founder. What's your story that made you the entrepreneur you are today?

I am Chefdivah. That is Divah with an "h" because I am a hustler and stand outside of the other Chef Divas. Growing up, my maternal grandmother had a significant influence in my life. I spent most weekends, summers, and holiday breaks with my grandmother. She taught me how to cook and bake, let me experiment in the kitchen without reservation; plus, she taught me how to make tamales. Where I grew up, local liquor stores were miles away on the lake. So my grandmother sold beer and alcohol to the local community. It was like a bar with an atmosphere of the old television show *Cheers* vibe, but at your auntie's house with all the crazy relatives over at any point. Everybody knew everybody; my uncles always had friends over in the backyard after work so it was easy to cover up. It was nothing more than family visiting family. We made real money every day from morning until late at night. Things were especially active late at night when they could not get to the liquor store before closing. My hustle and drive were instilled in me at a young age.

My grandmother was big on making sure that her children and grandchildren got an education because she did not have an education of her own. She had to drop out of school to take care of her brothers and sisters since she was the oldest child. So in regard to us going to school, she was always there for us from co-signing loans to using credit cards or hustling up money for our books. I guess she did not have a formal education, but she was very well-educated in a way that helped her children and grandchild.

Overall, I am a DOPE female chef in my season working hard to manifest my dreams and make all of them a reality. I am also raising my son to be confident, leading by a positive example of what it looks like to accomplish goals. I want him, along with other youth, single mothers, and anyone who has ever struggled, to see me do extraordinary things. This lets them know that all things are possible with faith, prayer, consistency, and hustle with drive.

What have been the key factors to your success and why?

Five key factors to my success are staying positive, remaining focused, planning my goals and visions, living by the Law of Attraction, and surrounding myself with the right people. It is essential to keep a positive mindset and remain focused on your goals. As the old saying goes, "keep your eyes on the prize." While doing so, check your goals so that, as you accomplish things, you can cross them off your list. I believe the Law of Attraction is real and all things that you want to accomplish will come to the light. Finally, you are about as good as the company you keep. Iron sharpens iron, so it is crucial to surround yourself with people that are doing what you are doing or better. You always want to pick the brains of those who have been where you are and are where you are trying to get. One thing I've learned is that people who have achieved a certain level of success will always want to genuinely see you succeed. Therefore, they will do anything and everything possible to help you reach that success.

What has been your worst decision and how did you bounce back and still get to where you are today? How did this failure prepare you for your current success?

I think one of the worst decisions I have made professionally is spending and wasting money on business opportunities that I knew were not a good fit for me. These failures helped me to realize that all money is not necessarily good money. If you are not passionate about what you are doing, there will be no genuine joy in making money. When you are truly doing what you love, the money will come to you. You will not have to chase the money.

What has been your best decision and why?

One of my best decisions in life was to become a high school teacher. I know the burning question of many will be, "Why become a teacher? You don't make the money you should make for what you put up with each day." Or my favorite comment is, "Poor thing, I don't know how you put up with it." I always laugh because I am one of those teachers who does not have those types of problems. I am an old school firm but fair person. My students know who to play with, and it is not me. They LOVE their chef and reference me as their school mama. I am relatable; I am a person they can talk to and confide in, and I can give them some direction. Most of my students are not loved the way they want to be loved at home and they know I will love them, yet I will also get on their behinds! I am that teacher that, when my fellow co-workers have problems in their classes, they will say, "All right! Don't make me email Chef Larkin and tell her how you are acting!"

Outside of the obvious, such as working with youth, making a difference, and positively impacting their lives, being a teacher on a school schedule has given me the flexibility and opportunity to build my brand and business concepts over the past seven years. No working nights or weekends, paid holidays, and paid summer breaks make up a hustler's dream job to moonlight and strategically plan to put things in place. Long hours are the first things that burn out a restaurant chef. I run the culinary program, so I have complete freedom to dance to my own tune and do my own thing with unlimited potential of creative thinking on various aspects of my business. Unlike working in the food service industry, there are many limitations compared to when I was a restaurant chef for eight years.

What is an unusual habit you have as an entrepreneur that helps you succeed?

An unusual habit of mine is to keep late nights and have early mornings. These times are my genuine moments of solitude, and it appears all my creative juices flow late at night. I get all my light bulb moments from 10 p.m. - 4 a.m.

With the knowledge and experience you have now, what would you have done differently if you were to start your entrepreneurial journey again?

If I had to start again, I would have had more mentors earlier in life, learned to be more vocal, networked more, and would not have feared rejection. I would also have stepped out on faith instead of being scared because "Scary Money Don't Make No Money" (a slogan from my clothing line). By nature, I am a quiet person; however, I know how to talk to get what I want. As I got older and built my confidence, I came into my own.

What do you do when you feel demotivated and overwhelmed?

When I feel demotivated and overwhelmed, I take a moment to relax and meditate. Self-care is important and most likely whatever is overwhelming or demotivating me is not what truly needs to be done nor needs my energy. I need to focus on the moment. I am a massage connoisseur, as I have been told, and will promptly book a massage appointment along with other things to relax such as manicures and pedicures. Because I work with my hands and am on my feet for long extended periods, I must take care of them because they are my money makers. I de-stress to get my mind right and regain focus.

Discuss a crisis situation (2008 depression, 9/11, COVID-19) that you/your company were in and how you overcame it.

COVID-19 has been nothing less than a blessing in disguise for me. While some business owners unfortunately struggled quite a bit during the pandemic, I was blessed that my business took off and skyrocketed! It is cliché to say that we can make lemonade out of lemons, but that is exactly what I did. I truly took lemons, squeezed them, and pulled things from the pantry and fridge to make whatever I possibly could. I created different flavored lemonades, Lemon Cream Cake, Lemon Pie, Lemon Cheesecake, Gelato, Lemon Pepper Wings, and Lemon Detox Water. I mean, you name or think of anything with lemons in it, I made it! When we first had to go into quarantine, I was out of the classroom on Spring Break. This goes back to one of the best decisions I believe that I made in life, which is to be an educator. I was already on a holiday break from work and did not have to return for the rest of the school year. Guess what? I was PAID IN FULL the entire time that I was out of the school building from March to August. That money lasted until school resumed for the 2020-2021 school year. So imagine that I received a full paycheck just as though I was reporting to a brick and mortar workplace, yet I am actually able to be in the comfort of my own home. Everyone was scared to leave their houses, but they were also becoming tired of cooking. They missed having someone to cook for them at a restaurant. Do you see how this was a great business opportunity for me? I then cleaned out my freezer as I do from time to time. That turned on a light bulb for me and I came up with Quarantine Cuisines for meal prep. This covered a wide range of special occasions: milestone anniversaries, birthdays, proposals, or just because someone wanted to say I Love You. I also found a way to be very creative for those who were doing Quarantine Dating. That is where I perform in-home meal preparation service: breakfast in bed, a three-course dinner, or brunch for a group of good girlfriends that miss each other. You know that last group well. They are the ones who are about 3.5 seconds from losing their minds because the kids and their significant others are pressing their absolute last nerves! I created a menu for each of these scenarios, posted pictures and videos, sent text messages, and then bam! It only went up from there.

I saved the best concept for last. I also make tamales as an homage to my grandmother. She was one of the #1 hustlers I knew, God rest her soul. This period away from traditional school allowed me more free time to crank out tamales. So, amid quarantine and brainstorming new flavors, I came up with Oxtail, Smothered Chicken, Smothered Pork Chop, and Nacho tamales. Then I took it further and did loaded tamales. I came up with three Shrimp Etouffee (three tamales topped with rice pilaf and Shrimp Etouffee), Crawfish Etouffee (three tamales topped with rice pilaf and Crawfish Etouffee), and the "It Is" Tamale (three tamales topped with rice pilaf and smothered chicken, collard greens, macaroni and cheese, and puree candied yam drizzle). All of these have been added to the meal preps. During the time from March 2020 to July 2020, I cleared over $15K, not to mention figuring out the most cost-effective shipping aspect. Game over! Black Girl Tamales is successfully being shipped across the country and I am even working on getting onto store shelves, partnering with restaurants to manufacture and franchise the concept on a larger scale.

What is that one secret to your business success that would be helpful to current and aspiring entrepreneurs?

One of my old bosses used to say, "LaToya you goin' have to stroke 'em." Then, as he broke it down, it made total sense. You must learn the psychological aspects of dealing with people and the art of persuasion. Be nice, be consistent, smile often, and build long-lasting relationships with people. Who wants to do business and spend their money with someone rude, unprofessional, and always mad with an attitude? You master the "stroke" and there is nothing you cannot get from anyone you come across in life.

What's your advice for entrepreneurs who are still struggling?

I would tell these individuals to operate with an open mind, with the willingness to do something different, and to get something they have never had. Struggles will come about in business as they do in life. However, when they come, be open to change. Have the clarity and focus to know when it is time to do something different and not be so antiquated and stuck in your ways. Learn to take constructive criticism from someone that is doing what you are doing. Better yet, when someone says something to you that you do not like, do not get in your feelings because you have too much ego and pride. Instead take advice from that person who has achieved what you want to achieve, regardless of if they are older or younger.

I have had experiences with so many older people in my career. Before I started teaching, I worked for school districts as a consultant for child nutrition. Many of the cafeteria workers have been in their respective schools since they put the first brick in the buildings. The district hired me to advise them on how to improve their programs. Some would have preferred their teeth pulled without Novocain rather than to listen to me because they were older than I was. Many of them had children my age. However, I was hired to help increase revenue, make the kids excited about school lunch and breakfast, and to help the employees keep their jobs.

Unfortunately, I was viewed as someone who could not possibly have a wealth of experience. Maybe it was because I was younger than those that I trained. Maybe it was because I was female and men are traditionally seen as more reputable with knowledge in their field. Or maybe it was that I was a young black woman who had multiple degrees and I was working in an area that was likely traditionally biased towards people of color. It surely ruffled some feathers! There was someone who once shared with me that my co-workers and I were looked down upon by the people that we trained. They saw us as "a bunch of highly-paid, over-educated Negroes" who tried to come in and change what they were doing. I know that the language I have chosen to use may seem a bit harsh, but the way that it was conveyed to me was much worse than this. The interesting part is that without the training that my team and I were able to provide, many of the employees who resented us being there would have not stayed long at all. Most of the programs were at the point where they could not afford to keep some employees and were on the verge of letting them go. I saw that those who valued their jobs quickly got on board with what we wanted to share with them while others were still reluctant due to their personal biases. My takeaway from this is that you should always be open. Do not be so quick to shut down an idea from someone that you think is not on the same level as you are. That person could actually be an asset instead of a hindrance.

When you started your business did you have support? How did you handle the naysayers?

There will always be naysayers! I was blessed because I had unwavering support from my parents, my grand-mother, family members, and a few close friends. It was a tough pill to swallow when I realized that people say they are proud of you but then pass up every chance to support you while they support everybody else in a heartbeat. Honestly, most of my support came from total strangers, people I never knew.

This taught me to whip out that long-handled spoon, develop a tougher skin, and not get in my feelings so quickly just because everybody is not going to be excited for me. If someone is not where they want to be in life, how are they going to be happy and excited to support you when you shine bright? The reality is that they cannot. I remind myself that this is my dream, so never stop believing.

Underdog

Elisabete Miranda

Elisabete Miranda is president and CEO of CQ fluency, a global language services company that specializes in culturally relevant translations for life science and healthcare industries in over 170 languages. The company works to customize and translate the meaning and feeling of messages to facilitate real connections and true cultural understanding between people who don't speak the same language. The company is based in Hackensack, New Jersey, and information can be found online at www.CQfluency.com.

Tell us about you as the owner/founder. What's your story that made you the entrepreneur you are today?

I am originally from Brazil and am the youngest of three daughters whose mother died when I was only two years old. I have always had an incredible work ethic, most likely because I began working at age twelve. By age sixteen I was alone and homeless for a short time. Fast forward, after owning twelve small businesses at different periods of time, due to the economic turmoil in Brazil, in 1994 we packed ourselves up in only three suitcases and moved to the "land of opportunity" with our six-year-old daughter. Like many immigrants, I arrived in the US with very little money, not speaking one word of English, with the hope of providing a better life for our family! The biggest challenge that I had when I moved to the US was not only the language barrier but the cultural differences, especially in the healthcare space. It was clear from the start that my "why" and life mission would be to "improve lives."

Within six years of being in the US, I had learned English, finished my college degree, and became a partner in a business with my sister-in-law that was then Translation Plus, LLC. This company evolved into CQ fluency, a fast-growing, successful, and certified woman- and minority-owned and operated business.

All the challenges I have had in life have made me firmly believe that almost everything can be overcome when you want it bad enough and tell yourself, "I GOT THIS!"

What have been the key factors to your success and why?

I have always said that with passion, you can do anything. If you are not passionate about what you choose to do with your life, you are limiting your potential. Also, I would never be where I am today without hard work and persistence along with an eternal "can do" attitude. I am a certified workaholic or a "work lover" as I prefer to think, and always give 110% to go above and beyond. One of my secrets to success is to put myself in the other person's shoes. That perspective gives me the confidence of knowing the right thing to do.

What has been your worst decision and how did you bounce back and still get to where you are today? How did this failure prepare you for your current success?

One of the decisions that I regret was not making a decision that was needed. As a small company, I made the mistake of not focusing my business on one industry from the start. As with many small businesses, there is little success when you try to be all things to everyone. You need to know your niche and position your company based on the area of business that you do well.

After identifying that most of our revenue already came from the healthcare industry, we made the decision to focus our expertise on healthcare. This has enabled us to be where we are today. A clear, focused vision laid the groundwork for our success

What has been your best decision and why?

My best decision has been to not only obtain minority certification for the company, but also to get very involved in diversity organizations. I'm very active in the National Minority Supplier Development Council (NMSDC), the Women's Business Enterprise National Council (WBENC) and Diversity Alliance for Science (DA4S) and I participate on different boards and committees. These organizations have made it possible for me to cultivate an incredible network of like-minded people over many years. I have been able to leverage my involvement by promoting diversity and inclusion and have amazing relationships with people who started out as prospects and potential clients and have now become my friends. An incredible number of business opportunities have resulted from these networks, some of which took over ten years, but were all worth the wait! If I hadn't participated in the Center of Excellence program through the New York & New Jersey Minority Supplier Development Council (NYNJMSDC), I would never have met the people who became my biggest supporters and advocates. It was through these relationships that I was encouraged to apply for the EY Entrepreneurial Winning Women Program™. Being chosen as a Winning Woman in 2010 was a HUGE moment, and I almost died when I won. Oh, my goodness, it changed my life in so many ways, mostly by teaching me to think big and be bold and believe that anything is possible. Being singled out by such a prestigious organization was a huge honor for me personally and for our employees. I saw the award as recognition of my hard work and accomplishments, but it was even more significant as a tribute to what we achieved as a team. I simply wouldn't have been considered if our company wasn't successful.

What is an unusual habit you have as an entrepreneur that helps you succeed?

At the start of each new year at CQ fluency, we always select a "word of the year" to create a focus for positive change. It is a practice so fitting to our culture and contributes to our success. This year our word is "gratitude." I have never felt entitled, and that is why I work so hard. I always identify the silver lining despite the circumstances, by consciously practicing positivity, treating everything as an opportunity to learn, and always feeling grateful.

With the knowledge and experience you have now, what would you have done differently if you were to start your entrepreneurial journey again?

I would have started to think big a lot sooner. It's known that *we become the average of the five people we spend most of our time with*. So, I would have joined entrepreneurial networks earlier on, and surrounded myself with people smarter than me to be inspired by. You can't be what you don't see!

What do you do when you feel demotivated and overwhelmed?

I rarely feel demotivated because I know the value of hard work, and to be a successful entrepreneur, you need to work harder than everyone else. But when I feel overwhelmed, I reflect on my "why," which is to improve lives. I have never been motivated by money, because I believe that as humans, we have a moral obligation to do whatever we can to improve the lives of everyone we touch. One of the ways I do this is by creating jobs in an environment where people can be happy while also supporting their families. When I remind myself of this, it makes me feel that all the hustle is worth it because it allows me to help many others along the way!

Discuss a crisis situation (2008 depression, 9/11, COVID-19) that you/your company were in and how you overcame it.

In my personal life I had to overcome many challenges when I lived in Brazil, and this gave me the certainty that I can overcome anything. But what keeps me awake at night during a crisis is my moral obligation as a business owner to protect my employees. This is what makes me work harder and do everything in my power to keep the business thriving, so I can protect my people and my family.

What is that one secret to your business success that would be helpful to current and aspiring entrepreneurs?

You can't grow your company if you can't grow yourself. Be bold, think big, and don't feel afraid to ask for advice. Knowing when you need a partner, an extra resource, and how to collaborate is critical to growing a business. Something I always say, because I believe it, is *you don't get what you don't ask for*. Ask anyone on my team! It's my advice, and my go to, and now most of theirs, too!

How would you describe the culture of your company? Did you develop your company consciously or did it just happen?

It's been said that if you don't define your culture, your culture will define you! I'm obsessed with developing a good culture and as a leader, it's my job to set the tone.

I hold myself to the same standards to which I hold my employees, and there is not a single thing that I would ask my employees to do that I wouldn't do myself.

When I reflect on the reason for our company's success, I attribute it to our team. You can't grow a company alone! CQ fluency is a purpose-driven company and we exist to improve lives. *We are passionate about having a positive impact in every life we touch, through our work, our interactions with each other, our clients, our vendors, and everyone around us!* We describe ourselves as a "people-centric" company, and we live by that.

We are a diverse company by nature. The diversity and inclusiveness of our people contribute to the tone of our culture. Everyone knows that they should bring their true selves to work, just like I do. We really embrace that and it creates an environment so amazing that it's difficult to describe without experiencing it.

While our core values are passion, respect, integrity, diversity and inclusion, and being exceptional, there are some characteristics that I use, or reiterate, when describing our overall culture:

Positive attitude. I'm convinced that a positive attitude is a big differentiator. Nothing is impossible if you have a "when" not an "if" mentality. I once heard, "you have more value in your attitude than in your bank account." I'm not implying that this is easy. Sometimes, regardless of what you do, encouraging people to change their attitude and have a positive outlook on life can be impossible. Some people are just happy being unhappy. My issue with this is that negativity is contagious and often a stronger force than positivity. As leaders, we need to be able to identify negativity as quickly as possible and act fast to diffuse it, because it is very easy for one person to contaminate your culture.

Passion. In our company, we are passionate about people; meaning, we value our customers, but equally value our employees and vendors. I truly believe that without their happiness, they can't make our clients happy. We have a caring and passionate culture, and we have fun, we laugh, and we celebrate achievements, big and small. In 2015, we achieved a big revenue milestone; to celebrate, we took the team and their families to Mexico. It was a wonderful bonding experience. We had a blast and team spirit went through the roof.

At CQ the expression TGIF is not allowed. I firmly believe that life is precious, and you need to do something that makes you happy. If you live your life to be happy on only the two days of the week that you don't work, then you need to look for a job that makes you happy. I don't want to be responsible for anyone's unhappiness. We have adopted the same policy as Zappos – when we hire a new employee, we offer $3000 for them to leave voluntarily after three months if they are not happy. We only want people who want to be with us.

Integrity. We want people who do the right thing even when no one is watching. Mistakes and s**t happen; how you deal with them is what makes the difference. We approach EVERYTHING we do with integrity and it is one of our most important core values. Our commitment to integrity permeates the entire organization. Our clients know it, too. It's one of the reasons they trust and stay with us for as long as they do. We have a "no ego zone" to ensure we have authentic conversations without defensiveness so the whole organization wins. This is how we consistently deliver on our promises and, on the rare occasion we get it wrong, we do whatever it takes to correct and improve as a team.

If you don't know, LEARN! It's impossible to know everything, but I believe that it's our job, especially as underdogs, to learn. New experiences are at our fingertips all the time, literally. Just ask "Uncle Google" and, with a simple search, we can become experts on a number of topics. Believe me, I don't have enough fingers and toes to count how many times I have become an "expert" overnight. Again, knowledge is power, and without being resourceful it's impossible to grow.

What's your advice for entrepreneurs who are still struggling?

It's okay to be the UNDERDOG! Most entrepreneurial, diverse companies can be regarded as small, and not a threat to their larger competitors. Use this as your advantage. Bigger doesn't always mean better, but typically it's the credibility in the marketplace that gives the bigger companies the competitive edge. The best thing to do is not to think of your company as an empire in the making, but rather as the underdog; the one who is always going to work harder, be agile and flexible, is nicer, kinder, and humbler. People want to work with nice people who are driven, demonstrate their enthusiasm with the prospect of working together, and are grateful to do so.

Be bold! We must grow ourselves before we can grow a business. Growing a company is not easy. You constantly deal with things that you don't know and are frequently out of your comfort zone. Don't be afraid to ask for advice; you will be surprised by how many people are willing to share. A perfect example is all the contributing authors in this book! Be hungry for knowledge and become a life-long learner. Knowledge is power and power gives us the courage to be bold. Once I moved to the US, the fact that I didn't speak English had a big impact on my self-esteem. As my English improved, so did my self-esteem and I started to be bold again and I was able to yield great results and grow, both personally and professionally. While I constantly rely on data and facts to make informed decisions, I frequently deviate from the "didactical way of doing business" and always consider my gut instinct (I tend to follow my heart).

Even though I am motivated by purpose not money, I don't ever underestimate the competition or overestimate financial risk tolerance. It's crucial to closely monitor your business from a financial perspective and know when to adjust if needed.

Becoming too emotionally invested in a single idea can blind an entrepreneur of reality. You need to be willing to make necessary, sometimes even painful, corrections to increase the chances of success.

Don't let the fear hold you back and don't give up if you fail. You cannot have success without making mistakes. You will get hurt, you may lose an opportunity that you so desperately wanted, or lose an important client. By being bold, you will have the strength to bounce back and learn from the mistakes. The people that never fail are the ones who don't try in the first place. Be okay with falling; when you get up, **dust yourself off,** and **start again**! **Be bold!**

Lead with your heart. As an underdog, it's always a challenge to be "heard" and for me, it's an even bigger challenge because I have the added struggle of being somewhat unconventional. It's not that I don't know the traditional way of doing business, it's just that sometimes I decide not to follow it. For me, it's more important to be true to myself. I always say that you need to bring your true self to work, and I lead by example. I believe that we are "one person," professionally and personally. I know that suggesting you lead with your heart might sound crazy to some, but against all odds I can say that I have achieved success, and it worked for me.

The most important person in my life is my daughter; she is my greatest blessing. Because of how much time I focused on my business, I often felt she was short-changed because I didn't get to spend as much time with her as I always wanted to. It has been something I deeply regret. Recently, after listening to an important business call, my daughter shared with me how proud she is of me for working so hard and being true to me. All along, without me even knowing it, I have been her inspiration. This proves that with love in your heart, everything eventually comes full circle.

Anything is possible if you value the right thing(s), and for me, the right thing is love! I put love into everything I do in my life, and it has never failed me. With love in your life, you will attract good people in business and in life, just like I have. With good people surrounding you, you can do anything!

Whether it be making decisions, winning the big client, or building your culture, use your status as an underdog as a competitive advantage. Take the risks, be bold, dare to be different. Your business can be compared to a ball of clay: it's yours to mold into what you believe it needs to be, it's your "art" to craft. That's where the true beauty of success is. Don't give up on your dreams, work harder than everyone else, be passionate about what you believe, and follow your heart! YOU GOT THIS!!!

Responsible Culture

Chukwuka C. Monye

Chukwuka C. Monye is managing partner of Ciuci Consulting, a leading execution focused management consulting firm that specializes in the optimization of business operations through innovative strategies and consumer intelligence with a focus on socioeconomic impact. He is an innovation strategist, corporate development and consumer intelligence expert, and has experience in several industries including financial services, healthcare, agriculture, telecoms, media, entertainment, Fast Moving Consumer Goods (FMCG), retail, and the public sector in Nigeria and the United States. Ciuci Consulting is one of the fastest growing consulting firms in the Middle East and Africa, and has an international presence in Africa, North America, and Europe. The company is based in Lagos, Nigeria, and information can be found online at www.ciuci.us.

Tell us about you as the owner/founder. What's your story that made you the entrepreneur you are today?

I am an innovation strategist, corporate development, and consumer intelligence expert. My experience covers several industries including financial services, healthcare, agriculture, telecoms, media, entertainment, FMCG, retail, and the public sector in Nigeria and the United States.

I have a Master's in Business Administration (MBA) and a PGD in Strategy and Innovation, both from The University of Oxford, UK. I also have a Bachelor of Arts in Business Administration from Warner University, Florida where I graduated with honors and was also the university's first black student union president. I have received several awards including "Who's Who" in American Universities and Colleges and the United States Achievement Academy Award given to top students in the country. I also received the United States Golden Bridge Award for Most Innovative Executive of the Year in 2018.

I am passionate about the development of the African continent, which was why I returned to Nigeria a year after I received my bachelor's degree. When I interacted with executives on my return, most of them mentioned "people problems" as one of the challenges faced by businesses in Nigeria. I saw this as a gap because the development and use of human capital are crucial to economic productivity and growth. This led to the establishment of Ciuci Consulting. Our two objectives: to provide advice to businesses in Africa and to develop locally-based human capacity amidst a challenging educational and economic environment.

I have also led the development of several social impact initiatives aimed at taking the capacity-building focus to corporate Nigeria and the society at large in sectors such as agriculture and healthcare on a pro bono basis as a sign of Ciuci Consulting's commitment to its ideals. I have been involved in the incubation of several successful products and companies including the City of Lagos edition of the Monopoly board game and the Healthcare Leadership Academy (HLA), a leadership institute for the healthcare sector with collaborators such as Cambridge and Duke University.

I have been featured as a keynote speaker at several business and youth conferences focused on the youth, capacity development, education, and entrepreneurship. Many of my published materials have been featured in several media platforms including the Nigerian Guardian, CBS, NBC, and Huffington Post.

I am currently the Director General of The Delta Economic Summit Group, a private sector led think tank focused on influencing and delivering positive and strategic change, most especially economic development, in Delta State, Nigeria. Through this platform, I led the establishment of the "Unsung Heroes Awards," an awards ceremony that celebrates individuals that have impacted their communities in significant ways with little or no recognition. Each edition has moved the audience to tears as they marvel at the amazing work being done by the honorees, from providing free eye surgeries to taking care of orphans with limited resources.

I believe entrepreneurs cannot achieve true impact if the impact that they desire is not tangible. This is what makes entrepreneurship worth it, fulfilling, and purposeful.

In thirteen years, Ciuci Consulting has executed over 350 projects with significant social and economic impact and published over 150 research reports and articles. The firm consists of ethically-driven professionals who strongly believe in integrity and partnership as key ingredients for delivering high-quality results to clients.

While Ciuci Consulting started out in the telecoms and banking sectors with strong competencies in research, analytics, strategy formulation, and capacity building, it has developed robust proficiencies in consumer intelligence, human capital development, interim management and advisory services, business planning, business turnaround and restructuring, financial management system, and feasibility studies. Today, Ciuci Consulting has a fully diversified client base in the private and public sectors and a world-class analyst training program for its consultants.

Ciuci Consulting has developed a solid legacy of adding real value to its clients. It has been recognized by many as a market leader: Jobberman, the largest job placement in sub-Saharan Africa recognized it as one of the ten most innovative companies to watch out for. It won the Stevies Award for the Middle East and Africa Category for its contribution to social and economic impact in Nigeria through human capital development and several social interventions; and also won the Middle East and Africa Category for its innovative solutions for clients.

The firm played a prominent role in the COVID-19 response in Nigeria by managing strategic assets including a molecular testing center, a 200-bed hospital, and a 340-bed treatment center.

What have been the key factors to your success and why?

Great leadership and great businesses are always defined by three critical components – vision, good systems, and people.

My vision has been very clear, thereby making my convictions easy as I am not easily swayed or distracted.

First, the principle of systems thinking helps me achieve quality outcomes in projects and situations. It emphasizes the relationship among a system's parts rather than the parts themselves. This includes the willingness to see situations more holistically; recognize that they are interrelated; acknowledge that there are often multiple interventions to a problem; and utilize unique insights and discoveries to develop interventions that will dramatically change the system in the most effective way. Through systems thinking, I have learnt the inevitability and imperative of delegating tasks. The focus is always about the overarching goal.

Second, People Matter! People Matter! People Matter! Despite the educational system and challenging economic environment, I have been able to successfully build a strong base of talented professionals. This has been a major competitive edge – building an organization that believes that people matter.

One of the initiatives that I have led includes The Analyst Training Program (ATP), an annual in-house capacity building program for entry-level analysts. This six-month program equips participants with the required skills, knowledge, and exposure to analytical, strategic thinking, problem-solving, communication, business acumen, financial modeling, interpersonal and leadership proficiencies as well as other relevant technical expertise.

Another initiative is iQube, an organization designed to engage the youth and foster knowledge-sharing, collaboration, and out-of-the-box thinking. It is founded on three I's – Innovation, Inspiration, and Insight – and plans to address specific socioeconomic development needs in Africa.

What has been your worst decision and how did you bounce back and still get to where you are today? How did this failure prepare you for your current success?

The worst decision, which in retrospect was a necessary decision, was when Ciuci Consulting took a bet on a major public sector project. This project was the largest deal we had done and a number of variables such as change in government were out of our control. We were optimistic that our payment was guaranteed despite a possible change in government. Unfortunately, irrespective of the impact of the project, the new administration did not pay contractors and consultants that worked with the previous one. It was a demoralizing experience as we had engaged both local and foreign professionals who had to be paid. Although this was a major financial setback for the firm, it taught us how best to structure similar deals and mitigate certain risks. We have since successfully carried out various projects in the public sector.

This experience had the potential of making me depressed, as it was a very difficult time. How do you explain to all the local and foreign experts that were staffed on the project that you cannot pay them? My reputation was at stake. While a number of people tried to convince me that this happens and there was really nothing I could do until the client paid, I was restless and very uncomfortable with not fulfilling my end of the agreement so I sold some of my assets to pay all the experts. My approach to resolving this crisis, though not popular at the time, felt like the honorable thing to do. I have had to be at peace with myself and, since then, several opportunities have come my way. My word is my bond. It may cost me relationships but, ultimately, I owe it to myself to be true and honorable.

What has been your best decision and why?

It was the decision to move back to Nigeria to establish Ciuci Consulting and influence so many young people.

This, for me, is fulfilling especially because many business owners and entrepreneurs are less interested in capacity building. It is rewarding when I see people's lives change because of the support I give.

I am proud of what Ciuci Consulting has become in thirteen years. Not many companies survive beyond five years in difficult business climates like we have in Africa. We have developed strategic solutions for both public and private organizations in Africa. Having carried out over 350 projects, with eighty percent of them focused on Small to Medium-sized Enterprises (SMEs), Ciuci Consulting has developed significant capabilities that have enabled it to support several SMEs thereby impacting the economy in major ways.

What is an unusual habit you have as an entrepreneur that helps you succeed?

"You must have Business Voodoo." This is what a client said to explain how well I was able to articulate his requirements for a potential project. This ability is something that I have exercised over the years. My colleagues have often argued that it is a gift and not an acquired skill. On a number of occasions, I have been able to not only articulate a client's problem but also help to depict clients' visions.

For a society that can be religious and believes in "spiritual" sources for insights and solutions, this ability makes me somewhat qualified to be "believable." Combining this with technical and analytical skills creates combined assets that become really powerful. I can then reel out "spooky" (intuitive) and non-spooky capabilities to deliver cutting edge solutions to my clients.

Another habit I have is transparent leadership. This is not a common leadership style. Some say it is a style that is not appreciated by people in Nigeria, where being secretive, bossy, and mostly dictatorial is believed to be the style that is effective.

On the one hand, I appreciate some cultural nuisances that are centered on "respect for elders," however, the expression of this culture tends to undermine subordinates or team members. It often suggests that if you are a team member and not the leader then you are meant to listen and not share your opinion. This cultural element is also seen in the process of problem-solving where the leader is the moderator and solution provider in a brainstorming session. I believe that no man is an island and that problem-solving is comprehensive when it incorporates inputs from several people. I can recall when a security guard was engaged to contribute to the development of a survey instrument for a research project. The team developing the survey found the questions suggested by the security guard to be most valuable.

This leadership style is ultimately linked to an important essence of entrepreneurial existence that I shared earlier – people matter!

With the knowledge and experience you have now, what would you have done differently if you were to start your entrepreneurial journey again?

I would not change a thing because everything we have done was required and necessary in making us who we are today. Sometimes I am tempted to say that perhaps raising money upfront would have helped. But I think a lot of the grit the company has today is because resources weren't readily available and we had to be innovative and creative.

A quote by Thomas Edison says, "The most certain way to succeed is always to try just one more time." For us at Ciuci Consulting, we remained firm and continued in the course of action in spite of the difficulty or opposition.

What do you do when you feel demotivated and overwhelmed?

I listen to inspirational music. I am quite sensitive to music, so it helps me. The messages in the songs I listen to are typically powerful and positive. It may also make me dance, something I really enjoy, too.

I also immerse myself in things that reinforce my vision because when it is reenacted and reinforced, I begin to work towards it again. I am a visionary so if demotivation has reduced the visibility of where I am going, I speak with other like-minded entrepreneurs to make it clearer again.

Discuss a crisis situation (2008 depression, 9/11, COVID-19) that you/your company were in and how you overcame it.

During the time of the consolidation of banks in 2009, Nigeria experienced significant economic contraction and a lot of professional services firms struggled. In this period, Ciuci Consulting had a strategy session and identified financial services as a profitable sector. Consequently, we executed a number of financial services projects. One of our strengths is that we are nimble and very strategic, so we used the situation to our advantage.

What is that one secret to your business success that would be helpful to current and aspiring entrepreneurs?

We simulate environments and situations to prepare us for difficult moments so that employees are ready and better prepared when they encounter similar conditions in the future. Using this approach, we mirror real-life challenges that teach employees possible scenarios the business can face. This enables the management team to identify weaknesses in the system and evaluate its responses to different types of disruptive events. As a result, we are able to make improvements to our systems and procedures based on test findings. Employees, on the other hand, are able to improve their conceptual knowledge and gain a better appreciation of business strategy and the systems of business management.

What's your advice for entrepreneurs who are still struggling?

It is very important that entrepreneurs evaluate why they are struggling. Most times, they forget that perhaps they were not meant to be entrepreneurs in the first place. I am not of the school of thought that suggests that entrepreneurship is for everyone who desires to build an enterprise. Entrepreneurs should evaluate if they are meant to be entrepreneurs; if yes, then they should find mentors that can provide necessary guidance and begin to tackle the prevailing issues. Remember – no man is an island.

From Vanity to Sanity

Jessica Moseley

J essica Moseley is the CEO of TCS Interpreting, Inc. The company is a woman-owned small business and nationwide provider of sign language interpreting services. We are among those awarded the nation's largest federal contracts for the provision of on-site and video remote interpreting services. TCS Interpreting, Inc., fulfills its mission by providing world-class language access to the Deaf community, nurturing and developing competent practitioners, and partnering with organizations to develop best practices for interacting with Deaf individuals. The company believes robust, native language access is a human right, and envisions a world where everyone has the autonomy to determine their own native language choice. TCS Interpreting, Inc., is based in Silver Spring, Maryland, and information can be found online at ww.tcsinterpreting.com.

Tell us about you as the owner/founder. What's your story that made you the entrepreneur you are today?

As the CEO of TCS Interpreting, Inc., I wanted to create an organization that provided equitable access for the Deaf community. Many of my clients have learned to adapt and be proactive about their education and pursuit of equality and look to my company for high-quality content and communication access. I strive to speak the truth and communicate that being Deaf isn't a disability – it's simply a different language. This was modeled to me at a young age as I watched my parents, who were entrepreneurs, when I was growing up. Seeing their own struggles, both personally within their own families and professionally in business, created a fire in me to make an impact in the world by demonstrating what the Deaf community could do.

What have been the key factors to your success and why?

I believe that my ability to listen to others and my mindset around failing have been key factors in my success. By listening, I can understand all sides of a story from multiple perspectives and make sure everyone at the table has a chance to share their story. I have learned the value in acknowledging and interpreting multiple points of view, especially coming from a background where I grew up feeling like I never really belonged. The more I reflect on my journey, the more I understand and value all three of my communities: Deaf, Hearing, and Child of Deaf Adult (CODA). I am blessed to understand each one of these groups. Another major component that has led to my success was my lack of fear regarding failure. I believe the only way to get stronger is to fail as it allows us to know where to learn and how to grow.

What has been your worst decision and how did you bounce back and still get to where you are today? How did this failure prepare you for your current success?

As a young COO and later CEO, I was unfamiliar with the interpreting industry, but my lack of experience or education didn't stop me from jumping right into the entrepreneurial life. After some trial and error, I understood that in order to run the company successfully and earn the respect of both the Deaf and interpreting communities, I needed to quickly surround myself with industry and community veterans. I wanted to be sure I had a strong team to lean on to help guide me in making the best decisions I could to ensure I was leading the business towards success.

I accepted my lack of expertise and made it my goal to implement a management team comprised of seasoned industry professionals, educators, and a general counsel specializing in accessibility law. In addition, I sought out national certification and acquired my National Interpreting Certification (NIC) with the Registry of Interpreters for the Deaf, in 2016.

We steadily grew from $800k to $5 million in less than three years. Not having formal interpreting or business education, I was very focused on the vanity part of growing a business and I felt like I was on top of the world. Little did I know, I was unable to see that I was working 80+ hours a week in my business just to make a small profit which was not enough to sustain. As our client base increased and our workload tripled, we grew at a pace that we couldn't keep up with and our expenses were out of control! That led to carrying expenses for years we could not afford and employees getting the short end of the stick. This included a reduction in benefits and no pay increases until I was willing to make the hard decision and let people go. Looking back now, I realize that my time working *in* the business should have been spent working *on* the business.

What has been your best decision and why?

Staying true to the company's core values while experiencing rapid growth, letting go of fear, and embracing what I don't know have been some of my best decisions. This allows me to raise awareness about what language access really means while ensuring that our community can rely on TCS Interpreting for the language access they need to live an empowered and enriched life. This has allowed me to grow the team and business in ways I didn't expect.

What is an unusual habit you have as an entrepreneur that helps you succeed?

I am very old fashioned when it comes to note taking, to-do lists, reminders, and scheduling. I put everything down on paper. There's something special about writing pen on paper, even when it comes to little inspirational notes. My sticky notes, lists, and calendar are all on paper and for some reason it just helps me to get organized better than having it all on my computer. I also am a big fan of journaling and positive inspirational readings. I often look at some of my previous journalings, write more, and read some positive quotes, articles, etc., to combat self-doubt and work hard to get on the other side of it.

With the knowledge and experience you have now, what would you have done differently if you were to start your entrepreneurial journey again?

I would advise my younger self to embrace the detours and obstacles that accompany an organization's growth. Success is not linear. Challenges alone do not define a business or the leader, it's the attitude and subsequent actions that shape and define your path. I would also inform my younger self that passion and commitment will sustain me through uncertain times. I would tell myself to trust my decisions, be comfortable with making mistakes, and making decisions that are not favorable. I would say that while making the right decisions are tough, they are simpler than dealing with the wrong decisions that at first look so easy. I would remind myself that I would rather do it well and with grace than do it bad only to be nice.

What do you do when you feel demotivated and overwhelmed?

As I am sure most entrepreneurs experience, there are definitely times of loneliness and self-doubt. Learning to trust my decisions and being comfortable with making mistakes is a work in progress. I get inspired by my past knowing that I've made it through similar moments before so I can make it through again. I also realize from time to time that there are some areas of the business that will outgrow me – and I am okay with that. Proud of that, actually! Having a coach and mentor in my life who helps me to take a step back and see things from a different perspective helps a ton, too. I rely on those I trust in my close circle to bounce things off of. I work regularly with a coach, a therapist, a trainer, and a hypnotist. All of that self-care allows me to adjust my mindset when life presents roadblocks.

Discuss a crisis situation (2008 depression, 9/11, COVID-19) that you/your company were in and how you overcame it.

Every entrepreneur knows what it is like to have money problems. I learned early on what it felt like to rely on my business as my sole source of income. As I mentioned above, as a young COO and later CEO, my lack of experience led to some interesting financial situations. While working 80+ hours and with expenses growing out of control, it wasn't until I had finally accepted that I would have to make the tough decisions that things started to turn around for both myself and the company. I had to let people go. While it was not easy, I learned how to accept both my lack of experience and the steadfast advice of others. While it was a difficult experience overall, both me and the company came out of it stronger.

What is that one secret to your business success that would be helpful to current and aspiring entrepreneurs?

Be intentional about building your tribe. Be clear on your personal and professional core values and be sure you choose people who will embody and hold you accountable to those values. Whether that's in the form of a mentor, a resource, or someone you can be one-hundred percent vulnerable with, make sure they are somebody you can share both the ugly and beautiful sides of your entrepreneurial journey with. When it comes down to it, those values and your tribe will be a beacon and sustain you through the inevitable challenges.

What's your advice for entrepreneurs who are still struggling?

My best advice is to be certain that you aren't being defined by a crisis. Apply what you have learned during hard times so that you can be defined by your growth and successes. Make sure the definition you have of yourself and your business is measured by your level of resiliency, commitment to learning from challenges, and willingness to embrace necessary course corrections.

Your willingness to show up again and again for the people you serve speaks volumes about your business. The best investment I made was in myself for this exact reason; it has changed how I was looking at every crisis. This past year has had a lot of change, and with it came a lot of growth. It's easy to get frustrated when things change and life throws curveballs at you. These are the times I step back and focus on the only thing I can control: my reaction.

I have tried to focus on more awareness of who I am; I had lost that focus over the years and it has all led to this moment. Without the countless hours spent on my self-care, with my coach, therapist, and tribe, I might not be where I am today. Investing in yourself shows up in your business every day and creates a ripple effect through your employees.

How would you describe the culture of your company? Did you develop your company consciously or did it just happen?

I believe our commitment to providing equitable access for all sets our company culture apart. Programs such as mentoring, professional development, recruiting, and our accountability metrics contribute to a more engaged workforce. In addition, we have implemented six core company values: Level the Playing Field, Learning Never Ends, All In, Got Your Back, Do the Right Thing, and Make A Way. These company values demonstrate our commitment to maintaining integrity throughout company operations. I would say overall that developing the culture we have now was a conscious decision. We changed our values from aspirational to attainable to reflect what we are already doing.

Not Your Average Creation

Dr. Tamara L. Nall

D r. Tamara L. Nall is the president and CEO of The Leading Niche (TLN), an award-winning and internationally recognized company known for using data and cutting-edge consulting to deliver actionable intelligence. The Leading Niche supports commercial and government customers in domestic and international markets, including the United States, Canada, Europe, and Africa. The firm provides big data, cyber-security, intelligence, health IT, regulatory/compliance and investigative/examination consulting. TLN also has a research arm, NALL-EDGE, which curates intellectual capital driven by data and research. The company is based in Washington, D.C., and information can be found online at www.theleadingniche.com.

Tell us about you as the owner/founder. What's the story that made you the entrepreneur you are today?

I've been an entrepreneur since I was a child. My sister and I had several businesses, which included babysitting, a lemonade stand, and even a home-based library (yes, we charged late fees!). Our parents gave us twenty-five cents for an A, so that wasn't working in our minds. Our most profitable business was what today would be called an administrative services company. We categorized and filed invoices for a meatpacking company in Bessemer, Alabama. I went into my father's office and boxes of papers lined the hallway. I asked him what was going on, and he explained what was in the boxes. That next week, I pitched my business idea to him and his supervisor, and our new business began. I made over $30,000 as a teenager. My first employee was my younger sister, and we still disagree on whether she quit or I fired her (LOL!). She is an organized person so the endless boxes of invoices drove her crazy; for me, I saw opportunity, so I seized the chance.

Despite these entrepreneurial ventures, there was one defining moment that solidified in my mind that my life's mission was entrepreneurship. As a teenager, my father was eventually laid off from that same company. We no longer travelled as much or ate out; my parents bought our clothes and Christmas gifts from the thrift store. Overnight, our lives changed. Yet my friends, whose parents were entrepreneurs, continued with life as usual. My friends' families did not have to make the same choices that we did. I did not know what an E.N.T.R.E.P.R.E.N.E.U.R. was, but from that moment, I knew that I would be one because I did not want a company to control my professional destiny. My future would be determined by me (and God, of course!).

What have been the key factors to your success and why?

Several factors have allowed me to get to where I am today. The number one factor has been God and my spiritual life. Entrepreneurship is not for the faint of heart. There are some really tough days, and being the leader of an organization is a lot of responsibility. I put everything in the hands of the Lord. I pray over everything. My mantra is actually a quote from the Bible: "To whom much is given, much is required." I use this to guide me in both my personal and professional lives. I believe that we are created with a unique fingerprint, talents, gifts, and a special calling. One of my purposes in life is to be an employer. My faith allows me to wake up each morning knowing my mission, and helps me enjoy my rest each night. I actually have a printed list of all my customers and employees, and I call each one by name every morning during my prayer and meditation. Every morning I feel blessed to employ people and contribute to their welfare.

The number two factor contributing to my success is hard work with a passionate spirit of excellence. There are so many companies that say they focus on their customers, but do a poor job at execution. I require my employees to have high standards of excellence. I lead by example. Anything that we produce must be high quality, and if we make a mistake, we own it immediately and analyze how to avoid it in the future. Your work standard is your brand. It's that assurance of quality that allows you to grow. Always make your work shine. That's how customers remember your name.

The number three factor is planning. If you don't plan ahead, you're playing defensively. When making new plans, I ask myself, "What will make it easy for us to grow rapidly? What will we do if the worst-case scenario happens?" I always have a Plan B and a Plan C.

The number four factor is human connection. It's my nature to help people. My employees, my clients, and network are like my family. If someone needs a contact, I'll put them in touch. If someone has questions about the industry, I'll take time to speak with them. What I give comes back to me exponentially. There are hundreds of people I've helped who I know will help me in the future. The key to a strong network is that you actually have to love people and get to know them. What are their likes? When is their birthday? What are their dislikes? How can I help? These are questions I think about when meeting a person. Everyone has a story, so my goal is to figure out that story. The trick is you don't succeed at networking by trying to network. You succeed by loving and caring about people. I try to know everybody's family, their kids' birthdays – because I enjoy people.

What has been your worst decision and how did you bounce back and still get to where you are today? How did this failure prepare you for your success?

The worst decisions I've made have been those where I ignored my gut. It's hard for many entrepreneurs to trust their intuition. We spend our lives hearing that we must abide by the judgment of our bosses and our customers. But when you're the founder, you're the expert. You know your industry and company better than anyone. You have a responsibility to listen to your gut, or suffer the consequences. Whether related to a new employee, an investment, a project, or any major decision, you have to listen to your entrepreneurial voice that will guide you. I often seek the advice of others, but at the end of day, the final decision falls on me as the CEO.

Specifically, I hired employees that exhibited red flags during the interview process, but I let the pressure of growth take over my thinking. I knew immediately when I made the wrong choices. With one senior hire for a director position, she had different morals and a perspective on customer delivery that did not align with The Leading Niche's core values, vision or mission. My heart was not settled during the process, but I needed someone quickly. When I interview a potential employee and I'm not in love with them, that's a red flag. Now, I have my team of managers serve as a sanity check when I express doubts over a potential employee.

In another situation, our company missed an opportunity to pursue a larger contract we would have definitely won. My vice president of strategy at the time recommended that we not pursue it. My gut said "yes" but I trusted her and wanted to allow my management to make independent decisions. We did not bid on the contract but found out that the winning score was lower than our preliminary score. We would definitely have won the contract! This would have propelled us forward. I was hard on myself for two years after until my mentor told me to let it go and focus on learning from the experience.

Go with your gut. If it doesn't feel right, it's not right!

What has been your best decision and why?

My number one best decision has been hiring and making the necessary investments into the company. It's hard to grow if you're doing everything yourself. It's easy to be anxious about trusting someone else with your client's satisfaction. But soon you're spending hours each day doing things that other smart, capable employees can do, and spending very little time leveraging your most valuable skills. By delegating tasks, I free up my time to leverage my expertise most efficiently. I also bring added value to clients by delegating to people with expertise that I *don't* have. This is extremely hard for entrepreneurs who start as a one person company. We hired more people and made the investments that paid off exponentially.

What is an unusual habit you have as an entrepreneur that helps you succeed?

I speak things into existence out loud. I wake up each morning repeating affirmations, listening to uplifting music, looking in the mirror to speak positivity to myself, and on some days, dancing around my house. I proclaim, "The company will hit this milestone." "I will do a TED talk." "I will be a best-selling author." If someone overheard me, they'd think, "Oh my, she talks to herself." But I believe it's not enough to just *think* about your goals. You have to speak them into reality. The walls have to hear it. You have to claim your dreams and goals and have the faith they will happen. Proverbs 18:21 states (in my own words) that the tongue can bring death or life, so speak life and reap the benefits of positive thinking. Speak it into existence!

With the knowledge and experience you have now, what would you have done differently if you started your entrepreneurial journey again?

I'm going deep and personal on this one. If I could do it over again, I would spend more time focused on my personal goals. Yes, success and wealth are there, but who else will enjoy it and will I enjoy it? Prior to starting The Leading Niche, while working for a large management consulting firm, I missed every special day in my life. I was home for the holidays, but while my family enjoyed each other's company and the festivities, I was behind a computer. Then, when I started The Leading Niche, I worked so hard that I never turned off, even while on vacation. The last twenty years of my life flashed by so quickly.

I'm also in my mid-forties with no children. While I have frozen my eggs, I wish I'd thought or planned for children earlier and focused more on nonprofessional aspirations. So, whether female or male, young or old, family or not, take time to decide and plan for your personal goals as well. Do you want to run a marathon?

Visit every country in the world? Build a family? Appreciate the family you have now and participate in all of your children's activities? Write a book? Whatever it is, take time to work on you just as much as you work on your business. We have only one life to live, so live your best FULL life!

What do you do when you feel demotivated and overwhelmed?

It's important to know how to recharge when you're feeling down. Sometimes, you have to be selfish and just focus on yourself and do things that re-energize you. There are three things I do when I feel this way.

First, I call my nephew. He is the brightest little boy ever, and he loves me. He yells my name (Aunt Teat!) whenever he sees me. You've got to tap into people who love you unconditionally. He reminds me of why I am focused on building a sustainable enterprise and a legacy. Since I don't have children, he may someday take over my company. He gives me hope for the future.

Second, I recently focused on self-care, and that is different for everyone. For me, I get massages and facials, plan staycations, go on short international trips to the beach, eat nice dinners and catch up with friends. Since COVID-19, however, all of these methods have become impossible. Therefore, I had to improvise. I gave myself home facials. I also created beach-like settings at my home to mentally take me to the beach. I put on a swimming suit and coconut/mango lotion and sit on my balcony with a cocktail and music. I had to bring the Caribbean to me. So, find your self-care zone!

Third, I love to laugh. Growing up, my family laughed a lot, so I was nurtured in a supportive household who loved God, family, forgiveness, love, and laughter. I look for media that makes me laugh. Laughter is accessible at any time. You've just got to remember to look for it.

Discuss a crisis situation you or your company have been in and how you overcame it.

At one point, the federal budget for one of our business areas was slashed. We lost a third of our government contracts overnight. That was the only time we had to lay off a large number of employees. It was heartbreaking. I knew each of my employee's stories: new home, family illness, their spouse's job loss, a mortgage. They were family and many were with me from the start of our government work. It was devastating. I had a meeting with each and teared up because, to this day, it remains the hardest decision I had to make for the company.

I never want that to happen again, so I've diversified our service offerings. I realized we needed to have many *types* of customers. We would never put the majority of your revenue in one market. By diversifying, we ensure that we still have work if one sector takes a nosedive. I also doubled down on scenario-based planning. What is the worst-case scenario? How do we respond? This allows us to drive goals for growth and make sure we can adjust for any change in the market. This exercise is incorporated into our annual strategic planning process.

What is that one secret to your business success that would be helpful to current and aspiring entrepreneurs?

One secret is to move into your customer's networks as soon as possible. Although most of our customers were in the federal government, I didn't know many people in the industry, nor in the D.C. area. It took time to realize how much tapping into those networks could increase my business. When I looked at the growth of my competitors, their companies grew through their networks. They could make calls to find partners or potential employees. You can't choose what social group you're born into, but you can authentically navigate yourself into any circle with a little strategy. I wish I'd put more effort into entering the D.C. circles earlier. It would have made it easier to establish my company's reputation and resulted in more' growth. I've always taken my connections seriously and focused on what I could do for others but not so much on the government side. I encourage all aspirational entrepreneurs to create a relationship map to assess gaps mapped to where you'd aspire to go. You might find some gaps you should cover as you build your network. I would also say to build genuine networks and not those with the sole goal of what you can get out of them. Put something in and let that be your focus.

This secret is tied to successful networking. Make as many connections as you can. You never know who, from your local networking event or virtual happy hour, might need your business. Get to know people and their families. If I know someone, I know how they conduct their personal lives and how they treat people outside of the office. I'm more willing to do business with someone if I trust them in that way.

What's your advice for entrepreneurs who are still struggling?

There's no reason to go at it alone. There are always people you can consult with who have fought these battles before. You may find a solution in a half-hour phone call that would take months to find on your own. Find a mentor or a champion who believes in you and your dreams. You need someone you can reach out to for questions or concerns. Join an entrepreneurial mastermind of like-minded individuals who will encourage you throughout the process. As you grow and move to different stages, these mastermind groups might change. The more you put into and contribute to these forums, the more you and others will learn.

How would you describe the culture of your company? Did you develop your company consciously or did it just happen?

You have to actively manage your business to create the company culture you want. You have to lead by example, by action. At The Leading Niche, we have five core values.

#1: **Business for us is all about trust!** We only do business with clients, partners, and employees that we trust. I've passed up more than ten million dollars in contracts because I didn't trust the partner. It's better to turn down a contract than to work with someone who may damage your reputation or your legal standing. At TLN, we build credibility through honesty and integrity; we never compromise the company's or customer's values, and we are committed to fair business practices and the highest industry standards.

#2: **We love to serve, and it shows!** We have a service attitude and feel that our job is to make our customers' lives easier. If we can help, we will. We love to serve our employees, our partners, our vendors, and our customers. We love to help every stakeholder to fulfill their goals in any way we can. This spirit of service comes back to us many times over.

At TLN, we believe in building relationships, not just building business; we raise customers' expectations by setting higher standards, and we provide our customers with the tools and technologies to make the right decisions.

#3: **Our growth comes from teamwork!** No entity can sustainably grow without people and support. We expect to help each other. At TLN, every team member is an integral part of the company's heartbeat and has quick access to senior management. We create a positive environment where efforts are appreciated and acknowledged, and we support continuous growth for our team members.

#4: **Creativity leads to innovation!** Some people feel that innovation has to be breakthrough and huge. However, innovation can be small incremental changes that make a difference. At TLN, we thrive on challenges and we love working with our customers to develop sustainable solutions. We create innovative solutions that result in unparalleled value, and we are an incubator for creativity, imagination, and ideas.

#5: **We open the door for communication!** Besides ethics, communication is one of the most important virtues we hold at TLN. Communication is also key to our success. We all need to know exactly what our team is thinking and feeling, and what is expected of us. This means honesty. People are encouraged to speak up if something doesn't feel right. It also means ensuring clarity. We have a "two email rule." If something takes over two emails to explain, we need to get on a call and talk things out. We believe in being open and direct. At TLN, we believe in respectful, candid and productive conversations; we strive to communicate openly with our customers, employees, partners and other stakeholders. We "communicate often and early."

A Journey Guided by Empathy and Steered by Innovation

Nish Parikh

Nish Parikh is the cofounder and CEO of Rangam, a minority, woman, and disability-owned workforce solutions company. Rangam's philosophy of "Empathy Drives Innovation" influences everything they do. As one of the fastest-growing professional staffing agencies, the company specializes in attracting and retaining talent globally for IT, engineering, scientific, clinical, healthcare, administrative, finance, and business professional sectors while integrating veterans and individuals with disabilities into the workforce. Rangam's mission is to improve the quality of life for job candidates while providing exceptional service to clients. The company delivers an integrated and inclusive recruiting solution that combines technology, training, and education to candidates while providing clients with a diverse network of qualified talent. The company is based in Somerset, New Jersey, and information can be found online at www.rangam.com.

Tell us about you as the owner/founder. What's your story that made you the entrepreneur you are today?

Throughout my career, I have developed products and services with the mission of helping people overcome barriers and find opportunities for success. I have always focused on efficiency in terms of speed, productivity, and flexibility. As I grew as an entrepreneur, I also learned how to scale my products and services to make a bigger impact on a broader canvas.

I came to the United States in 1992 with a dream to start my own business. The dream came true three years later in 1995 when my wife, Hetal Parikh, and I co-founded Rangam. My entrepreneurial venture began in 1997 when I launched GetItDelivered.com, an e-commerce portal for delivery of food and wine. At that point, e-commerce was on the rise and I wanted to seize the opportunity. As the co-founder of a small business, I was also aware of the daily challenges that come with being a small business with limited resources and so I wanted to build something that other small businesses could benefit from. I started working on web-based content management solutions for small businesses. Among all the solutions that I put my mind into back then, EduTeamPlus and HRTeamPlus would later define the course of *Rangam's* business.

EduTeamPlus offered technologically advanced educational programs for young students, specifically those with special needs. I worked with a highly skilled team at Rangam and built EduTeamPlus as a supplemental tool for teachers. It paved the way for an app-based program (iLearnNEarn) for both teachers and parents.

In 2010, Rangam received funding from the Verizon Foundation to run a research pilot program of iLearnNEarn. The research was focused on validating the effectiveness of the Applied Behavior Analysis (ABA) based intervention technology that we developed to teach children with autism. Upon successfully completing the research project, we continued running programs in local schools in New Jersey. Then in 2013, we received half a million dollars in prize money from Verizon in their Powerful Answers Award competition. The award-winning idea was based on how an entire community works together to help a child on the autism spectrum become independent. We now had the money to build on iLearnNEarn and we did it through hard work, collaboration, and a passion for innovation. ColorsKit, an advanced version of iLearnNEarn, was launched in 2013. ColorsKit is a collaborative tool connecting all stakeholders from the special needs ecosystem for enhanced intervention, better assessment, expedited learning, and data collection.

HRTeamPlus was a basic web app that could manage a limited number of HR-related activities. We enhanced it to build SourcePros™, an advanced talent management solution driven by artificial intelligence and machine learning algorithms. While SourcePros™ gave us what we needed to efficiently manage Rangam's recruiting processes, we had to build a similar tool for disability hiring.

In 2015, Rangam launched The Spectrum Careers portal in partnership with Autism Speaks. The platform connects service providers, job seekers, and employers at the national level. In 2017, we learned that companies were looking for end-to-end solutions to support disability inclusion programs. Based on market trends and needs, we developed the SourceAbled™ program. Through SourceAbled™, we are helping corporations to not only hire people with disabilities on a large scale, but also retain talent by creating a natural support system and a culture of inclusion and empathy.

What have been the key factors to your success and why?

I have always had a healthy curiosity to identify and solve problems, along with an entrepreneurial spirit of persistence in the face of adversities. And I never stop learning and improving.

What has been your worst decision and how did you bounce back and still get to where you are today? How did this failure prepare you for your current success?

Around 2002, following the burst of the dot-com bubble, I got an opportunity to take up a construction project for a federal government agency. At the same time, I was working as a consultant and was satisfied with my performance. Soon I realized that I was not a good fit for the construction industry; it was not an area of my expertise. Besides, I was frazzled from trying to balance two commitments. I failed in the construction business, but not before learning who I am and what I truly wanted to achieve as an engineer-turned-entrepreneur who likes to put skin in the game. In hindsight, I would call it a journey of discovering myself.

What has been your best decision and why?

My best decision was to build SourceAbled™, an end-to-end commercial solution to disability hiring. It remains my most impactful venture to solve the societal challenge of unemployment and underemployment for individuals with disabilities.

What is an unusual habit you have as an entrepreneur that helps you succeed?

Strange as it may sound, I lack attention to detail. However, this habit helps me move fast towards a larger goal without getting stuck in the "perfection" loop. I do not obsess over perfection, nor do I sacrifice an idea because it appears flawed or incomplete.

Thankfully, though, I am surrounded by people who pay great attention to detail and help me stay on track.

With the knowledge and experience you have now, what would you have done differently if you were to start your entrepreneurial journey again?

If I were to start all over again, I would remember that novel innovation does not necessarily mean practical innovation. There were instances in the past when I got too preoccupied with the novelty of a solution and overlooked the practicality of it.

What do you do when you feel demotivated and overwhelmed?

There are three primary factors that cause me to feel demotivated and overwhelmed. They are individual, circumstantial, and strategic. When it is individual or circumstantial, I step away from work and distract myself by listening to music and appreciating nature. When it is strategic, I go online and read something or watch videos pertaining to technology and contemporary business solutions. I try to learn as much as I can to replenish my energy so I can start afresh with a positive attitude.

Discuss a crisis situation (2008 depression, 9/11, COVID-19) that you/your company were in and how you overcame it.

Rangam started by serving the IT industry with enterprise tools while providing highly skilled talent for various technology projects of its clients. Committed to creating jobs for individuals with disabilities, we then set up a technology subsidiary, Rangam Technologies (formerly WebTeam Corp), in New Jersey to design, develop, and deliver game-based skill development programs. A mobile app development and recruitment center in India was established prior to the 2008 recession that triggered a rapidly crumbling US economy characterized by an unprecedented number of layoffs and IT spending cuts. However, Rangam's growing workforce expertise opened new doors even in those adverse circumstances. The team focused on building new technologies for data collection and establishing International Organization for Standardization (ISO) standards to get business from tightly regulated industries. Rangam has since successfully expanded its footprint across North America, Europe, the Middle-East, and Asia.

As the circumstances surrounding COVID-19 are limiting us to interview and onboard candidates, our IT team is working around-the-clock to make quick and drastic changes to the SourceAbled™ technology platform. SourceAbled™ now has an enhanced dashboard and a dynamic data analytics module to monitor mission-critical data pertaining to the urgent needs of our customers. In addition, we have adopted a totally new strategy to identify autism- and disability-friendly remote jobs. We have started implementing it for all of our existing and new clients to cover both onsite and offsite jobs.

Given that most companies are going to operate on a restricted budget over the next few months, we are building a self-serving technology version of Source-Abled™ that can be tweaked for customers of all sizes and financial profiles. We have also adopted a parallel development strategy (as opposed to linear) to expedite the delivery of our products and services to our clients.

What is that one secret to your business success that would be helpful to current and aspiring entrepreneurs?

Be empathetic to your customers and employees. Empathy is the glue that binds people together and helps build lasting relationships.

How would you describe the culture of your company? Did you develop your company consciously or did it just happen?

The philosophy of "Empathy Drives Innovation" is woven into the fabric of who we are at Rangam. It is part of our DNA, shaping the organizational culture and competency. We believe that understanding and sharing the values of our customers, clients, and candidates motivates us to perform better by doing well while doing good. The pillars that support "Empathy Drives Innovation" are:

Accountability: A culture of accountability stimulates proactive thinking and action. We at Rangam are intrinsically motivated to take initiatives and become more invested in the future of the organization, especially as we focus on building rewarding and sustainable careers for people with disabilities and finding jobs for military veterans. We recognize that highly engaged employees are personally accountable for their actions and do not wait for others to deliver results.

Diversity: Working from both sides of the Atlantic and also from Asia, the basic tenets of cultural diversity and social inclusion have become integral to Rangam's identity. Our people, who come from different ethnolinguistic backgrounds, bring a truly unique set of perspectives to drive business results globally. When it comes to supplier diversity, we invest time and resources to raise awareness about the importance of supplier diversity internally with our human resources personnel and program managers, as well as with our clients. We work with top managed service providers and attend various supplier diversity expositions and roundtables nationwide to foster collaborations and accelerate the growth of Minority and Women-owned Business Enterprises (MWBEs). The partnerships we have built over the past two decades have really made a difference for us as we compete for corporate procurement contracts.

Integrity: Integrity is doing the right thing when nobody is watching. It is a priceless value that we attach to everything we do, not only as a company, but also as individuals with a strong moral compass. We strive to do our best in life, whether it be helping someone find the best jobs for autistic adults or pursuing a personal quest.

Loyalty: We are proud to have a "people first" policy, which recognizes that our employees are the ones who produce the products and deliver the services of Rangam. This also means that our employees carry the reputation and image of the organization squarely on their own shoulders. They take ownership and promote our brand to the outside world. We appreciate those who have become an indispensable part of Rangam.

Responsibility: We started our journey as a small homegrown business. With goals of connecting people to jobs and improving the way mental health is managed in schools, homes, and workplaces, we knew from the outset that it was imperative for everyone to foster shared values and responsibilities in order to prioritize better. The tradition continues to this day.

Teamwork: Rangam delivers an integrated workforce development solution involving a synergy of technology and partnerships. We train and educate our employees and consultants while providing our clients with a large, diverse network of qualified personnel options. All of this, and much more, stems from teamwork and collaboration across different groups within the organization.

Trust Your Gut

Lynn K. Petrazzuolo

Lynn K. Petrazzuolo is president, CEO, and Senior Environmental Scientist at Avanti Corporation. The company is a small Native American woman-owned business that provides environmental science, engineering, and data management services to federal agencies, including the Environmental Protection Agency (EPA), National Oceanic and Atmospheric Administration (NOAA), the Department of the Interior, and the National Institute for Environmental Health Sciences (NIEHS). Avanti Corporation staff provide studies, data analyses, and public outreach strategies to support effective environmental regulatory programs and human health protection. The company is based in Alexandria, Virginia, and Raleigh, North Carolina, and information can be found online at www.AvantiCorporation.com.

Tell us about you as the owner/founder. What's your story that made you the entrepreneur you are today?

After receiving a degree in the new field of environmental sciences in the mid 1980's, I have worked my entire career in a field I am passionate about. I have learned from all my jobs, starting with selling entry tickets to a county park at age fourteen, that I have always enjoyed and worked hardest at jobs where everyone is treated with respect, top management is approachable and engaged, and growth is encouraged and nurtured.

I took over as CEO of Avanti over fifteen years ago after the company had been "dormant" for five years. I immediately was led to believe by others in the industry, including our bank, that I was not qualified to run a company. It was when I was exploring the potential sale of the company to a man that I would partner with, that I realized that I had the knowledge, experience, contacts, and (most important) the vision of what Avanti could become with me as the leader. I got my first subcontract within three months and never looked back. (And I found a new bank.)

What have been the key factors to your success and why?

I have never tried to be something that I am not. And, by extension, I have never tried to sell clients on services that I am not completely confident we have the ability to deliver and exceed expectations. Not that there haven't been moments of "Oh cr*p, we won it! How are we going to get it done?" If we offer it, promise it, or sell it, I am confident that I can do it, manage it, or find the right person to get it done to my standards.

I have stuck with what I know – how to team with other firms, track and win government contracts, and deliver to federal agency clients. I have explored state and local or commercial contracts but always come back to what I know. It's not just about staying in my comfort zone; rather, it is doing what I am good at and recognizing what that is.

What has been your worst decision and how did you bounce back and still get to where you are today? How did this failure prepare you for your current success?

My worst decision was early in my tenure when I teamed with a company that I did not completely trust. I relied on a verbal agreement and they pulled out at the last minute. They had made another deal with my main competitor for the opportunity. It took me out of competition for the contract because the Request For Proposal (RFP) had been released and all the players had picked their teams. From that experience I learned to know who you can trust, listen to your gut when you think something isn't right, and get all teaming agreements in writing.

I also learned that I was too trusting. I am generally an open and honest person so I tend to assume that everyone else is that way, too. I don't think I have become overly distrustful of everyone, but I have learned to be more cautious about others' motives.

What has been your best decision and why?

Moving the office out of my home has been my best decision. My home is not big enough that I had a separate office – rather it was a corner of the family room.

Because of that, I was always at work. The computer, emails, just one more peek at something online would always pull me to my desk. Getting work out of the house helped define that boundary.

What is an unusual habit you have as an entrepreneur that helps you succeed?

I think I am unusual in that I do not dwell on setbacks, losses, or disappointments. I don't stay awake all night worrying about work issues (except for rare occasions), and I am able to compartmentalize so that when I leave the office, I leave work. I believe that you get worn out, and often burned out, if you work all the time. That doesn't mean that I don't work some long days, nights, holidays, and on vacations. But that is more the exception. I think building a business while raising a child helped me make the distinction that you have to put your full attention on wherever it is needed at the time – you cannot multitask the two effectively. Too often, I felt like I was failing at both until I learned to focus on one at a time.

With the knowledge and experience you have now, what would you have done differently if you were to start your entrepreneurial journey again?

I would not have applied for the Small Business Administration (SBA) 8(a) program so soon. I applied and was approved in sixty days, before I had won any work. It was not a bad thing to have right away but I could have leveraged more work during those nine years if I had more experience, more existing clients, and a better understanding of the power of the program. A lot of companies think that the 8(a) program is a ticket to getting contracts, but the truth is for many companies it is a ticket to grow your existing business with clients that already know you.

What do you do when you feel demotivated and overwhelmed?

When feeling demotivated, I look for a new opportunity to pursue. Proposals and the hunt for new work motivate me. When overwhelmed, I try to take a short break. I walk, move around, or run up and down the office stairs a couple of times so that I can think while shaking off any anxiety that comes from being overwhelmed. I also am a list maker and putting the tasks on a list helps because crossing items off feels like progress.

Discuss a crisis situation (2008 depression, 9/11, COVID-19) that you/your company were in and how you overcame it.

Under one of our first prime contracts a large business subcontractor was not performing very well and was discussing project details with the client behind our backs. I spoke with their project manager and suggested that we work together to find a solution to the performance issues so that the client would be happy and our team would look good for finding the fix. The project manager agreed to look into the situation but they continued to perform poorly and go behind our backs.

I huddled with our staff and explained the situation that if we took the work away from the subcontractor to correct the issues, we would have to out-perform this large business from Day 1 or we would lose the confidence (and business) of this important client. The team assured me they could do it.

Shortly after notifying the subcontractor to stop work, and informing the client of our plan, we were presented with a letter that asked us to restore the subcontractor and explain our actions. The letter was clearly the work of an "old-boys network" trying to keep the work with the large company. I knew that what they were doing was wrong and I knew that I could not let them push us aside so easily.

I wrote an extensive response to the letter and booked a flight to deliver it in person to the contracts administration of the agency. I had a 1 p.m. appointment with my Contracting Officer (CO) so I also made an 11 a.m. appointment with the small business liaison. I gave him the letter and asked that he share it so that the CO would have time to review it before our meeting. When I came back into the office for the 1 p.m. meeting, the CO, the CO's boss, and her boss's boss joined us for the meeting. We discussed the origins of the letter delivered to me, the responses in my letter, and the additional details that I did not want to put in writing. This was a huge risk and I felt I had to let them know what was happening in their agency and defend our integrity.

The upshot of the meeting was that the inspector general was contacted and after an investigation, some federal staff reassignments occurred. We completed the contract with excellent reviews, still perform this work ten years later, have worked again with that large business in other teaming arrangements, and I established that my company plays fair and demands that others do the same.

What is that one secret to your business success that would be helpful to current and aspiring entrepreneurs?

Find your "tribe." This is the group of other professionals (formal or informal) who can give constructive advice or discuss business issues. This is not your board of directors because you have to answer to them. They should be other business owners who might face similar obstacles and are not (and probably should not be) in your particular area of expertise. I have "tried out" several professional associations and some were better fits than others. I also have found I have outgrown some groups and have moved on to others.

What's your advice for entrepreneurs who are still struggling?

If you have a service or product and you know there is a market, why are you not getting sales? Probably because you are newer than other companies and have not yet gained your potential clients' trust (i.e., gotten their business). I have two thoughts for getting established and reaching new clients: differentiation and relationships.

If you have a product or service that you are selling, chances are that you have already found there is a need for this product or service and know who your target audience is. If not, you might need to read a different chapter first. But if there are buyers out there, your challenge is to get them to want you instead of whoever has been around the longest, is the biggest, advertises the most, etc. Realize that nobody likes change. Many clients would rather complain or work to change a problem than switch to a new vendor. What is it that you have or do, that would make someone take a chance on a different or new vendor? You need to not only figure this out, but you also need to be comfortable and confident in your answer. If you don't believe it, they won't either.

So, why choose you? If your selling point is that you can do the same as the other choices, you have not differentiated yourself, even if your price is better. You have to tell customers not only that you are better, but *why* you are better. Do you have a new process or a better solution? Are you the expert? Did you improve the product – if so, how? If there is a cost savings, demonstrate how the service or product will be better *and* cost less. Find something that makes you and your product stand apart from the other options.

Do your research or simply ask the potential client what is their current need? What keeps them up at night? What could they use to make their life or job easier? What's not working as well as it should? Figure out your target clients' biggest problems (pain points) and demonstrate why you are the best at solving those problems. Present your case concisely and use facts or figures to substantiate your claims.

Assume that the person you market to, or meet with, is not likely to be the ultimate decision maker. So, do that person's work for them and give them the tools to justify to their management that their company needs your product or services. The person you meet with will ultimately become the agent who has to sell you further up the ladder. Think about ways to make this person look good to their superior when they take your information forward. Your job is to leave them wanting to sell you and your company to their management. Give them the ideas and facts they need. Offer to help them prepare whatever is needed to take your information forward in their organization.

Think about how that person will sell you and your company to his or her boss without you in the room. Did you provide enough information on why they need you or why your company is the better option? Don't expect them to figure out how to make your case – arm them with the facts and figures to ensure you are differentiated from their current supplier and all other choices. Give them clear, concise, and direct images and information that tell your story even if you are not in the room.

Not every sales meeting or proposal will result in a sale. However, you should create a relationship with each potential client whether or not they buy from you. Once you have the relationship (and calling or sending numerous emails is not a relationship), do not dump the person if you don't make the sale. That person can still be an agent for you by referrals. Ask for feedback on why the sale did not occur. If it was lack of funding, dig further to see if there isn't some way that your product or service would actually save the client money. Ask if your contact knows anyone else who might be interested. If you were successful in convincing the person that your product or service has value, they will offer to make other introductions.

There is also great value in learning to walk the tightrope of not being persistent enough and being a pest. Learn to read people and cut your losses if the person you are talking to is not interested or not going to be interested. Trust your gut to know when you are wasting your time, don't spend a lot of time on the hardest nut to crack. Leave your contact and product information and move on. But always say thank you and keep the door open. I have had people shut me down or make small talk while looking over my shoulder for someone else in a room full of people only to end up in a conversation with them later as part of a group. Somehow, I gained credibility once they saw I was not an "outsider."

It's tough to break into any business. Grow your contact list every way possible and be someone who people want to work with. Even if they cannot use or buy your service or product, they may know someone who can. That is the introduction you are working for; change is hard but getting an introduction is just as good as an endorsement. Distinguish you and your company as credible, build those relationships, and be ready to confidently make the case for why you are the one to choose.

How would you describe the culture of your company? Did you develop your company consciously or did it just happen?

The culture of Avanti Corporation has evolved over time. We have had some good, fun, and cohesive groups and we have had phases that were not so good. Currently, we have a great company culture even though it has been disrupted by COVID-19. We are actively working to capture and foster that culture and to make additional improvements so that when we come back from working at home we can pick up where we left off.

I did not consciously create a culture for Avanti for many years and we have both enjoyed and suffered the results of that lack of intentional direction. For the longest time, I believed that setting the example of my expectations and values would somehow magically transfer to the hearts and minds of all employees! I wanted and expected everyone to work hard, be professional, and to treat everyone with respect. For the most part, that happened. But, when there were lapses, I would be disappointed in the person rather than see the signs that I have to actively cultivate the culture. It doesn't happen organically, no matter what example you think you are setting.

Several improvements to our culture have occurred over the last few years and Avanti's culture is now one where employees feel valued, expectations are clearly defined, and good work is rewarded.

One of our first steps towards consciously creating a great culture was to more clearly define our core values. With assistance from our management coach, senior managers developed a list of core values that described the behaviors, attitude, and ethics that we were expecting employees to embody. Through these values we more clearly defined our expectations and our culture. I felt senior managers were demonstrating these values, but it was not flowing down to have an impact on our culture. After defining this list, all employees were invited to a discussion to talk about what each one of the values means and how they might be demonstrated in our work and daily activities. Getting employees to verbalize the meaning of these values helped establish a more defined culture of hard work and mutual respect. The values are now listed on the conference room wall.

We also incorporated the importance of our values into our hiring process to continue building a culture of like-minded people. We frequently hire staff who are recent college graduates and the job is often their first "office job." Previously, because the job is entry-level, we did not evaluate each candidate with as much scrutiny as we might for a more senior hire. Did they have a degree in a field related to our work, did they get decent grades, do their references vouch for their willingness to learn, and do we think they will show up? Now, we begin interviews in the conference room where candidates are seated to face toward the wall of values. We discuss that these values define our culture and we ask candidates to tell us how they demonstrate some of these values. Previously, we selected a few candidates for interviews from resumes and hired "the best of the candidates we had," rather than wait for the perfect fit. Our process now for entry-level hires has more emphasis on our gut feelings about a candidate's sincerity and ability to fit into the culture we have. We have learned patience and to no longer hire anyone who we "think" might work out. To reinforce our culture of mutual respect, we also include more of our current staff in the interview process. We want everyone who might work with a candidate to have an opportunity to weigh in on their suitability for the job.

Our core values also have been incorporated into the annual review process to reinforce their importance in our corporate culture. Rather than list accomplishments for the past year, we have employees demonstrate how they have exhibited the core values through their actions. We ask for the same in peer evaluations. My favorite part of the annual review process is reading the complimentary remarks staff provide about their colleagues. I believe it helps foster a greater sense of appreciation for each other when you are asked to recall and share examples of good behavior or performance. All supervisors are more likely to notice the good, and not just the bad, when they are reminded to do so.

After written reviews are received, we hold face-to-face discussions to discuss goals for the next year. The last item for each discussion is to ask every employee what the company can do to help them advance, learn, grow, etc. I want all employees to feel valued and this question is a reminder to me to support each employee and their individual goals.

The most recent reinforcement of our corporate culture is occurring just as we are preparing to move to new office space. For many years, I have always looked for the most economical space, furniture, and equipment. I expected staff to be all right with older desks and chairs because, "Look – mine is that way, too." I believed that being economical demonstrated that I was not "wasting" money on overhead costs. However, a good, hard look at our office revealed that my "cost-effectiveness" could also be viewed as miserly. I believed that as long as it was equally distributed – my desk drawer is being held shut with tape just like others' – it was fine. Nice offices are for impressing clients and our clients never come to our office; we go to them. Employees were "making do" with what we had to offer, and I realized that I was not conveying my appreciation for them. When I started shopping for new space, I realized that our employees deserved a nice space that they can be proud of and feel valued.

Our lease is ending at the end of this year and I have informed staff that we are *not* moving any of the furniture. I hired an interior designer to help convey the culture of our company through professional, inviting, and upscale finishes. My staff have weighed in on furniture options and décor. I have finally found it is OK to have nice things because that shows staff that I want them to have nice things and I want them to be proud of the office where they work. As far as our culture, I believe that the new office space will not be a factor in changing our culture, but rather a reflection of our consciously created culture.

Select Hard, Manage Easy^{SM}

Kimberly Rath, MBA

Kimberly Rath, MBA, works every day with entrepreneurial leadership as well as leaders of long-established organizations across the globe to help them create a leadership legacy and assure a bright future. She co-founded talent management consulting firm Talent Plus in 1989 and today serves as its cochairman. Over those three decades Kimberly has cultivated tremendous visibility among the organization's clients and their leaders, many of which are large healthcare organizations, hospitality providers, and luxury retailers. She is obsessed with creating organizational cultures where people tap dance to work, where individuals get to do what they are good at and enjoy and have the opportunity to work with great leaders, mentors, team members, guests/customers, and a great brand. She's a recognized leader in the field of executive development and human resources in the United States and Asia. Being an entrepreneur, she is in kinship with those starting up new organizations and is fueled by their enthusiasm to be disruptive and/or bring a solution to the market that is either new or an improvement.

Talent Plus is the premier global human capital and talent management consulting partner. As experts at each critical inflection across the talent lifecycle, their evidence-based solutions *scientifically* assess, select, onboard, develop, coach, engage and retain the right people with the right talents to grow and gain a profound and sustained competitive advantage over industry peers. Information can be found online at www.talentplus.com or by calling 1(800) VARSITY (827-7489).

Tell us about you as the owner/founder. What's your story that made you the entrepreneur you are today?

I have always been fascinated with studying people. I was part of a mentoring program, today known as NHRI Leadership Mentoring, that Dr. William E. Hall cofounded at the University of Nebraska – never knowing one day he would be a business partner. Through this program, I became intrigued with studying what's right about people. Putting that into solutions at Talent Plus has been a natural place for my passion for how people grow and develop. When we started Talent Plus, we believed we could change the workplace. We have always had a passion for focusing on what people do well and matching them with a job with the right fit for their talents, team, manager and culture. Doing this changes the culture of an organization where people are celebrated for what they do well. Today, we see client partners building these types of organizations, Talent-Based Organizations ®, and the outcomes go right to their bottom line.

What is good for people is good for business, and these organizations are better able to take care of their end users and improve their customer/guest/patient experiences.

I have a vista of the importance of relationships in my personal life as well as my business life. Putting people first and providing incredible customer service when it was just the original founders. We did it all, answered the phones, sold, and serviced! What we did not realize was the foundation of customer service we created – the importance of client urgency that remains a value today – providing thirty plus years of client relationships and referrals that keep going strong.

What have been the key factors to your success and why?

Great leaders truly care about their employees and extend themselves to help employees succeed and thrive. Caring habits include asking employees about their weekends (or other days off), remembering birthdays and anniversaries, flexibility when issues arise, teaching, coaching, and working hard to meet employee needs.

What has been your worst decision and how did you bounce back and still get to where you are today? How did this failure prepare you for your current success?

I do not spend too much time looking in the rear-view mirror. Entrepreneurs know success and failure become part of your DNA. My dad had his own business and I saw the customer service he provided his clients. I'm devoted to our colleagues and clients and spend a great deal of time thinking about them. I hope that they see that out of mission and dedication comes the ability to make a difference.

What has been your best decision and why?

"To whom much is given, much is required." The better Talent Plus does financially, the more we are able to share with the communities where we work. Our corporate promise is to be a compelling partner for colleagues to grow, clients to thrive, candidates to engage, and communities to prosper.

Several years ago, we decided instead of spreading our corporate social responsibility gifts across every organization that approached us, we wanted to engage a process to make a more significant impact. To that end, every spring, our colleagues vote on four organizations (pillars) they are interested in supporting throughout the year with our talent, time, and treasure. We have an individual who leads a team of colleagues who have a passion for social responsibility and engage all our colleagues in these initiatives.

Over the years, through focusing our time, talent, and treasure in these ways, we have been able to make a sustainable impact. We are committed to corporate social responsibility at Talent Plus and we have fun doing it. We "plant" our colleagues along the way as we move to new pillars and support colleagues who serve on not-for-profit boards, as well as individual colleague involvement.

Additionally, we use our holiday party as a fundraiser (to the tune of $12,000) to fund a nearby school's Backpack Program through a local foodbank. Further, each week of the school year, three associates visit that elementary school to provide food to the children through this Backpack Program.

We also provide and serve dinner for a shelter kitchen for the homeless in our community. Colleagues and their families quarterly set up, serve, and clean up, serving one hundred individuals.

We have always encouraged our colleagues to take time to volunteer, understanding much of that takes place during a workday. Last year we added a full day that each colleague can spend volunteering for their favorite non-profit organization.

What is an unusual habit you have as an entrepreneur that helps you succeed?

One of my habits has been to start and end every day with top performers. My doing this gives me momentum to "tap dance" to work daily, largely because I make my first interaction with someone hitting it out of the park – a big project, a client, or a new solution. As I make my way out of the office, I do the same thing – conversations with someone at the top of their game, leading a team, etc. My passion is creating platforms for individuals to grow and see brighter futures, whether our leadership team, Subject Matter Experts (SMEs), or leaders among our client partners. I engage with those who are struggling and needing insight. I simply try not to start and end my day there.

With the knowledge and experience you have now, what would you have done differently if you were to start your entrepreneurial journey again?

Stay on a learning journey. I would have gotten a Master's in Business Administration (MBA) at Pepperdine University earlier as it has helped me see opportunities and possibilities for our organization in a refreshed way. I would have augmented that with subsequent coursework focused on elements such as strategy, UX/UI and design thinking, knowing additional learning helps you stay relevant. Every individual needs to keep advancing their skills and knowledge. Staying on a learning journey keeps you current and relevant in the workplace. With four different generations in the workplace, exposing yourself to new ideas helps you stay in the mix. It also allows you to be more open-minded to divergent views and have more context for them.

What do you do when you feel demotivated and overwhelmed?

This does not happen to me very often because I am a lifelong learner. But this last year has been one of change. One thing I have done during the pandemic is to stay connected virtually. I have participated in learning sessions and panels to understand other people's perspectives.

I spend time with family, their significant others, and my friends. It's an opportunity to invest in them and feel more centered and grounded.

I connect with our client champions. Their stories reignite my energy on why our business is so important and the difference The Science of Talent® makes in an individual's life and organizational culture.

Discuss a crisis situation (2008 depression, 9/11, COVID-19) that you/your company were in and how you overcame it.

We just finished celebrating our thirtieth year in business and there have certainly been tough times. During these, all we could do was demonstrate care and concern for our client partners. We have broadened our horizons and looked at additional industries invested in the end user experience.

To survive an economic downturn, hardwire your organization. We have seen our clients bounce back faster after economic downturns. They have carefully selected individuals, using a validated assessment, hardwired to be resilient, growth-oriented, resourceful, and optimistic. These traits help overcome difficulty.

What is that one secret to your business success that would be helpful to current and aspiring entrepreneurs?

Take time to get every selection right. There is so much change afoot in the workplace today and when change occurs, individuals who have **grit, flexibility, resourcefulness and optimism can take on change and adapt to** workplace changes. Using a validated assessment looks for qualities essential to your business and culture to stack your organization with individuals who can move forward. **Create a culture where change is embraced, accepted and celebrated**. The attributes of success encompass what many would term as softer skills and those are strengths I have found to be successful – **taking an individualized approach, modeling a culture of kindness and caring, envisioning the future with appreciation and openness**.

What's your advice to entrepreneurs who are still struggling?

Select Hard, Manage Easy.^{SM} It is perhaps the most concise way to describe the revolution of talent selection in the world today. Its true meaning, however, is more than meets the eye. So, just what does it mean to "select hard?"

Every hiring manager faces a common dilemma. You know your organization gets better or worse with each hire so selection decisions must be carefully considered.

And today there is a larger than ever pool of highly trained, qualified individuals from whom to select.

One candidate might be a highly educated individual with over ten years of experience who offers a smile, charisma, and an ability to think quickly on their feet in their interview. Another candidate has a strong track record and seems genuine and friendly. Both have excellent references and seem to possess the characteristics of a strong salesperson. You want the candidate who can generate the most sales while fitting best within the company's culture. It's a 50/50 shot. How can you select hard so that they can manage easy?

By using an evidence-based talent assessment system, you can understand the talent of each candidate and their potential – both in the role and in the organization's culture. By ensuring each potential employee's talent is weighed along with potential fit, organizations can be assured they have the right people in the right places.

You have taken the time to select hard, so can you really "manage easy?" Is there really such a thing? Yes, there is, and it's best reached on a continuous journey called "relationships." While the selection of each team member is critical, their onboarding is tantamount to the importance of their selection. Knowing what you learned in the selection process creates a platform for that management.

As well, having a mindset of continually recruiting is one way to have a constantly filled talent bench. Your talent bench is made up of external candidates who have the right talent to be a good fit for your team, but for whom you do not have a position today. To create a strong bench, continuously recruit, whether you have openings or not. Keep in touch with these individuals. Make them an envoy for your brand while working outside your organization. Do not simply rely on the person who has HR on their door. Instead, create an organizational culture of individuals who are always on the lookout for great talent that would be a fit in your organization.

In my own journey as an entrepreneur, I, along with my co-founders, took the selection of each employee seriously. When we were a small organization, we placed a great deal of intention on selecting the "right" person and continue that foundational discipline today. This must always be front and center to build a sustainable culture. Great leaders use science to select and determine fit and invest in the talent they have selected, creating a basis for growth. It allows one to continue that mantra, "Select hard, manage easy."

How would you describe the culture of your company? Did you develop your company consciously or did it just happen?

Culture is shaped by the people an organization selects, develops, and retains. With each hire, your culture becomes better or worse. And, when you are growing an organization from a few people to a larger endeavor, every selection shows up. Several years ago, I led a mindset within our organization that Talent Plus would be our most important client. We use our own talent assessments and development tools with all our colleagues. In other words, we eat our own cooking. If it works for us, we know it will work in application for client partners.

We have a culture that discovers and develops human potentiality; it's our mission and our purpose. Having a mission and a purpose improves employees' lives. It creates an authentic culture. While organizations might have nap rooms or unlimited vacation, it makes these benefits simply part of what culture is built around and not just a temporary fix to creating a great culture.

Each of your brand ambassadors goes home each day; they wear your T-shirts, they meet with your customers, they talk about open positions in your organization. Create a place where they get to go each day, do their best, be celebrated for contributing, are made to feel significant, and the ripple moves way beyond your building and your balance sheet.

The Courageous and Creative, the Small Business Employer

Dr. Angela D. Reddix

Angela D. Reddix is the president and CEO of ARDX, a multimillion-dollar healthcare and IT management company, and the Chairman and Founder of Envision Lead Grow, a Norfolk-based national nonprofit organization aimed at aspiring girls of all ages. She develops programs that teach them the critical skills and dedication it takes to accomplish their dreams through entrepreneurship. The spirit of the organization is chronicled in her first book, *Envision Lead Grow - Releasing the Boss Within* as well as her TEDx speech, "The Power & Promise of Little Girls Who Dream." Her companies are based in Norfolk, Virginia, and information about ARDX can be found online at www.ARDX.net and information on Envision Lead Grow can be found online at www.envisionleadgrow. org.

Tell us about you as the owner/founder. What's your story that made you the entrepreneur you are today?

I would describe myself as a visionary and innovative thinker with global perspective and entrepreneurial drive. As a passionate mentor and advisor to the next generation of young girls and women, I am a leading advocate for entrepreneurship as a way of creating positive transformation in the world. My own entrepreneurial drive led to the formation of ARDX, a multimillion-dollar, award-winning healthcare management and IT consulting firm. The company has more than one hundred employees who are dedicated to improving the lives of our nation's most vulnerable populations.

I endeavor to inspire greatness through the lessons of my own story, and have been honored to receive the Old Dominion University's Entrepreneurial Hall of Fame, the Humanitarian Award presented by the Virginia Center for Inclusive Communities, the Women of Achievement Award presented by Old Dominion University, ODU's Entrepreneur of the Year and Founder's Day Regional Service Awards, the Leading Ladies of Hampton Roads Award the US Chamber of Commerce's Big Blue-Ribbon Award, Inside Business' Women in Business Award, STEM Innovator Award, Pepsi Historically Better Award, and many other notable achievements.

As a trusted community leader, I serve on a number of Boards and task forces.

Committed to lifelong learning and achievement, I am the Director of Norfolk State University's Hodge Entrepreneur Center. I received my bachelor's degree in business administration in marketing from James Madison University, a master's degree in organizational development from Bowie State University with a focus on training, a graduate certificate in healthcare compliance from The George Washington University, and a Ph.D. in business administration from Oklahoma State University.

I was born to be an entrepreneur! From a very young age, I loved to plan and sell others on my concepts. One of my favorite things to do was to create business plans. I was a student of dance, ballet, tap, and jazz. I calculated how much it cost to be in the number of classes that I took a week and determined that would be a great business. Before I had finished my freshman year in college, I created a business plan for a dance studio. After graduating the entrepreneurship bug continued. A college friend recruited me to sell Mary Kay and I loved every moment of it. The principles learned in Mary Kay were second to none. After marrying my college sweetheart, the entrepreneurship bug continued and we launched an African American Parenting Magazine "Our Pride & Joy". We grew the magazine to a circulation of over fifty-thousand and were successful in attracting major sponsors and advertisers, until 9/11 hit and the sponsorship dollars came to a complete halt. This led me back into corporate America where I was able to progress quickly up the corporate ladder due to all of my experience in organizational development, marketing, sales, project management and domain expertise in healthcare. After spending almost a decade running a major division for a large government contractor, I decided to relocate back home from Washington D.C. to Virginia Beach, Virginia. At this point we were parents to three children. I decided to take some time to focus on family and became an independent consultant. Because I had established a reputation in the industry, I quickly received requests to form a company and received 8(a) certification. The company was formed in November and by March we were 8(a) certified. Record speed! In November, I was a subcontractor and by April of the following year I received my first large prime contract. ARDX was born out of demand not by desire. That demand came from always remembering to make my customer shine and they always call me for more.

What have been the key factors to your success and why?

I believe two overarching factors that have allowed me to succeed are my insatiable ability to dream and laser focus on executing my vision. These two factors are elaborated on in my book *Envision Lead Grow - Releasing the Boss Within* through what I call seeds.

Seed #1: **Consider what makes your heart sing.** I find that adults have been conditioned to see barriers more often than opportunities; therefore, I make every attempt to create a space to go back to the little girl in me. That is where I find the purity of what brings me peace and joy. When I start from my core, I find that I am fully able to innovate from an authentic place.

Seed #2: **Put pen to paper.** Personally, this is setting goals. Writing the vision on paper makes it real.

Seed #3: **Speak it and bring it to life.** Announcing my vision to my organization, friends, and potential customers means I must make it happen. I believe in saying what you are going to do and doing it. No excuses!

Seed #4: **Inhale and exhale.** I am careful to place the right people in the right place on my tree of life. It is so important that I ensure that those who are closer to my root and trunk truly provide nutrients for the growth of my vision. I have learned to discern those who bring life into my vision and those who suck the life out of it. This has been a hard lesson, but knowing pays dividends.

Seed #5: **Delve into the details.** I have often heard the phrase that "the devil is in the details," but I believe that the details are the gift. When we spend time rolling up our sleeves and researching before moving, we save time and money. There lies the gift.

Seed #6: **Plan your success.** Planning is the fun part for me, but I recognize that most people don't enjoy creating charts and task lists. I see planning as the insurance policy to protect individuals and organizations from unnecessary catastrophes. We all know that neglecting to plan is planning to fail.

Seed #7: **Reevaluate your plan.** Planning is done with the best available data. As more or different data becomes available, the plan must be adjusted.

Seed #8: **Stop and smell the roses**. This is from the seeds you have planted. This is simple; enjoy your success and marvel at what you have nourished and grown.

What has been your worst decision and how did you bounce back and still get to where you are today? How did this failure prepare you for your current success?

I believe the worst decision any leader can make is to not make a decision, so I would have to say that I don't have a "worst decision." However, the decision that has been most detrimental to my organization was bringing on a group of five executives all at once. To complicate matters further, we outgrew our office space. So not only did I remove myself from the daily interaction with the staff by adding an additional management layer, but I also physically separated myself from the staff by moving my office to another building.

While I engaged the mid-level leaders in the interviewing process and believed that I had received buy-in, I really underestimated just how critical it was that the staff continued to feel connected to the founder of the organization.

Bouncing back from this was not easy and it took years before there was recovery. I increased the intensity of communication through regularly scheduled corporate newsletters, town hall meetings, and CEO Chats to ensure the staff received messaging directly from me. I emphasized with executives the importance of understanding and embracing the spirit of the organization. For those who could not align with the spirit, I had to accept that they were not a match for the organization. In time, the trust was repaired and the organization grew stronger because of this experience.

Now, almost six years later, I have a cohesive leadership team. Through those early experiences, I became crystal clear regarding the winning characteristics of an ARDX executive. While the lesson was painful, it was impactful.

What has been your best decision and why?

It is interesting that the closest thing to a "worst decision" was rooted in the best decision. For years, I was the center of the organization. I was the technical expert, the customer relationship manager, and the chief decision maker. Wearing all those hats was a necessity during the early years, but as the company grew, it became impossible to do all things, and do them well. I was becoming the single point of failure.

Our sustainability as an organization was dependent on getting solid senior leadership. The decision to continue to seek the right individuals that could propel the organization forward has allowed me the opportunity to benefit from trusted advisors and offered me the opportunity to expand into areas that bring me greater personal satisfaction.

What is an unusual habit you have as an entrepreneur that helps you succeed?

I would say that my unusual habit is journaling my lessons learned for the day. I find that I cannot control how people will react to decisions or circumstances, but I can learn from every discussion, observation, and experience. I honor myself and continue to grow by not taking offense, but instead gaining at least one lesson each day.

With the knowledge and experience you have now, what would you have done differently if you were to start your entrepreneurial journey again?

If I were to do one thing differently, I would have started this organization with a partner. While I am sure there are hardships that occur in partnerships, I believe the emotional tax paid is so much greater when you face the dark days alone. I believe it would be nice to have an opportunity to drop the baggage for a moment and know that someone is there, with as much skin in the game, to carry the load for just a few moments.

What do you do when you feel demotivated and overwhelmed?

When I feel demotivated, there are two things that reenergize me. First, I read entries from my journals. I am reminded of just how far I have come over the last fourteen years. Second, I listen to messages from my children. Their voices motivate me as I know what I am doing today creates their legacy for tomorrow. The perspective of the past and the promise of tomorrow fuels my motivation every time.

When I feel overwhelmed, the only thing that centers me is prayer and scripture. No matter where I am or the position I am in, I have learned to pause and pray. Without fail, my prayers are answers.

Discuss a crisis situation (2008 depression, 9/11, COVID-19) that you/your company were in and how you overcame it.

Our company has been fortunate as we doubled our sales during the 2008 financial crisis. Even during the COVID-19 pandemic, we were positioned to continue to maintain our business without disruption. Most notably, the social unrest during the inhumane murder of George Floyd was a crisis that became unbearable. As an organization, I am proud of the diversity of race, age, and sexual orientation that we have attracted. However, it was unconscionable for me as an African American CEO to not create an atmosphere that allowed staff to discuss their feelings regarding racial injustice.

I held a CEO Chat and shared my own story. I believe that the only way we can move forward is by giving our staff a license to have a conversation, provide education, create awareness, and then move to action. Telling our stories through conversation offers a perspective that I couldn't possibly expect someone to understand if they have not walked in my shoes.

That CEO Chat was an eye-opening experience and I received heartwarming letters from staff, ranging from fifty-eight-year-old white men to thirty-year-old black women, who felt that they were not liberated. They received permission from the CEO to become comfortable with having the uncomfortable conversation.

That was just the beginning, but it was a tremendous step forward in creating a culture that allows our small business to be a light in our community.

What is that one secret to your business success that would be helpful to current and aspiring entrepreneurs?

I believe the secret to success is congruence to your mission. I find that people are busy doing things, but many times those things support someone else's mission or someone else's vision for your mission. I have observed that people are easily distracted by the latest trend or what their neighbor has accomplished. Years later, they look back and see that they have lost years chasing someone else's mission. When you are an aspiring entrepreneur, it is critical that all actions are congruent, that you are your mission.

What is the best investment you've made and why?

I believe the best investment of money and time was obtaining my Ph.D. in business administration from

Oklahoma State University. The program offered me the opportunity to gain a greater understanding of the value of making decisions based on sound quantitative and qualitative data. This has proven critical to decreasing waste and increasing productivity. But bigger than the impact to the company is how much I learned about myself. During the program, I learned theories regarding expert performance and deliberate practice that ignited a spark in me that has now become my lifelong mission. In 2017, I founded a 501(c)(3) nonprofit organization called Envision Lead Grow. This organization helps transform communities of poverty into communities of prosperity through encouragement and support of middle school girls. Through entrepreneurship training we impact self-efficacy, self-control, and delayed gratification. What began as my dissertation has blossomed into a longitudinal study with more than one thousand girls in forty-eight states. In 2021, the program will go global.

The dollars and time invested in obtaining my Ph.D. were significant; however, I have received an immeasurable return on investment each time one of our girls believes that they bring value to this world.

When you started the business did you have support? How did you handle the naysayers?

When I started the business, I had the moral support from my close circle (grandmother, husband, children, and close friends). Because most people could not really understand the industry that I was in nor what I did, they had no understanding of what it took for me to be successful. I find that when people don't know the business, it is very difficult for them to see the vision. Therefore, their comments appeared to be negative and overly critical.

By year three, I began to recognize a key factor. If everyone was given the gift of the vision that was planted in me, everyone would have this business. The best way to handle the naysayers is to recognize their limitations and continue to move toward greatness. Many of yesterday's biggest naysayers are today's loudest cheerleaders.

Be Curious, Stay Humble, and Do the Work

Ryan A. Rickert

Ryan Rickert is the owner and founder of Clean Slate Group, part of a collection of specialty companies that work together synergistically. One of the divisions of Clean Slate is The Wrap Agency. These companies were born out of a desire to create beautiful public art that also was graffiti resistant. After approaching $3M with ideas, Clean Slate Group was able to help develop a laminate that resists graffiti and also creates products for general commercial purposes. These companies have been running for nearly a decade now, and continue to have bright futures. The company is based in Bozeman, Montana, and information can be found online at www.cleanslategroup.org.

Tell us about you as the owner/founder. What's your story that made you the entrepreneur you are today?

My first entrepreneurial venture was selling lemonade and Snickers® on a construction site during the workers' lunch and smoke breaks. I was seven years old and visiting homes in my neighborhood that were being built, accompanied by my father. From there I ordered candy and toys from catalogs to resell to my classmates. One of the most memorable sales of my youth was one hundred and forty-four sombreros that sold out in under an hour at a Cinco de Mayo party at a local restaurant. I've been blessed to be able to see, from an early age, gaps in the marketplace and/or better ways to create or deliver products and services.

What have been the key factors to your success and why?

The three most important factors to my success are personal ethics, grit, and tenacity. In terms of personal ethics, I am unwilling to compromise my integrity or my character just to close a deal or win a client. As for grit, I have a willingness to get up and out of bed when I don't want to, an ability to do the work when I don't feel like it, and an inability to sit and feel sorry for myself. I am also tenacious and willing to go the extra mile or do more than anyone else.

What has been your worst decision and how did you bounce back and still get to where you are today? How did this failure prepare you for your current success?

My worst decision was a hire I made in the very early years of one of my companies. But in a way, what happened was less the fault of this bad hire and more my own fault.

I was very good at negative self-talk. You know how some people say that there are "numbers people" and "verbal people"? I don't believe this anymore, because I've come to see that you can develop basic competency in many things with just a bit of effort. When I was younger, however, I bought into the idea that I was "not a numbers guy" or more specifically "not an accounting guy" (whatever that means). As I think back on it now, it's shocking, because you can close down entire career fields in your mind due to a faulty belief that seems real and true to you when you're young and inexperienced.

That belief continued on into college, where I had to take two accounting classes. I did what I needed to pass, repeating the same old script: "I don't like math" (and I'm no good at it). What do you think happened when I went into business? I wasn't proactive with my finances. I was reactive. I used "bank account bookkeeping," if there was money in the bank, my business must be successful, right?

This led to situations in which people would say, "Hey Ryan, don't forget to invoice me." They were being kind, but what they really could have said was, "Hey dummy, do you know how to run a business?" By using the terrible metric of "bank account bookkeeping" I was preparing myself for a world of hurt.

That hurt came with an employee who I thought was going to solve these problems for me. He was an older gentleman in my personal network who showered me with compliments and who also happened to be an expert in accounting. I didn't do my due diligence (another key principle of accounting - see what happens when you don't pay attention in school, kids?) and essentially gave him the keys to the kingdom.

Fast forward seven months and when I happened to be looking at the bank account, I saw a check amount I didn't recognize that was written by "me". I dug deeper, then deeper. At the end of this paper trail was the very first unauthorized check he wrote to himself "from me," which dated back to his third week of employment. The cost of my negative self-talk, lack of due diligence, and unwillingness to face up to what it took to run a business was $77,000.

Now, I'm not going to tell you that my revenge was that I went and got a finance degree and am now a CFO, but I did educate myself a lot more and am pretty dangerous now around Profit and Loss Statements (P&L), balance sheets, and any other standard financial reporting a company needs. And all it cost me was $77,000 and a few servings of humble pie. You may wince at that number (trust me, so do I), but in a way I'm glad I made that mistake early on, and at such a relatively low cost compared to what might have happened years later.

What has been your best decision and why?

In 2015, I heard a series of sermons that really pushed me to be more intentional with my time. You can always make more money, but you can't make any more time...unless you become very intentional with your schedule. This meant saying "no" to a lot of opportunities but "yes" to a lot more time with those I love and a dedicated focus to my companies. There are months that get off track, but for the most part I've been enjoying more time ever since I reclaimed my schedule. It's still paying dividends every day.

What is an unusual habit you have as an entrepreneur that helps you succeed?

Jocko Willink has popularized early morning rising, and it is something I value as well. Before I go to bed, I quiet and empty my mind by putting all my to-dos down onto a list. I can then sleep more easily knowing there's nothing that hasn't been considered. When I get up (sometimes as early as 3 a.m.) I'm able to focus (no one else is in the office) and beat the email game (even the time zones ahead of me haven't woken up yet). When I told a friend about this habit he shared a quote of Emily Bronte that I agree with: "A person who has not done one half his day's work by ten o'clock, runs a chance of leaving the other half undone."

With the knowledge and experience you have now, what would you have done differently if you were to start your entrepreneurial journey again?

When I was young, I was very money-oriented. I was chasing the big bucks. That can also lead you to fear losing what you've earned and, when done for the wrong reasons, is a foolhardy pursuit. If I could go back to younger me today with my hard-earned wisdom, I'd tell him to realize that no matter what happened, things would be okay. If I lost everything I owned tomorrow, I'd still have my family and my faith, and I could start over. My value isn't in my bank account or my possessions, but in the great gift of life I have been given. There's always another day to redeem a bad day that's gone before.

What do you do when you feel demotivated and overwhelmed?

Hal Boyle has a quote that resonates with me: "What makes a river so restful to people is that it doesn't have any doubt - it is sure to get where it is going, and it doesn't want to go anywhere else." When I can't focus or am feeling off my game, I retreat into nature. I adventure and I pray. This might be casting a fly to catch a trout, or foraging for wild mushrooms, or shed hunting for antlers that I can later carve into gifts for family, friends, and associates (yes, I live in Montana and carving decorative eagles, words of encouragement, and names into antlers that I find, is a normal hobby for me. I also find mental clarity in restoring old axes, hatchets, and panning for gold from my setup in my backyard. Yes, really!). It allows me to recalibrate and effortlessly be present with whatever I am doing. After a while, without rush, I find myself recharged and ready to get back in the game.

Discuss a crisis situation (2008 depression, 9/11, COVID-19) that you/your company were in and how you overcame it.

In one of my earliest businesses, the very first employee also had become a dear friend. It was a great working relationship...until it wasn't. I made a business decision to create another business, which he took very personally, and then, behind my back, went to poison the well with half of my team (there were seventeen employees besides me). He made an attempt to force me to sell the business to him, and part of me wanted to give in, because I thought I was going to lose the company. But I didn't. I stood up to the threat, and the poisoner left. I had an individual conversation with every employee to get us back on track and some felt that they needed to go. The ones who stayed had now made it through a fire with me, and hence our relationship grew stronger.

What is that one secret to your business success that would be helpful to current and aspiring entrepreneurs?

Dale Carnegie, the granddaddy of personal development, enunciated as one of his principles: "Be genuinely interested in other people." Before I learned this principle, I practiced it instinctively. I would find out and learn people's names, the important relationships in their lives, their hobbies. This allowed me to build real relationships and make sure I wasn't just creating superficial transactional "friendships" that could fold at the slightest touch. Be curious and don't be afraid to ask people about what matters to them.

What's your advice for entrepreneurs who are still struggling?

Be good to people and go out of your way to help people in need....and prioritize people over money.

Run all decisions through your mental checklist. My checklist includes these questions: Is this honorable, fair, and wise? Will I be proud of this decision? Will my wife and kids be proud of this decision? Is this creating value? If all the boxes aren't checked, don't do it. As I said above, when I was younger I was very money-oriented. Once I created my mental checklist, I struggled less in every way. I benefit more people. I have more meaningful relationships. I have more margins in life. Unsurprisingly, I make more money, too.

When the chips are down, remember that all you can do is live for *this day*. Focus on showing up for *this day* and whatever you are doing, do it to your best, with honor. Take a breath, begin with gratitude for the breath in your lungs and the challenge ahead, and then keep putting one foot in front of the other. Do your best to make decisions that will bear fruit for tomorrow.

How would you describe the culture of your company? Did you develop your company consciously or did it just happen?

Culture has always been a big deal for me, as I've been part of good company culture, GREAT company culture, and really bad company culture. With each of my companies, I seek to build value for businesses and people, with honor and integrity. I value integrity, humility, heart, and hustle far more than a fancy degree (or any degree, for that matter). Historically, my companies have had incredible culture in large part because we hire for cultural fit above all else. I can train people in certain systems or get them up to speed with various skills. But I can't teach them cultural fit. It doesn't mean those people are bad or incompetent: just not good fits for us (which ultimately means we aren't what they are looking for, either).

Whenever I've gone against this principle, and hired someone because I thought they were incredibly competent in a particular skill or were "exactly who we needed" at the moment, I've regretted it. It's never worked out, over more than a decade of businesses and over one hundred hires to date. The result? We have a very talented, creative, and ethical team, which creates a perpetual self-fulfilling and self-refilling culture across all of my companies. Outside of my wife and three sons, this is one of the parts of my life that gives me great joy and pride.

Every Problem Is an Opportunity

Dr. Carrie Singer

Carrie Singer is the executive director of Quince Orchard Psychotherapy, a group mental health practice with locations throughout the Washington D.C. metro area. In five years, she went from being a solo practice psychologist to employing thirty clinicians bringing in $5M in revenue. In an era with so many in need of mental healthcare and so few good practitioners accepting insurance, her practice made a mark for itself by partnering with physicians and managed care companies to increase quality and accessibility of care. The company is based in Rockville and Frederick, Maryland, and information can be found online at www.qopsych.com.

Tell us about you as the owner/founder. What's your story that made you the entrepreneur you are today?

I never set out to be an entrepreneur. I saw a gap in our community that needed to be filled and kept taking the next right steps to bring it to fruition. In hindsight though, I never much liked having a boss, always had quirky ideas for inventions, and never settled for being told no. I'm a firstborn child, the "class mom" in my kids' classes every year, the type to start petitions and write strongly-worded letters when something is unjust, and the family planner of all tasks requiring organization. So you could say I'm fairly confident and assertive. But that wasn't always the case.

I was a rebellious teen, to put it mildly; arrested for drugs, kicked out of three high schools, in and out of multiple rehabs. The final rehab stint was two years at an all-girls therapeutic boarding school in the wilderness of Montana. The highlight reel there included routinely being forced to cross-country ski twenty miles at midnight, building a huge in-ground fence for months, shoveling horse manure, and carrying a backpack full of rocks around as "therapy." A disproportionate amount of the students later committed suicide or overdosed and others filed lawsuits for abusive practices until the school was finally shut down.

Having experienced what bad therapy was and being more aware of my own issues, psychology became a field of interest. After finishing high school and launching on a course for a new life, I was scared straight and found a recovery community, got my act together, finished undergrad in three years, and went right into a doctoral psychology program. Being raised by two successful physicians, I knew that private practice was the best option for income and flexibility. A few years into solo practice though and I was feeling burned out. There were too many people who needed help and only so many hours in the day. After having kids, time became even more precious.

One of the things that I enjoy most about being a psychologist is solving problems. Working as a pyscyhologist, I could only help a limited quantity of people with their personal problems. I figured if I could launch a group practice overseeing other helpers, we would be able to help thousands with a broader reach solving problems on a regional scale. I was so scared to hire my first employee, worried that we wouldn't have enough work for them. Of course I totally undersold our potential and the needs of the mental health market because we have experienced exponential growth year after year and still have hundreds of clients on a waitlist. Sometimes I look back and wonder what would have happened if fear kept me from taking that first step.

Becoming a leader has been a joyful but, of course, stressful experience. It invariably exposes inner strength you never knew you had and magnifies flaws you hoped no one would ever notice. Having no previous real business experience, I became an avid consumer of every book, webinar, and blog post on marketing, finance, and human resources I could find. I invested in business coaching and joined a number of entrepreneur groups. Trying to figure it out on your own can only get you so far.

Instead of letting my rocky background, lack of start-up capital, and fears about not being good enough to do something bigger with my career dictate my future,

I leveraged my personal experiences to understand my ideal client, create a vision and culture for our company, and possibly change the landscape for affordable mental health care in our local community. My future goals are to chip away at our broken mental healthcare system on a national level by leveraging technology to help link patients with the right help. Every problem is an opportunity waiting to be solved. Turning pain points from blind spots to passion to progress is how entrepreneurs see the world differently.

What have been the key factors to your success and why?

I used to just tell people I was in the right place at the right time, but really it was a lot of blood, sweat, and tears. Weekends spent driving a moving truck to set up a new office and having twenty-four hours to furnish and decorate six thousand square feet before opening day. Taking irate customer calls at all hours and talking them down. The gut punch of realizing there was a billing error and we had one month to pay back $60,000. Business is not for the faint of heart! It requires research, marketing, hiring the right people, developing standardized operating procedures, constant networking and most important, not giving into self-limiting beliefs. There are no "get-rich-quick" schemes that work; they all take time and dedication. Even as a cynic by nature, I tend to believe that when you are optimistic about what you can accomplish and put that positivity out there, the universe tends to respond. We try to emanate positivity in our customer service approach with clients and our employee-centric work culture and enjoy long-term relationships in return.

What has been your worst decision and how did you bounce back and still get to where you are today? How did this failure prepare you for your current success?

For the first few years we were so focused on scaling, that we didn't have the right infrastructure in place. We had no bookkeeper, no budget, no cash reserves, no plan for company culture, and most decisions were made on the fly without proper forethought. I started out paying people too much because we wanted to attract good talent, but our margins couldn't support it and we had to decrease pay, which impacted morale and turnover, of course. The trade-off was that we could then afford to offer benefits, which led to hiring new staff who were excited to settle down where they could build a career. Trying to wear "all the hats" and fill all of the administrative roles was exhausting and unsuccessful. Building the right management team has finally allowed me to enjoy my business instead of resenting it as I did in the earlier years.

What has been your best decision and why?

I can't decide on one "best" decision. I think it's the accumulation of small decisions that are most important. "Should I spend a little more on marketing this month because the summer is coming and I'd like to offer the staff more paid time off if we can increase our revenue a bit? Should the receptionist who was just diagnosed with a chronic medical condition be shifted into a different position she can perform remotely? Should we give that patient who just got laid off a cost waiver and if so for how long?" Our leadership is reflected in the small caring choices we make daily that demonstrate our true character and commitment to values and culture. For the bigger decisions, I consult with my business team and trust my instincts and the best data available at the time. Overanalysis is paralysis!

What is an unusual habit you have as an entrepreneur that helps you succeed?

Impulsivity, for sure! When I get excited about something, I can't rest until I hit a wall with it or the process is initiated to actualize the idea. Can't tell you how many notebooks I have filled with late night musings, web domains I have purchased, and Doing Business As (DBA) names I have filed for.

With the knowledge and experience you have now, what would you have done differently if you were to start your entrepreneurial journey again?

If I had to start over again, I would probably actually do it the way the business books tell you to: create a business plan, secure funding, hire a good attorney and accountant, and consult with a seasoned mentor to develop a blueprint for the architecture of your ideal company's framework. Most business owners underestimate the amount of time and personal capital required. I sure did!

What do you do when you feel demotivated and overwhelmed?

As a therapist, I know all the right answers to this question. As a human, my practice of self-care is far from perfect. I usually suffer from too much motivation and juggling too many ideas at once, but every few months that adrenaline rush wears off and I'm happy to wind down and regroup. Overwhelmed is a pretty frequent state, though. We have two small children at home and have to cram in at least sixty hours of work each week around family schedules, often meaning that sleep is sacrificed. Hiring a Director of Operations and an Executive Assistant definitely helped, although turning everything over was hard at first. We also asked the cleaning lady to come every week and signed up for a healthy meal delivery service because I'd rather outsource the tasks I don't enjoy to maximize the limited quality time that exists. Usually it's about slowing down and prioritizing the importance of tasks, being diligent about reinforcing time boundaries, patting oneself on the back for how far you have already exceeded your wildest dreams, and remembering that things usually always work out and that obsessing about an unforeseen outcome invariably invites more stress and may actually impede goal achievement.

Discuss a crisis situation (2008 depression, 9/11, COVID-19) that you/your company were in and how you overcame it.

Given that we launched in 2015, COVID-19 has really been the only widespread crisis we have encountered.

We were lucky enough to have our industry spared as we quickly pivoted to telehealth and were able to continue to provide services. The more difficult part was that many of our patients lost their jobs and insurance benefits and needed mental health services more than ever. We provided as many pro bono services as we could and threw together "Coping with COVID" webinars and free online support groups. One webinar drew in two hundred and fifty attendees, a few of whom admitted to being suicidal that day and others insinuated they were living with domestic violence. So, the financial impact on our staff was small, but the vicarious traumatization was overwhelming and many therapists had to reduce how many hours they could put in. Working parents also had fewer hours they could pitch in, so our looming waitlist grew.

Since everyone was going through it together, though, a shared compassion emerged even between coworkers. The team found new ways to connect on a personal level, and we witnessed and metabolized the deep impact our work had on our community.

What is that one secret to your business success that would be helpful to current and aspiring entrepreneurs?

It sounds cheesy, but don't sweat the small stuff and believe in yourself. I see some business owners struggle because they don't invest in marketing and infrastructure, they don't trust or even like their employees, they give up too much of their time for too little profitability, and it makes them chronically grumpy and irritable. Some secretly from the start have misgivings about whether their concept is tenable and if they are really dedicated to the mission. You are your company's most valuable asset, so protect yourself. Protect from petty frustrations, lower-level work tasks that can be delegated, scuffles about money, defending yourself from ego bruises, etc. It's about the journey, not the destination, so enjoy the ride! In business, anything is possible. Work with a coach to define and harness your potential. It's lonely at the top and it really helps to have a trusted advisor and peer group.

Did you have to deal with tough barriers to entry?

Certainly not as many as some, but being a young female, I am often met with skepticism. When showing up for business meetings, I can't tell you how many times there has been a raised eyebrow and the inevitable questions: "Will anyone else be joining us? Are you the sole owner? Are you authorized to make this transaction on your company's behalf?" One time, I went to purchase office furniture and asked for a discount on twenty arm chairs and the store manager said, "Your boss was smart to send you." Hell yeah, she was! But I say ignore that noise, they'll never see you coming and you'll win with the element of surprise. Be the change you seek.

Did you ever experience a time you could not pay payroll costs?

Yes, two years into business with employees being overpaid and inadequate support staff, our medical biller left abruptly with one's day notice after we had just switched to a new electronic medical record system. The new biller struggled to acclimate, revenue hadn't come in for months, and employees were starting to ask if they should start looking for new jobs. I took cash advances on all of my credit cards and paid the minimum balance, didn't draw a salary for three months, and prepaid everyone's commissions. I do not recommend that. Always have someone who serves as a backup who is cross-trained for each essential role within the company, and operate with at least a three-month cash reserve.

Do the Joyful Thing

Jonathan Sparks, Esq.

Jonathan Sparks is the founder of Sparks Law, a national law firm specializing in business. Every day they register trademarks, and write partnership agreements, customer contracts, estate plans for business owners, and employment contracts. They offer creative legal ideas that spark the entrepreneurial fire! The company is based in Alpharetta, Georgia, and information can be found online www.SparksLawPractice.com.

Tell us about you as the owner/founder. What's your story that made you the entrepreneur you are today?

I started as an entrepreneur when I came up with the goal of saving $100 before my seventh birthday. At the time, I had a dollar a week allowance and had to hustle-market-sell my way to the goal within nine months. Most of the money I made was from doing random chores for the family and setting up lemonade, cookie, and homemade jewelry stand. By the end of it, I understood profits and losses with a sheet my mother and I went over together.

Since then, I've always been "entrepreneurial." I define this as strongly preferring that my income be tied directly to my *effort and creativity*, rather than the traditional seniority-based system that most employers use.

As a lawyer, I started at a big firm, worked my tail off, and quickly found that my employer had no incentives for noble, hard workers; it was a seniority-based system. There was a man that had been there for ten years that was in front of me in the line. I did twice the production that he did, consistently, but work productivity did not matter – he would inevitably get promoted before me.

Entrepreneurs working at "regular jobs" often feel stifled and put down in those environments; I certainly did.

What have been the key factors to your success and why?

I am creative and I will do whatever it takes to succeed. I am aware of my own mindset and the mindset of the people I spend time with. I can usually come at a problem from a new perspective that others haven't thought of. I stay away from doom and gloom thinking. I know in my heart that there are always opportunities. Once I find the opportunity in a situation, I pivot and I work to make it happen the way it needs to. I do whatever it takes.

There have been times that my entrepreneurial colleagues have given up when they see a problem. The old guard "solutions" don't work anymore in the modern world. They see problems as perfectly reasonable reasons to give up and they plan to fail. Their friends and family "understand" why they're giving up; everyone around them agrees that they should give up. Except me.

I am learning to be mindful of people around me, especially their perspectives and mindsets. I have a strong tendency to make choices based on what the people around me would agree with. That tendency holds me back if I'm around the wrong people. It can also propel me forward if I surround myself with the right people. In that respect, whenever I find an entrepreneur with a similar mindset, I befriend them and we build a community, brick by brick, of success-oriented individuals.

What has been your worst decision and how did you bounce back and still get to where you are today? How did this failure prepare you for your current success?

When I first started my law firm, I met a man that wanted to merge our companies and make a partnership law firm. He had about twenty-five years of experience, which, compared to my measly two, was pretty awe-inspiring. He had spent a lot of that time doing business law and was easy to talk to. I made the mistake of partnering up with the man thinking that (a) he'd be a mentor, (b) I needed a mentor, and (c) two heads would be better than one. I was wrong on all accounts. He was not a mentor. When I asked him for advice about how to run a business, make a sale, or even be a lawyer, his answer was primarily, "I don't know, did you Google it?" Instead of mentoring me, he took money out of our partnership bank account to pay for vendors that had *sold him their services* rather than us *selling them our services*. Apparently, guys that are great at sales are usually the easiest to sell to. Lots of entrepreneurs will waste gobs of resources (their profits) on services that don't add to profitability. The man hated budgeting and felt it was too constraining. The money we used to pay for these unnecessary services was always taken out of our account rather than resulting in profits.

I learned that most partnerships don't work out and if you're entering into one, to have a great partnership agreement in writing before a bunch of money comes rolling in. Money causes perverse incentives and makes people less likely to agree. Luckily, as business lawyers, we had written a great partnership agreement, and when we called it quits, the business split was smooth.

I learned that I didn't need a mentor. I had all the expertise I needed to run a law firm on my own. If anything, my being "fresh out of law school" gave me the advantage of knowing the new, more recent laws that had passed. I learned that having a single business owner that has the final say on everything is far better than having multiple partners. Reaching consensus is guaranteed to bog a business down. A great entrepreneur has novel ideas that have to be implemented quickly in order for that business to thrive. Unfortunately, if you have to get everyone's agreement on change before you can implement it, you tie the business's hands. The month after I split off from the partnership, my business grew by thirty-five percent and the month after that, we had more than doubled. The only real difference was that I was spending energy on growing my business, rather than worrying about my business partner.

What has been your best decision and why?

I decided to "do the joyful thing." When faced with the opportunity to do something that I really long to do (buy a 1955 Gibson Les Paul Goldtop, buy a wonderful home, hire a rock star employee even though I don't yet have a spot for her on my team, take time off for a bike ride on a mountain trail), I decided to do that thing rather than the other stuff that I "should do."

"Shoulds" will terrorize you and your company and I like to demolish them as much as possible. Often, after pulverizing a "should" and doing the joyful thing instead, I have a strong tendency to then knock the "should" out of the park in some way. Doing the joyful thing is ultimately a great motivator for me to do whatever it takes. There's this deal I make with myself that goes something like, "Okay man, I know you really want to do this thing, so we're going to do it, one-hundred percent. But then, we do the other stuff, cool?" I'm like a kid at Toys R Us in 1985! Doing the elated stuff ignites my ambition to do more for my company and gets me in the habit of acquiring more freedom; I feel so free and alive when I do a joyful thing. It's even sweeter when it's decimating a "should" in the process.

What is an unusual habit you have as an entrepreneur that helps you succeed?

I don't see problems as problems so much as opportunities that are hiding in puzzles that I get to figure out and then use to succeed more. This pisses some people off because they really want your agreement that a problem is a problem and that people should do things in response to that problem like plan to fail, miss the mark, and shut down. That's okay, though, that's just how they want to live.

The 2020 pandemic, for example, came with a mountain of untapped opportunities. Entire industries changed; some collapsed like the restaurant industry and some arose out of nowhere, like the testing and health care products industries. Many of my law firm owner colleagues chose to fail when facing the pandemic, but my team and I pivoted, found all of the new business owners that needed legal help because of the pandemic, delivered our services to them quickly, and everyone profited from it. I am now purchasing law firms that chose to shut down rather than see the opportunity.

Problems are just change. Change isn't good or bad. Change creates issues for things that are based on how it was before the change took place. It also opens up opportunities for things that are based on how the world will be after the change takes place, and that's the fun part. Entrepreneurs are visionaries. We can see far beyond what most people see. We can plan and project into the future and the more we're in the habit of doing that, of seeing the opportunities when everyone else is running around frantically finding the best way to fail, we're succeeding.

With the knowledge and experience you have now, what would you have done differently if you were to start your entrepreneurial journey again?

I would take bigger risks and make moves faster. I was very afraid to commit to paying an administrative employee for five hours a week at $12 an hour. I struggled to take my mind off of the amount of money I would be paying someone to do tasks that I could do myself. Although once I hired this person, I realized that every $12 I spent *bought me an entire hour* that I could use to bill $350 an hour, make my business plan, or be with my family.

There are many jobs that the business owner can do, and usually the business owner can do those tasks better than the person that's hired to do them. At least at first. Once they're trained, they should be better at it than you. Let's take sales, for example. Every company has a sales department and often the owner is the best person at sales. If I hire a salesperson, I guarantee that person will do a far better job selling legal services than I can possibly do while I'm out riding my bike on a mountain trail, jamming with my band, or putting my kids to bed. Hiring employees is buying freedom, and it gasses up your entrepreneurial spirit. Your business will only suffer through explosive growth if you don't take time to hire the necessary people.

What do you do when you feel demotivated and overwhelmed?

I take a beat. I usually do something outside or listen to music while journaling. It's important for me to write down all the thoughts swimming around in my head. Once I get them down, I no longer feel the need to attend to them; they're out there and I can leave them be. Usually, when in a demotivated or anxious state, it's difficult for me to think creatively. Anxiously, I worry that I might forget something. Writing that "something" down, however trivial it may be, allows me to let go of the anxiety I feel surrounding it and think creatively instead.

In a disciplined way, I do not allow myself to start thinking of solutions to issues until I am squarely out of that anxious state. I do this as a practice because most of the mistakes I've made came out of a worried mind.

Discuss a crisis situation (2008 depression, 9/11, COVID-19) that you/your company were in and how you overcame it.

In 2019, I had a crisis at my law firm. I was running my firm in the negative, meaning my expenses were over the money my firm was bringing in. My firm's bank account had dropped to about $5,000 and payroll came out in four business days, which would put the account deeply in the negative. I was sweating. I felt cold, I had gastrointestinal problems, my brain was fogging up, and I literally had trouble seeing straight.

I did a workout, and called up a friend who also owned a law firm. She kind of disregarded my fearful thinking and didn't really take much time to listen to my terrifying story about how the world was ending and this was it. I cannot thank her enough for disregarding my BS story and refusing to buy into it.

She then asked me what I could do to get out of the hole I was in. I told her I had an $80,000 line of credit that I hadn't used before. She started laughing so loudly that I had to pull the phone away from my ear. It was hilarious to her that I was being so fearful and had yet to use my line of credit. I then tried to tell her another story about how "good entrepreneurs" never use money from a line of credit and they bootstrap their company, yada yada yada. She, thank God, refused to believe that one, too. She explained to me, very matter-of-factly, that her line of credit was for $500,000 and that she often pulls hundreds of thousands from it and pays it off after six months or so.

Just hearing her say that, just hearing her experience, showed me an easy way to get out of the hole I was in. But if it hadn't been for her advice and laughter, I might have shut down my company entirely. In the end, I pulled about $15,000 from the line of credit and paid it all back within four business days.

What is that one secret to your business success that would be helpful to current and aspiring entrepreneurs?

Just do it. Most people believe that you can't take any action until you fully understand what you need to do, have all the things you think you need, and then you do it. The opposite is true. You literally can't understand how to do something until you do something. You will understand it in the end, but understanding is never a requirement for doing. We believe that our worried minds will come up with important solutions to what-if problems, but most of the time those what-ifs never take place and our worried minds wasted everything on speculation. How do you do it? You do it. You do it by doing it.

What is the best investment you've made and why? (Can be an investment of money, time, or energy.)

Self-development was a must for me. I had to get out of my own way and it took a great deal of head-stuff and guidance to do that. Like everyone else, my subconscious, or whatever you want to call it, has a very strong tendency to keep the status quo. I subconsciously hate change. But anyone that owns a business and has goals *wants change*. That means we're fighting our own subconscious. There are plenty of books about this and podcasts that I need to consume every day to keep my head out of the old and looking forward. There are also various personal development coaches out there that have helped me and call me on the things that are holding me back. If you hire a coach, make sure that any Kool-Aid served is vetted, legit, and has had plenty of sustainable and consistent success. Don't hire someone just because they posed on Instagram with a Lambo. Hire someone that gets you, and has the track record to prove that they can help you get out of your own BS and move forward.

When you started your business did you have support? How did you handle the naysayers?

To be honest, the biggest naysayer at the time was my wife (yes, we eventually got divorced). It became very clear to me that I had to surround myself with growth-minded individuals who humbly were able to challenge themselves and challenge others. We collectively taught one another to prioritize ego well below our business's goals and to make decisions with those priorities in mind. Often, there were decisions that served my ego that my growth-minded friends called me on. This allowed me to make the right moves, even if it felt uncomfortable at the time.

As a way of example, I egotistically really wanted to be liked by all of my employees, even when they were failing at the jobs they were hired to do. My ego would try and keep them on payroll because they were more likely to "like" me, but the business needed to part ways with them. Once I recognized that my business was going to tank if I continued to pay these people, I fired them. They clearly didn't "like me" when that happened, but my business became very successful and efficient. I quadrupled the business's profit margin, and reinvested in a more talented team. This, in turn, caused my company to grow even more, all because I prioritized my ego and my need to be liked well below my business's success.

Differentiate or Die

Solomon Thimothy

Solomon Thimothy is the founder and president of OneIMS, a Results-Driven online marketing agency specializing in lead generation and customer acquisition programs. The company was founded in 2006 with the mission of designing and developing the most effective and efficient integrated marketing solutions for clients.

Today, OneIMS helps growth-oriented U.S. and international businesses increase online visibility so they can reach and acquire new customers consistently. As a lead generation and customer acquisition agency, OneIMS creates powerful strategies and practical solutions for measurable and sustainable results for advancing businesses and their brands. The team strives to meet and exceed client sales and marketing goals by focusing on the core values of people, passion, and performance.

Using a 3C approach, OneIMS provides clients with the solutions, strategies, and tools they need to reach and engage their prospects and clients. They help clients attract and **connect** with their target audiences through owned, earned, and paid media channels. They help clients **communicate** their unique value proposition at every stage of the buying process. They help clients **captivate** their ideal buyers to take the next step through lead nurturing and sales enablement.

OneIMS is based in Chicago, Illinois, and information can be found online at www.oneims.com.

Tell us about you as the owner/founder. What's your story that made you the entrepreneur you are today?

Growing up in a family with many entrepreneurs, including my father, I felt called to lead from a very young age and knew that I would eventually strike out on my own. Though my parents always expected me to do well in school, they also fostered my independent spirit. They never tried to force a vocation upon me, never insisted I should aspire to be a doctor or lawyer or engineer. Instead, they allowed me the autonomy to choose my own course and made it clear that they would support me in whatever passion I chose to pursue. My brother, Samuel, was equally encouraging, my biggest supporter from day one and my guiding light, driving my business strategy forward to this day.

Despite their hands-off approach to my career goals, being the child of Indian parents did mean that one expectation was non-negotiable – I would graduate from college. I had always done well in school, so I didn't much mind this prerequisite and was willing to forgo the "entrepreneur drops out of college" story line to fulfill my parents' wishes. But even as I dutifully completed each credit hour, my independent spirit continued to flourish.

With my graphic design skills and a major in marketing, I decided I would figure out how to start a small venture building websites. But on a college student's budget, I couldn't afford the PC I would need to do such work, much less a Mac. So, my ever-supportive dad loaned me $2,000, essentially my first seed money, to buy my first Dell computer. I immediately started tinkering on the Dell and had soon taught myself Hypertext Markup Language (HTML). Once I had rounded up a few customers, my web design business was underway.

Nearly every Saturday, I would settle in with a cup of coffee at the nearby Panera Bread, crank out a website, and earn about $1,500 – a virtual fortune to an eighteen-year-old college kid. Though I still had to finish school, I was keenly aware of how much value I could deliver for my customers when I was able to do this work full time.

I started my company the very day after I graduated from college, initially just providing web design as a service out of my home. But when customers began to continually ask me for advice on how to draw people to their websites, I realized I would need to brush up on advertising and how to drive web traffic. I had no money to pay for formal courses, and in 2006 Google was only in its infancy, so my self-education required a good deal of resourcefulness. I attended conferences and webinars, read blogs, and learned a ton by simply trying things and failing. This process proved to me that, despite the conventional wisdom, formal education is not a requirement to being successful in business.

As the business began to expand, I outgrew my home office and, naturally, my dad went hunting for my first office space. Marketing gradually became the dominant component of our service offering and, today, it represents the vast majority of the services OneIMS provides. Though we still offer web design, marketing has become my real passion, and I feel privileged to help so many companies advance their business, market share, sales, revenues, and growth.

What have been the key factors to your success and why?

I owe a huge portion of the success of OneIMS to our comprehensive marketing platform, Clickx, a platform created by our team, for our team. Desperate to find a dashboard that would be a single stop for all of our data and reporting needs, we tested a few existing solutions, but none had all of the key components we felt we needed to accurately measure our clients' success. In the end, we hired an exceptional team of developers and set out to create our own solution.

Clickx was an enormous undertaking from day one, requiring thousands of dollars of investment and years of work to design and develop. With no venture capital investment for the project, we invested every dollar the company made back into development to help support what we were spending with developers. The idea seemed insane, it certainly didn't make sense in the short term given the amount of money we were spending, but I knew that in the long run Clickx would empower us to deliver more value to our clients than ever before.

Clickx delivered. Today, we have a truly comprehensive platform where we can track all of our internal and client data – Google Analytics, call tracking, number of clicks, team member tasks and productivity, client onboarding, and so much more – allowing us to work more efficiently and get a more complete picture of the performance of our clients' marketing campaigns. With all of our data literally at our fingertips, we no longer waste time on producing reports and instead invest that time into strategy, execution, and growing the company. With access to all performance metrics in one location, we can deliver value to our clients by giving them the most complete picture of the results of their marketing strategies. Thanks to Clickx, OneIMS has evolved from a service company to a truly integrated marketing firm with the Clickx platform as the foundation.

What has been your worst decision and how did you bounce back and still get to where you are today? How did this failure prepare you for your current success?

My worst decision was trying to wear too many hats, thinking I could be CEO, CTO, CFO, CIO, and generally the officer of everything at the same time. I failed miserably. Like whack-a-mole at a carnival, I whacked anything that popped up, be it emails, support tickets, sales calls, tech support, hiring and firing, and on and on. I had myself stretched so thin; I wasn't able to fulfill any of these roles effectively.

It is very difficult to manage and grow your business while trying to do everything yourself. This approach is a surefire route to burnout and detrimental to your business, as you can't focus on the overall performance of the business when you're focused on working in the business. Eventually I figured this out and did what was necessary to fix the situation – I fired myself. I stopped doing all the work and instead helped my team build the systems and processes they needed to do the work themselves.

What has been your best decision and why?

My best business decision has been to stick to my mantra of "differentiate or die." By this, I mean narrowing the scope of my company's services so that I could establish a niche and perfect our approach. Typical business strategy is addition, always adding more services, more lines of business, more revenue. In my experience, subtraction is often the better approach, limiting your scope and perfecting what you already do in order to differentiate yourself from your competitors. By sticking to lead generation and customer acquisition services, nothing more, OneIMS has created a highly specific identity that current and potential customers can easily resonate with. Because we are so specialized, we can speak very closely to a client's specific pain points.

Another great decision for me and my business has been my choice to never borrow money from investors or take out any other kind of loan. My dad always emphasized the proverb "it is better to give than to receive" when I was growing up, so in starting my business I had a learned aversion to borrowing money. What I have discovered over the years is that not borrowing buys you freedom. By not taking from investors, I have retained full autonomy in making decisions for my business. I can change the direction of my business on a dime if I wish without asking anyone's permission. I can focus one-hundred percent on solving problems for my customers instead of basing decisions on the need to deliver value for my investors.

What is an unusual habit you have as an entrepreneur that helps you succeed?

I believe "leaders are readers," which is why I never stop learning. I am constantly reading or listening to audiobooks or podcasts, trying to build my knowledge and get every little bit of edge that I can. Though I, of course, spend a lot of time studying new marketing trends and strategies, I also research a wide variety of other topics that will help me better manage my business, from leadership and sales to economics and psychology. Not only does continuous learning keep me sharp and up to speed, but it also stimulates my curiosity and keeps me engaged and interested in my work.

With the knowledge and experience you have now, what would you have done differently if you were to start your entrepreneurial journey again?

If I restarted my journey today, I would definitely be more willing to fail fast, as I call it, on ideas or strategies that weren't working. Blinded by my youth, naiveté, and idealism in the early days of the business, I would often keep pushing a dead idea long after it was clear that things weren't going to pan out. As a result, I wasted a lot of precious time on endeavors that didn't deliver any value to my clients. With experience, maturity, and a great team that helps me analyze new ideas more quickly, I can now change direction more swiftly and abandon ineffective strategies before they become a drain on company resources.

What do you do when you feel demotivated and overwhelmed?

I don't experience a lack of motivation very often, but when I do, I always try to deploy gratitude. I went through such a period amid the COVID-19 lockdown, and gratitude was what helped me through. By taking time to appreciate my team, my clients, and the connections and progress we were still able to make in spite of the lockdown, I was able to rediscover my natural optimism and keep my company moving forward.

Discuss a crisis situation (2008 depression, 9/11, COVID-19) that you/your company were in and how you overcame it.

COVID-19 has undoubtedly been one of the most challenging periods in the company's history. Being in the marketing space, OneIMS was particularly vulnerable as marketing dollars are generally one of the first items on the chopping block when companies struggle. Though we had to cut some hours and shave some costs, it was of utmost importance to me that we retain all of our team members. Finding good people that are the right fit for your team is extremely difficult even in good times, so I fully appreciated the value of my team and was not willing to lose them just to temporarily protect our bottom line. OneIMS has always been willing to go into the red in order to come out strong in the long run, and COVID-19 was the perfect testing ground for this philosophy. Thus far, it has worked to our benefit. Because we were able to retain our incredible team, we continued to serve our clients at the highest level throughout the pandemic and even established some new relationships.

What is that one secret to your business success that would be helpful to current and aspiring entrepreneurs?

Having passion behind your purpose is a powerful driver of success. Passion is a differentiator – we are almost instinctively drawn to people who are truly passionate about their art, their craft, or their career. Passion is also contagious. Those around you will become more excited about what you have to offer when they witness your enthusiasm. I am blessed to work with a passionate team because passionate people, in my experience, make the best problem solvers. Passionate people are driven to find solutions because they are truly invested in their work and the success of their clients.

My passion for marketing doesn't just drive my success, it makes me happier. I have often said that if I just wanted to make a lot of money, I would have gone into real estate. Instead I chose (and continue to choose) a career in marketing because it gives me immense fulfillment. I believe we live such short lives that it doesn't make sense to pursue something that you aren't willing to give your all. My slogan is "ALL IN not half in." I see so many people live their lives in a "half in" mode, many times with their feet in two boats rather than one, never really seeing what can be achieved if they row just one with all their heart.

What's your advice for entrepreneurs who are still struggling?

Always be in exploring mode and have the courage to try new things. Many of the strategies, projects, or businesses you begin may fail, but these failures are opportunities to learn and discover what works. If you wait for the perfect business plan with the perfect team and the perfect strategy, you will likely never go anywhere. Explore mode is the state in which we must operate in order to evolve, and evolution is critical to keeping your company relevant in the long run.

As business owners, it can be easy to get shortsighted and worry when things aren't working out in the short term. We put an enormous amount of energy into monthly, quarterly, and annual performance when we really should be focused on success over a lifetime. If you are struggling for a few short months or even years, it isn't fatal. Other opportunities will present themselves, so keep your perspective and don't get consumed by the struggle of the moment. One management strategy I often use when facing headwinds is to examine which aspects of the business are scaling fast and which are stagnant because of a strategy issue. When you have the right combination of product and market, selling comes easily. Identify where your sticking point is, be it the market, timing, pricing, or execution, and make adjustments accordingly.

What is the best investment you've made and why? (Can be an investment of money, time, or energy.)

My best investments have been my investments into the technology that supports OneIMS. For years, I had a scaling problem where every system we had wasn't built to scale, resulting in frequent issues and ultimately requiring a rebuild of some new system. Time and time again, we would eventually switch software and start over, just to get to where we left off. I had never dreamt of building a software company, but our infrastructure was in such dire need of improvement that I began a software company and slowly started to replace our off-the-shelf, Band-Aid software with our own tools and technology. With no IT background, no engineers on staff, no capital, and no Silicon Valley ensemble of mentors in my home city of Chicago, this endeavor was frustrating to say the least. Nonetheless, it was one of the best decisions I have ever made. The business now thrives on one system that handles everything – employee onboarding, project management, budgeting, reporting, and much more. Even better, other agencies now use it to grow their business. It can be easy to run scared from your biggest, most daunting ideas, but if you can persevere and see them through, they often deliver the biggest payoff.

Ground in Solid Rock: Your Day Is Coming

Theresa R. Williams-Harrison, MBA, PMP, CSM

Theresa R. Williams-Harrison is the founder and president of GEORGE STREET Services, Inc. (GEORGE STREET). The company is a woman-owned business solving the toughest technical challenges in the defense, intelligence, and cyberspace communities. GEORGE STREET is an action-driven digital services technology company that provides software and information technology services and solutions. For its customers, GEORGE STREET provides many railways of access to expert services and solutions. For its employees, GEORGE STREET is "Where Their Story Begins" and provides numerous pathways for employees to author their success. For the community, GEORGE STREET is a trusted partner, working to make our communities better with food donations, college scholarships, schools supplies, and financial donations. GEORGE STREET is grounded in providing the best to its clients, employees, and community. The company is based in Frederick, Maryland, and information can be found online at www.georgestreetinc.com.

Tell us about you as the owner/founder. What's your story that made you the entrepreneur you are today?

I'm the granddaughter of sharecroppers who bought the farm they once worked, and owned a local construction company and convenience store and built the church where many in the town worshipped. I'm the daughter of two of the wisest people I've ever known who have helped me make all key decisions in my life, are master logisticians who managed the love, education, upbringing, and movement of thirteen people, yet do not have high school diplomas of their own. I'm the sibling to ten, seven brothers and three sisters. Some are gainfully employed, some are underemployed, and some are unemployed. But all are committed to controlling their destiny. I'm the wife of my staunchest supporter who encourages me to always work towards reaching my goals and watching them grow. I'm the mother of two Historically Black Colleges and Universities (HBCU) college graduates who are making a difference in the world; one daughter has launched her company and my other daughter has decided she, too, wants to start a business, because it's all they know. I'm the grandmother of an HBCU Class of 2033 college graduate. I've always been focused on orchestrating and controlling my destiny. This is where my story begins.

What have been the key factors to your success and why?

I am intentional about spending one hour every day planning my company's growth to $50M. I am grounded in doing this daily at home to avoid distractions. I plan. I strategize. I scheme. I pray. I consider. I write down goals and thoughts. I rehearse. I apply, and do this every day.

I always have my big picture in focus as I work to map out the future of my company in stages, one scene at a time, one day at a time. I don't rush the process.

What has been your worst decision and how did you bounce back and still get to where you are today? How did this failure prepare you for your current success?

The worst decision I made was providing access to company proprietary and confidential information to an employee who was not yet vested in the company's growth and future. I now realize I was careless and opened the kimono to company information too soon. I was so happy to have the employee on board to off-load some tasks. I did not follow my gut that this was not the right person nor the right time to share information.

I created a vulnerable situation for my company because the person left, started a company, and took a lot of our employee and customer data. With the theft of the sensitive data, some employees were recruited away and I incurred some loss of revenue. However, many other employees were contacted but did not leave. As a result of this, I educated myself on how best to protect my company's proprietary information. I then put in place measures to control who has access, ways to track access to information, and limits to access. I secured my corporate data.

What has been your best decision and why?

The best decision I made was to start GEORGE STREET Services and live my passion.

I grew up in the most loving, supportive, encouraging community that provided everything a child could ever dream of. My public housing community was involved in my life and provided exceptional guidance and encouragement. They continue to do so to this day. My family and community shared the responsibility of raising me and others and left a lasting impact on my life. Because of this, I named my company after the street I grew up on in Baltimore: GEORGE STREET. This thought is so motivational to me.

What is an unusual habit you have as an entrepreneur that helps you succeed?

I celebrate my business journey. I enjoy this journey. The road traveled as a business owner is bumpy, long, tough, stressful, difficult, and lonely. I choose to document all milestones big and small along the way. I celebrated starting the company, getting my tax ID, winning opportunities, hiring employees, obtaining contracts, getting a line of credit, getting business cards. I celebrate! And I continue to have many reasons to celebrate.

With the knowledge and experience you have now, what would you have done differently if you were to start your entrepreneurial journey again?

I would watch who was at my table. I should have created guest lists for my dinner table earlier and I should have been more careful about who I invited to dinner, which is an important gathering in my life. The various people at my table represent people who are the circle of influence in my life. I listen to them. I spend time with them. I work with them. I live with them. I go to church with them. Everyone seated at my table has a strong connection to me and I am selective and strategic.

Don't just invite anyone to your table; give them a reason to want to be there because of what you have on your menu. On the menu, you should have real conversation, giving, openness, energy, honesty, discipline, authenticity, reciprocity, inspiration, connections, motivation, and creativity. Who is seated at your table? Who should you ask to leave your table? You must be willing to take control of your exclusive invitation list. It should be reserved only for those who will add value to your life and business and for whom you can add value.

What do you do when you feel demotivated and overwhelmed?

I'm determined to set and reach goals. When I'm demotivated or overwhelmed, I go to my bucket list and do something new. This helps broaden my views and interests and enhances my ability to see solutions to problems in a more creative manner. Adding a new facet or goal to my life requires focus and discipline and the journey is always fun. I've learned how to write a song. I've produced a song. I've run a 5K. I've taken Mediterranean cooking classes and now I'm learning Spanish. This process is rejuvenating for me. I consistently list things I want to do in my lifetime. Nothing is off limits. This demonstrates my ability to grow and helps mitigate feeling demotivated or overwhelmed.

Discuss a crisis situation (2008 depression, 9/11, COVID-19) that you/your company were in and how you overcame it.

I was diagnosed with an aggressive form of breast cancer in 2018. I had to go into treatment immediately which included chemotherapy, radiation, bilateral mastectomy, reconstruction a couple of times, many surgeries, two years of sickness, and too many side effects to name.

During this period, I had to rely on the leadership team I had in place. I have always been aware of my strengths and weaknesses. I have always known that I can't do everything in the company alone and I'm not good at everything. I had a team who were extremely complementary to my skills. I had people who were also committed and vested in my vision to grow the company and its culture. I overcame the impact of being out sick for two years because I had people who were good at what they do.

Because I overinvest in people, the company functioned without me. I hire the best people. Attract, motivate, train, and reward the best people. I overinvest with emotional currency. I give trust, independence, praise, freedom, and encouragement. People make things happen and they trust me, support me, believe in me, and respect me. They all gave back what they were given. Because of this, my illness had no impact on my company.

What is that one secret to your business success that would be helpful to current and aspiring entrepreneurs?

My ideas and services don't have to be perfect but I can't show that they are not perfect. If I waited to reach perfection before starting my company, I would still be waiting. There is no perfect time, perfect day, perfect customer, perfect products, or perfect services.

Allow yourself the opportunity to improve. The large companies all have products that have been improved over time.

If you feel a strong desire to present your product or service, do it now. Even if there's a better way, do it now, and work on getting it better.

What's your advice for entrepreneurs who are still struggling?

This is just where your story begins. Don't panic. Dig deep. Maintain control which is crucial to your employees and your customers. What you need, you already have. It's buried within. Dig deeper and refuse to give up. Dig deeper for more creativity. Dig deeper for a strategy which will move you beyond the obstacles that are overwhelming you. Replace struggle with progress, a move forward one step at a time. Dig deeper for inspiration from others. You must continue to succeed. You don't want to stop not knowing whether the next day will be your breakthrough. This is where your story begins and your day is coming!

How would you describe the culture of your company? Did you develop your company consciously or did it just happen?

I consciously developed the culture of GEORGE STREET. I reached a point in which I could no longer *not* be an entrepreneur. I had a sense of unwavering commitment and belief that I would succeed as a business owner. It's really easy to be comfortable working for others. It's really easy to be bound by golden handcuffs wedged into tight restraints, and restricted and controlled thinking; but this isn't fun. I worked for many years at a great company that granted me many opportunities to grow. However, unless my executive leadership left, there was no place for me to go, grow, and expand.

I realized early in my career that I craved the ability to create what I want and make it available for others. I needed to be liberated! I wanted to be challenged! I desired excitement in the workplace. I needed to create what I wanted, to be able to do what I wanted to do, in the way I wanted to do it. I'm doing just this with GEORGE STREET. This is a place where employees are the authors of their careers. They are encouraged to design their careers to include training and coaching. Employees are encouraged to review their career designs on a regular basis. The culture at GEORGE STREET provides employees with unwavering commitment from the company and belief in their success. The culture at GEORGE STREET grants the employees the opportunity to apprentice in challenging positions. GEORGE STREET is where opportunities are created for our employees. If one person fails at GEORGE STREET, we all fail. We are committed to ensuring everyone's success.

When the Stakes Are High, Bet on Yourself!

Diedre L. Windsor

Diedre L. Windsor is the founder of Windsor Group LLC. The company provides professional services and business solutions to federal government agencies and commercial entities. Windsor Group LLC has a wealth of experience in a myriad of areas including project and program management, IT support services, staff augmentation, and training and professional development. The company is based in Chevy Chase, Maryland, and information can be found online at www.windsorgroup-llc.com.

Tell us about you as the owner/founder. What's your story that made you the entrepreneur you are today?

I was very independent at a young age. A native of Detroit, Michigan, I knew growing up there was no money for college and I was certain, like most teenagers, I wanted to get going with my life as soon as possible. My mom was a single parent raising three girls. We had what we needed – food, shelter and each other. I have no qualms with my upbringing. Actually,

I can easily say I loved growing up in Detroit. I just wanted to see the world and make a better life for myself and help my mom. Because of her, my work ethic was strong. My mom truly had a 'hustler' spirit and did what she needed to provide for us. She was a nurse's assistant who also sold Avon, Amway and a host of other multilevel marketing inspired products on the side. From about the age of thirteen, I had a job; first working at the corner Ice Cream Parlor, Roscoe's, and later as a receptionist at a twenty-four hour beauty salon, Vantinus Hair Designs, where I got a front row seat to entrepreneurship at its best. Working there, I saw the possibilities. I saw what could be. Working in the salon made me more determined to make something of myself in order to create the life I wanted. In 1986, at the age of seventeen, I joined the Army immediately upon graduating from high school, giving me the independence I so desperately wanted. My time both in the US Army (as an enlisted soldier and commissioned officer) and later federal government (as a Senior Executive) prepared me, from a leadership perspective, for entrepreneurship. Having observed a myriad of leadership styles, I knew I wanted to create a company for which people would want to work.

What have been the key factors to your success and why?

Not to sound cliché, but I do believe a fair bit of our success has come from us simply making it known that we're open for business, ensuring we are prepared to participate in the procurement process and marketing our company. Other key factors include a willingness to work hard, clearly defined goals, flexibility, strong relationships, pursuit of opportunities and, above all, delivering results.

Entrepreneurship is very rewarding yet very hard. It's a labor of love. Put in the work on a daily basis - morning, noon, and night. Know and accept things will not always go your way. There will be wins and losses; learn from both. There will be doors closed in your face and, in some cases, the red carpet will be rolled out for you. Capitalize when those doors are open. And take good care of yourself. Take good care of your employees. Do what you say you're going to do. Keep going. As paraphrased from Ecclesiastes 9:11, the race is not given to the swift nor the strong but he who endures until the end. Don't give up.

What has been your worst decision and how did you bounce back and still get to where you are today? How did this failure prepare you for your current success?

While I wouldn't categorize it as a "worst" decision, hiring quickly without a clear understanding of the business's needs definitely taught me a few valuable lessons. I grew frustrated quickly because I couldn't see the value the new hire brought to the business and I didn't have the time to really carve out a place for him that would benefit the business. I learned that I needed to be more pragmatic in making hiring decisions. From then on, I turned to outsourcing which really changed the course of the business in a positive way. I outsource bookkeeping, business development, HR, and payroll, which ended up being one of the best decisions I've made.

What has been your best decision and why?

The best decision I ever made was quitting my good government job to concentrate on my business. It's almost impossible to maintain a full-time job and build a business enterprise simultaneously. Do it as long as you need to in order to sustain you and your family and then take the leap when you can.

What is an unusual habit you have as an entrepreneur that helps you succeed?

I once heard a business owner on a panel say that it's important to check your bank account daily. I agree. Since then, I've heard so many horror stories about fraud in business. Small businesses have very little recourse if they're victims of fraud so it's imperative to understand and have awareness of finances at a granular level. Obviously, having a good system of checks, balances, and oversight is key as well.

With the knowledge and experience you have now, what would you have done differently if you were to start your entrepreneurial journey again?

I wouldn't change a thing. I live by the adage, "Everything that happens is meant to happen." I've learned a lot of lessons through my experiences.

What do you do when you feel demotivated and overwhelmed?

I step away to regroup. Sometimes, I perform relaxation exercises; other times, I might take a short walk to soak in fresh air and sunlight and clear my head. Most often, I simply take a nap. I heard something a long time ago that stuck with me: When you hit a wall, it's time for a break, even if only for ten to twenty minutes. Set it down or sit yourself down. Let your mind rest. When I return to a project or task after a break, I usually complete whatever it is in a fraction of the time with a refreshed perspective. Naps are a powerful tool! Use them wisely!

Discuss a crisis situation (2008 depression, 9/11, COVID-19) that you/your company were in and how you overcame it.

We're a pretty young company so COVID-19 and a government shutdown are the only real crises we've encountered. We were fortunate on both fronts as we didn't lose contracts or have to stop work. That said, during COVID-19, I often considered other lines of business in an effort to establish multiple streams of income. Having people with families relying on us for their livelihoods adds a level of pressure, and I was very concerned with the idea of a single point of failure.

What is that one secret to your business success that would be helpful to current and aspiring entrepreneurs?

We outsource important functions which allow us to operate and present like a much larger company. This allows me to spend more time on the business strategy versus mundane tasks that could be accomplished somewhere else.

Did you ever experience a time you could not pay payroll costs?

Yes. My first payroll overdrew my account by over $5,000. I'd contracted with a Professional Employer Organization (PEO) and thought the first payroll was to be transferred by me on a certain date. This would have given me the opportunity to pull the money together. Due to a miscommunication, the money was withdrawn from my account with no notice. I remember it like it was yesterday. I was stunned. I cried right there in the bank. The bank teller, Ester, could tell I was overwhelmed. She tried consoling me and assured me things would get better. I borrowed from friends and family for the first few months. Thankfully, my only employee was none the wiser. She was paid on time every payday and often remarked how smoothly things ran at Windsor Group LLC. This made me chuckle, considering the lengths to which I went to ensure she got paid on time. She was oblivious to our financial woes. I didn't allow myself to get defeated. I kept my head up, stayed consistent, and kept moving forward. And I guess that's the most important thing: Realize that entrepreneurship is not easy, but it's certainly worth the sacrifice and effort.

On Just Getting Back Up Again

Pokin Yeung

Pokin Yeung is the founder and CEO of Absolute Games. The company is a casual games developer and their games have been downloaded over twenty million times. Absolute Games was acquired by Penn National Gaming and now operates as a wholly owned subsidiary. The company is based in Las Vegas, Nevada, and information can be found online at absolutegames.com.

Tell us about you as the owner/founder. What's your story that made you the entrepreneur you are today?

Some people talk of not knowing what to be when they grow up. That was never me. As far back as memory allows, I'd known I wanted to start my own business. My first business was selling candy in school. I bought bulk candy and resold it to classmates during recess. I did the same with batteries to teachers. But I didn't get it right at the start. In fact, I didn't get it right for a long time. My founder journey has been littered with failures, all of which influence my approach today.

My hiccups started in school. I was a solid C student. My Chinese grades were so poor my parents asked to put me in class with the foreign students instead of with the native Chinese students. The transfer was denied. It wasn't until I made friends with some honor students that I became motivated to level up my grades to join their classes. Going from C's to A's taught me that anything is achievable given the right circumstances.

My first job was with a multinational cosmetics firm. I logged long hours and weekends growing my brands. My products became best sellers. Despite their successes, I was never promoted. Eventually, my managers told me they didn't see me on the leadership track. That stung. I felt like I was performing well and demonstrated leadership traits. I didn't have the loudest voice, but I was coaching interns and guiding coworkers. I took in the feedback, and turned in my resignation. Looking back, I learned to recognize that potential existed in non-obvious ways. Reflecting on the burnout I felt working in a place where long hours were seen as a badge of honor, I realized the importance of taking care of my team and prioritizing their health and happiness. I'm glad everything happened the way it did, and overall, I look back fondly at my experience there.

Every bump is an opportunity for growth, and a further reminder that the world is not fixed. Conditions can, and do, change. It reminds me to be grateful even for setbacks, to evolve, and to take care of others while I have the opportunity.

What have been the key factors to your success and why?

By far, the largest factor to my success has been to say yes. I have an internal barometer; the more uncomfortable I feel about something (assuming it checks out ethically), the larger the potential learning opportunity. I think about my earliest phobia, a fear of phone calls. Realizing this might make being in business a little challenging, I volunteered to be a political canvasser. The experience was absolutely terrifying. I hung up on the first person I called – who called back understandably irate about being hung up on. I persisted through my list. Bit by bit, the fear dulled. Today, I make phone calls without a second thought.

Then there is turning towards seemingly bleak prospects. I sought an internship with a multinational mobile enterprise company, but performed poorly on the interview due to lack of knowledge about the industry. Rather than accept defeat, I spent time learning the concepts I didn't understand before writing in to "re-answer" the questions. Saying yes to one more try led to a product management internship, even without the computer science or engineering background that was typically required, and my work led to a patent.

Absolute Games was built at a hackathon, an event where the goal is to create functioning software or hardware by the end of the contest. My cofounder and I said yes to driving hours to attend the event, and then to launching what we built with many features still missing, into a crowded market. This game became the cornerstone of our business.

Selling our company, too, was about saying yes. We had no intention to sell, but said yes to a phone call. A year after we were acquired, I was given responsibility to manage an additional brand. Eventually, I became the general manager of the entire Social Games Division, where I manage a team of twenty-three.

That's how I try to approach life and opportunities. I never once felt qualified for what's come my way. If I allowed fear to rule, I wouldn't have had the experiences I have had. I live each day reminding myself to say yes and to embrace, instead of shy away from, any tough moment.

What has been your worst decision and how did you bounce back and still get to where you are today? How did this failure prepare you for your current success?

I used to believe success meant creating a venture-backable business. I focused my attention on building a company with the kind of metrics that would fit the venture mold. I concentrated on growth above monetization. How do we get more signups? Better user contribution rates? Monetization was an afterthought. If there were enough users, enough traffic, we could figure it out later.

While that strategy is necessary for a sliver of companies, and is especially important for companies that rely on network effects in a "winners take all" space, it is detrimental to most businesses. Instead of building a self-sustaining company, you become reliant on persuading others to your vision, leaving yourself vulnerable to changing market conditions.

My first business raised angel investment, but it was not enough. We had millions of engaged users, but never became profitable. I still recall the day I told our team we had to shut down. I don't want that experience again. Ever after, I evaluated businesses from a different angle. My criteria were capital efficiency, and low startup costs. I focused not just on building products that customers loved, but products they would pay for. I looked for recurring revenue models. Instead of selling something once, I sought products that were subscription-based or were consumable (like tokens in an arcade game). Rather than seeking out new customers, it became about returning the existing customers.

There are so many benefits that come from a cash-flow positive business. The security that comes from knowing you can walk away from any deal is powerful. My current business started with $500 and we were profitable our first month of launch. While uncertainty never goes away, solid financial fundamentals give you the confidence to take more business risks and make better bets.

What has been your best decision and why?

Aside from moving to the Silicon Valley (for a tech business), my best decision has been to be a generalist.

I'm not an expert in any one field but I do little bits of many things. If you meet your target market's fundamental need, there are many things you can get by with just being "good enough." I did the original game art in our game. It was pretty bad. No one cared. I did our accounting and marketing. My cofounder wrote the code for the actual product. We both handled customer service. Being able to do everything as a team of two allowed us to be incredibly capital efficient. Working across functional roles also allowed us to see the bigger picture better, pivot faster, and more readily realize opportunities for innovation. We were among the first in our industry to develop a fully integrated customer service platform. This close contact with our players allowed us to develop the loyal customer following that we still have today.

What is an unusual habit you have as an entrepreneur that helps you succeed?

My habits feel pretty pedestrian. The most unusual thing might be that my businesses have mascots. GeckoGo was a travel website, and its mascot was a gecko. The gecko represented an intrepid, inquisitive creature that was at once resourceful and curious about the world. Peer, a VR webcam, was a robot pal, while Abradoodle, a mobile game, is a puppy who just wants to be nice and play bingo. These mascots personify each brand. Creating a mascot helps me hone the voice, and craft more consistent, cohesive messages in my communication.

With the knowledge and experience you have now, what would you have done differently if you were to start your entrepreneurial journey again?

When I first started my founder journey, many well-meaning people advised me to stop and join a successful startup instead. "Work in the industry first; don't barge straight in," they said. I was impatient. I had an idea. I'd already worked for multinational companies. I had cofounders. In other words, I was going for it. I saw no reason to delay. In retrospect, they were right. While some founders make it on their first try, there are many shortcuts if you build off the knowledge of other successful businesses, especially those with the original founders still in place.

I now give that same advice. Is there somewhere you can "apprentice" first? Take the time to learn what works, what partnerships you need, where the efficiencies (or inefficiencies) are for that industry? The insights you glean and the relationships you build will more than make up for the detour.

What do you do when you feel demotivated and overwhelmed?

Being a founder is a test of emotional extremes. I still struggle to separate my sense of self from the business. On days with bad news after more bad news, when customers are complaining and sales are down, when features are taking long to release, it can become incredibly demotivating. The advice I've gotten is to embrace the lows. Running a business is never straightforward, and if you view both highs and lows as a normal part of the journey, it becomes easier to see the bigger picture. The only constant is that the feelings are fleeting. I like the saying, "You don't become who you become in the easy times." The lows and how you choose to respond to them shape your outcome.

Beyond that, I find breaking tasks down into bite-size pieces helps me mechanically get through rough spots. Instead of a project that might take a couple weeks to do, what's a task that can be accomplished in a few minutes? How much more concrete can I make the action? Developing a marketing campaign might get broken down as small as "write the subject of the email I need to send" or "find three sources of inspiration." There's usually a level of granularity where the ease of doing the task is higher than the feelings of inertia. And once there is momentum, it is easy to continue.

Discuss a crisis situation (2008 depression, 9/11, COVID-19) that you/your company were in and how you overcame it.

Absolute Games almost didn't make it through its first year. That is when I learned the importance of the work environment, clear communication, and work/life separation. In our first year, my cofounder (now husband) and I participated in Start-Up Chile. It's a program where you move to Chile. In return, you get an equity-free grant, but on a reimbursement basis. Ever cautious of cash flow, we lived and worked out of a studio apartment. Our kitchen counter doubled as a workstation. The counter barely fit two laptops, and our knees knocked whenever we both sat down. We quickly bought a second table, but the strain of constantly being together in the same small space in a foreign environment led to tense emotions and fights. Midway through the program, we called it quits. It was only then, in a time out, that we could realize the importance of giving ourselves permission to take breaks and step away. To this day, we maintain separate offices, and our business continues to grow with much less stress.

What is that one secret to your business success that would be helpful to current and aspiring entrepreneurs?

Don't get too attached to any specific idea or concept. While our core values of empathy for the customer and quality over deadlines stays constant, not being too attached to a feature or tagline allows me to look objectively at what the data is telling me without becoming personally offended or hurt if it doesn't work. I once spent three weeks debating the right shade of orange for our brand logo. Years later, I realized our logo colors of orange and green were not even great choices for some color blind populations. That effort would have been better spent iterating on product. I also believed our products *should* look a certain way. Then I updated our app icon to be less whimsical and more descriptive. Our downloads took off. I hate how our icon looks now, but I accept that it works.

Being open to change, and not getting too attached, is understated as a contributor to business success.

What's your advice for entrepreneurs who are still struggling?

My blanket advice is first to embrace the struggle. No matter the hardship, there is always a learning opportunity. The satisfaction of accomplishment is that much sweeter with a journey first. How much better is the mountain summit view after having trekked every step to the top? Stepping back, it's worth looking at *what* you are struggling with. Be candid. Evaluate whether to persevere, or whether it's time to pivot.

Let's assume you're struggling to gain traction on your business. Here are some questions to consider.

- Do you already have customers? How much are they actually willing to pay?
- What's your next best alternative to what you're doing?
- Does this business give you the margins to mess up? How many shots on goal do you have to get it right? (Maybe it's more than you think! Know your cash flow and run rate.)
- Are you playing catch up? Are you struggling to break past a plateau?
- How solid is your emotional support?
- What are your beliefs about this business and are they as immutable as they seem?
- What's the worst that can happen?
- Is what you're offering a need or a nice to have?

Years ago, I remember being introduced to the concept of the local max. The idea being, if you're trying to climb a mountain, first make sure you are climbing the tallest mountain. Otherwise you're limiting your potential. If you're struggling, ask yourself – is this the right hill to climb? And there's only one way to know. Stay close to the customer. See what their actions tell you. Don't be afraid to speak with them directly. I still respond to customers, even with a customer service team of six. In the end, if you don't get it right this time, it's just more knowledge for your tool belt. For now, just keep showing up.

Did you have capital limitations and how did you finance your business?

My first business focused on growth above profitability, and I was in a perpetual state of fundraising. The business never became sustainable, and eventually closed down. Subsequently, my priorities shifted to capital efficiency, preserving cash flow, and financial independence. I sought business models with low fixed costs and high margins. Mobile games fit these criteria. Our genre is "evergreen," meaning it's always in demand. We didn't have to have a hit; we only had to provide a solid experience. Development costs were low, allowing us to bootstrap our business from a $500 investment into an eight figure business. We ran one of the leanest teams despite being one of the top grossing games in our category. We kept our burn rate low by taking a DIY approach. We built the proof of concept on our own. Instead of hiring immediately, we outsourced at first.

I learned that it was important to be flexible on where you live. While I loved Silicon Valley, living in Las Vegas lowered our cash burn significantly. Talent, too, has been more affordable.

Be creative on where to find funds! We looked at accelerators and grant programs that didn't ask for equity. We earned our mobile development devices by winning hackathons. When there's a will, there's a way to get creative!

Acknowledgements

I want to send infinite virtual hugs to my tribe that helped make this project a success.

First, I have to give thanks to God who gave me the vision for this author collaboration, so that current and future entrepreneurs could be inspired through the stories in this masterpiece.

Second, I have to thank my father, Dr. Roe Nall, Jr., my sister, and my nephew who prayed for this book's success diligently for months. Although she is in Heaven, I want to thank my mother, Mayfred Jolinda Hughes Nall, whose life inspires me daily. I would like to also thank all of the authors in the book who allowed themselves to be vulnerable so they could share their stories and then trusted me enough to include them.

Special thanks to Alinka, Deborah, Dr. Zella Ondrey, and the Leaders Press team for making this process effortless and successful. A huge shout out goes to Tyler and his crew at Authors Unite for grabbing the baton in the final stretch for the book's win.

I would definitely be remiss if I did not say thank you to all of my friends and family who gave me words of encouragement and demonstrated excitement as if this book was their own. Last, but certainly not least,

I give appreciation to all of you as readers who will wrap yourselves in the pages of this book to read about phenomenal entrepreneurs who have shaped the world. I do not take your being here for granted. Love you all!

Dr. Tamara Nall

February 2021